D1595874

Freedom & Power

THE GOSPEL OF
Freedom & Power

Protestant Missionaries in American Culture
after World War II

❋ ❋ ❋

Sarah E. Ruble

THE UNIVERSITY OF NORTH CAROLINA PRESS
CHAPEL HILL

Set in Minion by Tseng Information Systems, Inc.
Manufactured in the United States of America

The paper in this book meets the guidelines for permanence and durability
of the Committee on Production Guidelines for Book Longevity of the Council
on Library Resources. The University of North Carolina Press has been a
member of the Green Press Initiative since 2003.

Library of Congress Cataloging-in-Publication Data
Ruble, Sarah E.
The gospel of freedom and power : Protestant missionaries in
American culture after World War II / Sarah E. Ruble.
p. cm.
Includes bibliographical references (p.   ) and index.
ISBN 978-0-8078-3581-4 (cloth : alk. paper)
1. Missions, American—History—20th century. 2. Protestant churches—
Missions—History—20th century. 3. United States—Foreign public opinion.
4. United States—Foreign relations—Public opinion. I. Title.
BV2410.R83 2012
266′.02373009045—dc23
2012007570

16 15 14 13 12   5 4 3 2 1

To
Betty Edwards &
Evelyn Johnson—
grandmothers
who did what was
true

Contents

Acknowledgments

In the years I have been writing this book, I have acquired many debts. It is a joy to acknowledge them, even though I will not be able to repay them.

I owe the idea for this book to Grant Wacker. Throughout the project, he has been an invaluable conversation partner as well as a constant source of encouragement. He remains the gold standard of mentors. David Steinmetz, Laurie Maffly-Kipp, and Julie Byrne all helped shape the direction of this project. Seth Dowland, Matt Harper, and Brantley Gasaway read early drafts and challenged me to rethink my central argument in the work's nascent days. It took me a while to see it, but they were right.

Elesha Coffman, Julie Gilbert, Brendan Pietsch, Kate Bowler, George Malkasian, Mary Solberg, Thia Cooper, and Jennifer Woodruff Tait read significant portions of the manuscript somewhere along the way. In each case, they offered insightful comments and encouragement to keep going when my enthusiasm flagged. Angela Tarango read the conclusion and, more importantly, refused to let me become a hermit. Lauren Winner read the whole book, asked tough questions, and gave me good advice. She also kept me from despair at key points.

Working with the University of North Carolina Press has made publishing a book much less daunting than I supposed it could be. Three anonymous readers for the press read the manuscript and commented helpfully. I appreciate the seriousness with which they took this work and hope that I can begin to do their suggestions justice. Tema Larter, Caitlin Bell-Butterfield, and Ron Maner answered questions and made the process smooth. Special thanks goes to Elaine Maisner, my editor. She supported the project through many years and some doubts. Her questions prodded me to greater clarity about my method and my argument. All writers should have such an editor.

My colleagues at Gustavus Adolphus College have been tremendously supportive as I simultaneously learned how to write a book, how to be a teacher, and how to be a colleague. They are teacher-scholars of the highest caliber and their commitments to their students inspire me. I am particularly grateful to the members of the Religion Department for providing a congenial environment in which to ply my trade. John Cha, our department chair, zealously protected my time as a junior faculty member so that I could write. When I was volunteering to take on extra courses, Garrett Paul saved me from myself (twice). At various times he, Mary Solberg, and Deborah Goodwin have added extra classes or extra preparations so that their junior colleagues would not need to do so. They are what senior faculty should be. Thia Cooper read drafts and cheered with me when I learned my manuscript was going to be published. Mary Gaebler has been a constant conversation partner. She, Eric Eliason, and Brian Johnson became a small community of friends who helped make Minnesota feel like home.

Two classes of students in my Missionary Impulse in America course at Gustavus entered into this topic with interest and insight. Their questions and concerns prodded me to think harder. Their astute reading of texts made me look at my own writing in new ways.

Historians depend on people who keep records. I am grateful for the wonderful staff at the Methodist Archives at Drew University, particularly Dale Patterson, Frances Lyons-Bristol, and Mark Shenise (who not only found me filmstrips galore but fixed the projector I broke so that I could keep watching them). Cathy Fortner and Kate McGinn helped me navigate the Free Methodist Archives at the Marston Historical Center. James Howell and the staff at Myers Park United Methodist Church in Charlotte, North Carolina, welcomed me to their church and let me make free copies. Norma Cathey, in a labor of love, long kept the archives at First Free Methodist Church and gave me free rein. It was good to be home again.

Other debts are more personal. Friends too numerous to count have enriched my life during the course of this project. My family has been a source of great joy. My parents, Mark and Karen Johnson, have read multiple drafts of every chapter in this book. They have cheered me and encouraged me. Their love continues to give me the freedom to take risks, secure in the knowledge that in their eyes I cannot fail. For that, and for much else, I am deeply grateful.

During the course of this book, my immediate family grew. Todd and Sydney came into my life as I was revising. They have embraced me—book included—in ways surpassing my every expectation. I am delighted by the laughter that now fills our house as well as for the quiet contentment of our life together. To Todd, particularly, I am grateful for the blessings of partnership, for sorrows shared, and joys compounded. I am amazed by the deep goodness of our life together and excited by the journey that awaits.

This book is dedicated to my grandmothers, two women who regularly attended missionary aid meetings and faithfully subscribed to missionary magazines. They also created families in which questions were welcome and where learning was celebrated. As a child I did not know that I was seeing in them a striking combination of faith and epistemic humility; I simply had a sense I was blessed to have them. I really had no idea how blessed I was.

THE GOSPEL OF
Freedom & Power

INTRODUCTION
✳ ✳ ✳

In 1959 James A. Michener published his first epic novel, *Hawaii*. Since World War II, Michener had carved a successful niche as a guide to the South Pacific. Rodgers and Hammerstein adapted his *Tales of the South Pacific* into the musical *South Pacific*. *Hawaii* never made it to Broadway, but it did become a best seller, a Book-of-the-Month Club Selection, and the basis for a 1966 movie starring Max von Sydow and Julie Andrews. As a novel that Michener intended to be "true to the spirit and history of Hawaii," the book narrated encounters among various peoples, such as native Hawaiians and immigrants from Japan and China, who by the 1950s composed a significant proportion of Hawaii's population. Large sections of the 937-page book focused on two other significant groups in Hawaii's history: the Calvinist missionaries who came to the islands in the 1820s and their descendants.[1] When Michener's novel became a movie, the missionary story constituted the entire plot.

While both the movie's and Michener's focus on the missionaries made sense in terms of Hawaiian history—the evangelists and their descendants had affected the islands—they also made sense in terms of the book's own context. *Hawaii* was published fourteen years after the end of World War II, a time that had solidified the United States' new role as a world power. The questions missionaries posed about the effects of encounters between different groups, particularly groups with disparate power, and what cultural changes the more powerful in a cultural encounter should advocate (or impose) were questions as germane to the 1950s as to the 1850s, if not more so. The questions the missionaries' actions raised posed ongoing concerns for the world's new superpower. This larger import became clear at the end of the novel when one of the early missionary's descendants traveled the South Pacific during World War II and compared the effects of colonization in Fiji and Tahiti (by Britain and France, respectively) with the changes wrought by the missionaries and their family dynasties in Hawaii. Through the missionaries, Michener explored the complexities of U.S. action in the world and what it would mean for the country to spread its way of life abroad.[2]

James Michener was not the only American considering missionaries in the decades after World War II. Although the missionary movement lost both public stature and visibility over the course of the twentieth century, missionaries remained the subjects of public discussion and debate among disparate groups of Americans. Mainline and evangelical Protestants, academics, and popular novelists all took part in public conversations about (and sometimes with) missionaries. Those conversations occurred in multiple venues, from Sunday morning sermons to anthropological monographs. The assessments also varied widely. For some, missionaries were stalwarts of faith, obeying God's command to preach the gospel to all people. For others, evangelists abroad paved the way for the decidedly nonsalvific gospel of Western capitalism.

The Gospel of Freedom and Power explores some of these disparate public conversations in their context, namely, the growing power of the United States from the end of World War II to the turn of the twenty-first century. Although not all conversations about missionaries referenced American power in the world explicitly, that power framed them. Missionaries, their supporters, the interpreters, and their critics lived in a world shaped by U.S. power and were implicated by it. Thus, while discussions about missionaries seemed at times narrowly focused on what evangelists should or should not do abroad, they were also discussions about how to be good global citizens while carrying American passports. In considering the role of missionaries, various Americans—many of whom would not think of each other as participants in the same sort of conversations—raised questions of cultural authority and normativity. Even as the conversations about missionaries promoted different views about evangelists, they performed similar cultural work. I argue that public discussions about missionaries reinforced a postwar American paradox: they explicitly asserted that people abroad deserved freedom but also (often implicitly) maintained that Americans knew what was best for the rest of the world.

Michener's *Hawaii*, for example, acknowledged significant problems with cultural imposition and encounters among people with unequal power. Hoxworth Hale, the missionary descendant traveling the South Pacific in World War II, concedes that the missionary dynasties were wrong to allow "our Hawaiians to lose their land, their language, and their culture." Yet the book largely places cultural imposition in the past and heralds what the missionaries and their descendants achieved. As Hoxworth travels, he sees the effects of English and French colonization in Fiji and Tahiti. The comparison makes him appreciate what his ancestors accomplished in Hawaii: "Health, education, building and the creation of new wealth . . . we are really far ahead."[3] Hoxworth also reflects on his great-grandmother, the missionary Jerusha Hale: "From her body came a line of men and women who would civilize the islands and organize them into meaningful patterns."[4] At its best, the civilization that the New England missionary dynasties brought paved the way for a multiethnic, well-run Hawaii. The book accepts the missionaries' standards (organization, civilization, wealth creation) as those by which any place (Tahiti, Fiji, Hawaii) could be judged. While the missionaries' desire to force Puritan ways on unwilling others is shown to have harmful consequences, much of what the evangelists and their descendants brought was depicted as universally good and the universal standard by which all places might be evaluated.[5]

Hawaii neither simply reflected prevalent beliefs about missionaries, Americans, and the United States nor simplistically formed them. As cultural studies scholars have argued, cultural texts do not exist in a vacuum but participate in a complex negotiation of ideas and attitudes. They neither mirror extant ideas nor stand apart from the culture and shape it. Rather, they acquire and make meaning as they interact with their context and with each other.[6] In the context of a postwar, nationalizing world, Michener's book made claims about Americans. Those claims acquired meaning in their context. They also participated in a larger cultural affirmation of America's supposedly universal values. *Hawaii*, for example, made claims that were echoed in other discussions about missionaries. The *Christian Century*, a major publication for Protestant mainline leaders, affirmed the supremacy of democracy and asserted the necessity of American Protestant world leadership as it discussed missionaries in the 1950s. Although the *Century* emphasized ecumenical Protestant leadership and *Hawaii* did not, both negotiated between a commitment to freedom abroad and a belief in universal values, particularly as those values were embodied by Americans. The concurrence does not prove that all *Hawaii* fans or all *Christian Century* subscribers thought about missionaries or America the same way. It does show that people encountered affirmations of the universality of American values in multiple places in the 1950s and does help to explain how the notion that people abroad deserved freedom and that Americans were arbiters of that freedom was contested, articulated, disseminated, and naturalized in the culture at large.

My focus on public conversations about missionaries differentiates my work from other scholarship on missions history. Rather than exploring what occurred in specific mission fields or studying mission theory, I analyze the public perceptions of and public conversations about missionaries in order to think through what messages different groups of Americans were generating and receiving about U.S. power and about how Americans should live in the world. *The Gospel of Freedom and Power* relies on the work of scholars who have delved into the vast archival material about conferences such as the 1974 International Congress on World Evangelization and who have poured over the minutes of mission boards. The pertinent sources for my argument, however, are materials available to people sitting in pews, reading academic journals, or browsing in a local bookstore. Moreover, I do not attempt a comprehensive analysis of any of the groups I cover. Not all Americans read *Hawaii*. The *Christian Century* spoke neither for nor to all people in the Protestant mainline. Yet the appearance of the paradoxical affirmation of autonomy for people abroad and of Americans' privileged wisdom in cultural texts from several different groups of Americans demonstrates the prevalence of this paradox throughout the culture. In other words, texts such as a Sunday morning sermon, an anthropological monograph, and a popular novel, put in their context and read in relationship to each other, suggest how ideas about autonomy and freedom, as well as the sense that Americans were fitting arbiters of both, became part of the cultural water.

The American Paradox

That conversations about missionaries reinforced and naturalized what I call an American paradox was ironic. For many involved in conversations about missionaries—particularly as the twentieth century wore on—the autonomy that people abroad deserved was particularly autonomy from the new global hegemon, namely, the United States. Yet those conversations echoed the paradoxical logic of the United States' foreign policy rhetoric—hence the "American" paradox. Just as participants in missionary conversations implicitly suggested that they (not the government but Americans nonetheless) were apt arbiters of how people abroad should use their freedom, the United States claimed that it wanted freedom for people abroad and that it was the best arbiter of what constituted freedom and who was using it appropriately. Again, participants in missionary conversations were not necessarily endorsing U.S. foreign policy, but they were reifying the paradoxical logic behind it—freedom for all but with Americans as arbiters of how others should use their freedom. They were echoing the United States' postwar Wilsonianism.

U.S. postwar rhetoric about its role abroad had three major sources. The Cold War with its Iron Curtains, three worlds, and evil empires provided one set of potent images. Yet the United States' belief that it had to lead, by action and not just example, preceded the onset of the Cold War. Another source of rhetoric came from the long-standing conviction that the United States boasted a special mission in the world. For much of its first 150 years, however, that mission was largely described as being an example of anticolonialism and republican democracy. Precisely because the United States was not an imperial power à la Britain or France, so the rhetoric went, it was an example worth following. Such a description was, of course, belied by territorial expansion in the American West, the Monroe Doctrine of intervention in Latin America, and, in the late nineteenth century, wars and occupation in Cuba and the Philippines. Moreover, as Walter Russell Mead has argued, the penchant for staying out of matters international has long co-existed with another impulse, namely, spreading American values. This impulse, the third source of postwar rhetoric, grew in the early twentieth century and became a foreign policy position, liberal democratic internationalism, more succinctly known as Wilsonianism.[7] Although President Woodrow Wilson could not bring the United States into his League of Nations or realize his dream of collective security, he did bequeath to the United States rhetoric that combined a belief in the United States' special role in the world with a justification for intervention abroad.

To ennoble America's participation in what appeared an ignoble war among power-hungry European nations, Wilson vowed that World War I would "make the world safe for democracy." A democracy-nurturing world would, according to Wilson, abandon imperialism and embrace national self-determination, allow free trade, practice collective security, and encourage all nations to adopt democracy. It would reject the previous arrangement for maintaining world peace, balance-of-power politics. Wilson averred that World War I proved not only that when the balance of power lost equilibrium it toppled violently but also that it lacked morality and an appreciation for human progress. To the disgust of realpolitik proponents (or partisans of a foreign policy based on a low view of human nature and a high view of the balance of power), Wilson publicly championed an international order based on American leadership, morality, and the belief that human beings could act rightly.

The twenty years following Wilson's presidency provided ample evidence that human morality provided a weak foundation for world order. The rise of fascism, the growth of communism, and the refusal of Wilson's own country to participate in the League of Nations did not bode well for Wilsonianism. But history takes strange turns, and reports of liberal internationalism's death during the "isolationist" 1920s and 1930s have been greatly exaggerated. Although Wilson's collective security dreams suffered defeat, his "Liberal Internationalist tenets informed the foreign policy of every administration after him."[8] After World War II, American leaders were deeply committed to Wilsonian rhetoric that equated the good of the world with U.S. interests. As a moral imperative, American leaders would make the world safe for democracy. They would encourage open markets and celebrate national sovereignty for people's living under colonial power. They would, in short, commit the United States to supporting economic and political freedom abroad—and, as the first and most powerful democracy, they would define true economic and political freedom.

Wilson's rhetoric resounded down the decades. By equating open markets and democracy, it justified the spread of American-style capitalism. During the Cold War, it turned what could appear to be a realpolitik-style fight between superpowers into an ideological battle between just and unjust political systems that must be fought wherever the two came into conflict. As political scientist Anders Stephanson notes, "Battle could, in principle, take place anyway, anywhere and anytime. And since the world was either white or black, every battle everywhere was by definition a victory for one or the other."[9] Thus military action in Korea and Vietnam, countries not normally associated with the United States' strategic interests, became morally imperative. After the end of the Cold War, the Clinton administration retained Wilsonian language. In a 1995 *Foreign Policy* article, Secretary of State Warren Christopher warned that with the end of the Cold War, the United States faced the same choice it had after both world wars: "Then, as now, two paths lay before us: to claim victory and withdraw, or with U.S. leadership to build a more peaceful, free, and prosperous world for America and people everywhere." Warren chose the Wilsonian option. "The United States has a remarkable opportunity to help shape a world conducive to American interests and consistent with American values: a more secure and prosperous world of open markets and open societies that will improve the lives of our people for generations to come."[10] To seize this opportunity, President Clinton sent troops to countries some observers claimed mattered little to America's national interest. Bosnia, Somalia, and Haiti, however, did need American support if they were going to become places that were safe for democracy. That logic said much about the history of Wilsonianism in the twentieth century. It evolved from a doctrine about making the world a place where American democracy could thrive to a doctrine about making the world full of democracies. Countries were to be granted their freedom by American troops so that they could benefit from freedom in ways acceptable to America so that America would be secure.

Many international affairs scholars contend that Wilsonian rhetoric beautified the ugly reality of a foreign policy guided much more by American self-interest than the rest of the world's good. That is to say that, although the rhetoric may have been Wilsonian, the policies were not always so.[11] Scholars point out, for example, that foreign policy insiders did not necessarily consider the Cold War an ideological battle. Rather, they saw it as an economic fight intended to destroy a system that kept markets closed to American goods.[12] The United States' willingness to work with authoritarian governments on the right bolstered their claim. Even "keeping the world safe for democracy" could be all about America insofar as it was a foreign policy designed primarily to make the world environment hospitable for one country. Interventions from Korea to Bosnia were not, according to this train of thought, concerned with the good of either Korea or Bosnia. Rather, interventionists had come to believe that only a fully democratic world (or a world full of countries ready to mouth democratic-sounding slogans and keep their markets open) would make the world safe for the only democracy America cared about.

For my purposes, Wilsonian logic belied by actual policies remains important because the logic was echoed as people considered missionaries—even by people who opposed the U.S. hegemony that Wilsonian rhetoric underwrote. That is not to say that the actual policies were insignificant. Far from it. Whether truly Wilsonian or not, the fact remains that after World War II, America did exercise significant world power. No longer content to be a city on a hill, a beacon of light for all to see, America took its light across oceans and borders. Missionaries and their supporters and critics lived in a world in which America soldiers fought in Korea and Vietnam, in which the United States aided the overthrow of "leftist" governments in Iran and Guatemala, in which American businesses aggressively sought new markets with the backing and aid of the government. Wilsonian, realpolitik, or otherwise, America was not simply a rhetorical hegemon: it was a real one.

Conversations about missionaries show how hard it was to escape the United States' power. As missionary supporters and critics alike considered the evangelists' enterprise, they acknowledged problems with U.S. power abroad. Yet they often reified the logic of that power in subtle ways. This book explores how and why they did so. The obvious answer to why—a widespread sense of American cultural superiority—is incorrect. It also misses the point. People who talked about missionaries did not necessarily claim that the United States knew what was best for the world. They did not repeat the Wilsonian paradox verbatim. Rather, they echoed the logic by claiming that *they* knew what was best for the world and did so for reasons particular to their group. By looking at a variety of sources from people across theological, political, and ideological spectrums, we can see how various people grappled with specific, concrete questions that addressed both America's and Americans' activities abroad. We can explore how world events, religious commitments, and disciplinary squabbles affected conversations differently or, in some cases, affected some groups profoundly without registering upon others, and how often separate conversations with different interests and objectives all reinforced the paradoxical logic of Wilsonianism.

The Missionary Movement and American Power

This book focuses on conversations about American Protestant missionaries serving abroad. I focus on Protestants because they, more than any other group, have been associated with power in (and the power of) the United States. Conversations about missionaries after World War II naturally invoked, remembered, and reinterpreted the long history of the American missionary movement, including the long relationship between the missionaries' cross and their flag. Thus a sketch of that history is in order.[13]

The American Protestant missionary movement abroad had multiple geneses. In an oft-told story, it began in 1806 when five students at Williams College organized a weekly meeting to pray for guidance and about the call one student heard to work overseas. During a rainstorm, the determined group met under a haystack rather than end their prayers and, that afternoon, devoted their lives to overseas missions. The impulse to mission, however, went further back. Early colonists described immigration to the "new world" as an errand to the wilderness done in the name of God. John Winthrop, a Puritan leader, famously claimed that his band of Calvinists was to be "a city on a hill." While the Puritans emphasized the exemplar aspect of their assignment, they gave nods in the direction of evangelizing the native peoples. The logo of the Massachusetts Bay Company featured a native man beseeching the English to "Come over and help us." In the colonial period, such attempts were sporadic and largely unsuccessful. Settler incursions into native lands were not a persuasive witness; the tendency of colonists to equate Christianization with the eradication of Indian culture was hardly more so.[14]

The rhetoric of a special American mission, however, survived the failure of the colonists to transform their neighbors into Christians. Both the continued sense of mission and the missionary failure at home played into the expansion of missionary work overseas. Colonial leaders, political and religious, claimed that independence from Britain further solidified the special role the new United States would play in God's plan for the world. For some Americans, overseas missions seemed a logical step in fulfilling that role. As Ussama Makdisi has argued, overseas lands also provided an opportunity to achieve what evangelists had not achieved among American Indians. Insofar as Christianization of a pagan population was part of the American mission, it had yet to be realized. Going abroad "presented a stage on which an original American mission narrative, and an original American promise of salvation at the frontiers of Christendom, might be re-enacted, and this time fulfilled."[15]

The part missionaries might play in God's plan for the world, however, did not lead all mission supporters to equate evangeliza-tion with Americanization. During the antebellum decades, mis-sion leader Rufus Anderson advocated a policy that emphasized spreading the gospel rather than American culture. Although Anderson boasted the power to enforce his policy, some of the missionary movement's most ardent supporters, namely, women, disliked it. Female missionaries were not allowed to preach. Any policy that made civilizing functions, such as teaching English, secondary to direct evangelism, subordinated women's work. In response to Anderson's policies, female missions supporters created their own missionary societies and celebrated "Women's Work for Women." They tended to assume that the subjugation of women abroad stemmed from the dual lack of Christianity and (Western Protestant) civilization, and they made it their mission to spread the benefits of both.[16]

By the end of the nineteenth century, women were not alone in assuming a close relationship between the spread of Chris-tianity and (Western Protestant) civilization abroad. That the ad-vancement of the one cause was the advancement of the other was a common assumption during the "high imperial era." Prot-estant Americans had long associated their religion with the United States' republican institutions. Celebrated preacher Lyman Beecher averred in the 1830s that Calvinism (his brand of Prot-estantism) "laid the foundations of the republican institutions of our nation."[17] Theologian Josiah Strong, in his 1885 call for the Protestantization of immigrants, *Our Country*, claimed that Anglo-Saxons were responsible for two developments, civil lib-erty and pure, spiritual Christianity. Because the two were conjoined, they would be spread together.[18] Whereas Strong was fixated on a domestic task, sociologist James Dennis wrote three ponderous volumes on the missionary task abroad. That task encompassed more than individual conversion, he claimed. Missions boasted "a larger purpose," namely, "to redeem that life that now is, so that the social desert of the non-Christian world shall some day bloom and blossom under the ministry and culture of Christianity."[19] The missionaries who went into the world to build schools, run hospitals, and establish Young Men's Christian Associations largely agreed.

By 1900, missionaries and their movement had grown both powerful and popular. That year, former president Benjamin Harrison, New York governor Theodore Roosevelt, and President William McKinley all gave speeches at the Ecumenical Missionary Conference in New York City. By World War I, more than 3 million American women belonged to some forty missionary societies. Movement spokesman John R. Mott participated in diplomatic negotiations under President Woodrow Wilson. Missions and their workers received wide approbation and possessed great cultural clout.

Yet, as the mission movement reached its apogee of cultural influence, it was fracturing, as was American Protestantism. Differing responses to new intellectual developments, such as evolution and higher biblical criticism, as well as to urbanization and industrialization, split Protestants into conservative and liberal camps. Missionaries on the theological left found themselves unable to disregard the validity of other religious systems. They moved away from direct evangelization and the demand that people convert to Christianity. While most still viewed Protestant Christianity as the apex of religious experience (and as the apex of civilization), they did not believe hell awaited those who did not convert. Other missionaries were unconvinced. As conservatives saw their colleagues hedge on the necessity of conversion, the reality of hell, and the divinity of Christ, they sounded an alarm. Denominational battles among northern Presbyterians and Baptists in the 1920s and 1930s, the well-known fundamentalist-modernist controversy, partly stemmed from concerns about what missionaries were and were not doing in the field. Conservatives within these denominations wanted all overseas workers to embrace doctrinal fundamentals, whereas moderates urged compromise, and liberals refused dogmatic tests altogether. The denominations resisted the conservative demands but lost people in the process. Some conservatives pulled out of denominational missions and joined young "faith missions," such as the China Inland Mission and African Inland Mission. The faith groups demanded the missionaries raise their own support rather than rely on denominational funding. Some early faith missionaries went abroad without financial backing, trusting that God would provide. Originally the faith groups understood themselves as complements to denominational work overseas. While denominations engaged in multiple tasks—preaching, teaching, and healing—the early faith missions emphasized direct evangelism. Yet, as liberals and conservatives split, the faith missions became less a complement to the denominations and more of an alternative. They maintained strict doctrinal tests and a firm conviction that non-Christians needed the salvation that came through Jesus alone. For those who wanted the fundamentals upheld, groups such as the China Inland Mission and African Inland became bastions of orthodoxy.[20]

For all of their disagreements on matters theological, however, both conservatives and liberals retained a sense of their special relationship with the United States. After the 1925 Scopes trial, conservatives seemed to disappear from American public life. As historian Joel Carpenter has shown, however, their disappearance was really a tactical retreat that allowed them to regroup and reorganize. Even in the midst of retreat, fundamentalists did not abandon their hopes to lead a Christian America or to spread their gospel abroad. Liberals, the purported winners of the 1920s battles, believed that they had settled the issue of who constituted the religious establishment in the United States. With presidents sitting in their pews and missionary leaders such as John Mott occupying positions of international prominence, they had many reasons for confidence.[21]

On Conversations, Sources, and American Exceptionalism

My study picks up the story in 1945. The first three chapters focus on conversations about missionaries among three groups: mainline Protestants, evangelical Protestants, and anthropologists. All of these groups boasted a significant interest in missionaries and a serious consideration of both their own and the United States' role in the world. In all three discussions, assessments of missionaries changed (not always in the same direction), and considerations of missionaries were intertwined with reflections on the need people abroad had for freedom from U.S. power. Still, in all three cases, the people engaged in the conversations repeated the Wilsonian logic of policy decisions they increasingly critiqued, for reasons theological, humanitarian, ideological, and practical. These chapters explain how such concerns played into the consideration of missionaries and U.S. action abroad. My fourth chapter looks at the missionary conversations and their Wilsonian echoes from another perspective, namely, gender. By examining how gender functions in sources ranging from church publications to popular novels, I demonstrate another way the logic of U.S. power was reified even as it was criticized.

The Gospel of Freedom and Power draws upon intellectual and cultural history as well as cultural studies in order to examine conversations about missionaries and about the United States during the postwar decades. I highlight ideas both easily accessible to and formed by a great swath of people, from tenured professors writing journal articles to casual readers of a Sunday morning bulletin. For example, when exploring conversations about missionaries among American evangelicals, I use articles in evangelicalism's flagship magazine, *Christianity Today*. These texts indicate what many evangelical leaders thought about missionaries and what a significant segment of evangelicals read. But because American evangelicalism comes in several hues, I use one denomination, the Free Methodist Church of North America, to see how the evangelical discussion was refracted through a particular lens.[22] I also attend to levels of conversation within the denomination. Publications, such as the Free Methodist *Missionary Tidings*, indicate denominational thinking about evangelists. To discover how discussion about missionaries—and, indeed, missionaries themselves—sounded to people sitting in the pews, I use rarely tapped archival sources, such as bulletins, newsletters, and sermon tapes, from a major Free Methodist Church. Likewise, I use the major mainline periodical, the *Christian Century*, as well as resources from one mainline denomination, the United Methodist Church (UMC), and archival material from a UMC congregation to explore how both leadership and laity talked about missionaries.[23] Again, these sources do not demonstrate that all evangelicals or all mainliners read the same texts or practiced the same politics. My goal is not to account for all missionary conversations among all evangelicals (to take one group). Rather, it is to show that a similar rhetorical logic could be found among disparate groups in America and to unpack the particularities of that logic.

By drawing upon these varied sources, I offer a description of multivalent discussions occurring among denominational officials, the women who diligently met on weekday mornings to sew bandages for missionary doctors, and the many people whose thinking about their country and the "rest of the world" was negotiated and shaped in their conversations about missionaries. That these sources give us insight into an ongoing conversation—one in which not everyone had equal power, and parts of which we have little access too—bears consideration. As scholars working at the intersection of culture and history have argued, texts are not necessarily truths. An article in *Christianity Today* cannot tell us what all evangelicals thought about missionaries. Nor can an article indicate how readers interpreted it. On the other hand, a *Christianity Today* article did have to win the approval of editors who saw their magazine as one of "evangelical conviction." Such an approved article can reveal something about what a group of people who wanted to set the parameters for the evangelical movement believed warranted discussion and what perspectives they wanted their audience to read. When read with other documents, such as sermons given at a Free Methodist Church, we can also see repeated patterns and how ideas were refracted through denominational and personal lenses. We get, in other words, a sense of the conversation: what ideas were on the table, how they changed as the conversation continued, and how various ideas bounced off each other and interacted with their historical context.

This methodological note is not simply an academic nicety. Recognizing that assessments of the United States, no less than assessments of missionaries, are produced in historical contexts and are influenced by a variety of interests militates against the American exceptionalism that the paradoxical logic of the conversations reinforced. American exceptionalism contends that the United States is qualitatively different from other nations, that it is, in fact, the example par excellence of the modern nation-state, and that it possesses a static essence. A host of recent works has criticized this view, showing that national identity is a construction and is dialogical. The foreign and the domestic constitute each other, which means that ideas of "Americanness" are informed by interactions with people abroad and change over time. Although many people involved in missionary discussions might have argued or assumed that there was an American essence, they actually helped to create an idea of that essence in their conversations. Some would have argued against exceptionalism but, again, reinforced it in their discussions insofar as they privileged Americans' interpretations of what was good for the rest of the world. The repetition of the logic of the Wilsonian paradox—that people abroad deserve freedom and that America (or Americans) are the arbiters of what freedom means and how it should be used— reinforced the idea of America's special place in the world. Again, the point is not merely academic. While American exceptionalism can be used to call the country to sacrifice and to abide by its stated principles, it can also be used to disguise colonial expansion (since exceptionalists would claim that the United States is inherently noncolonial) and justify self-interest (because exceptionalists can claim that what is good for the United States is good for the whole world).

This work on missionary conversations adds to the growing body of work that historicizes discourse about America and unpacks logic that (sometimes unwittingly) naturalizes U.S. power in the world. Like Christina Klein's work on the orient in the American imagination, Melani McAlister's study of the Middle East in the U.S. imaginary, and Ussama Makdisi's monograph on U.S. missionaries in the Middle East, I focus on a particular topic, a particular place to consider reflections on America and world power. In my case, as in theirs, particularity matters. The point is not merely to show the dialogic creation of the United States or simply to demonstrate that Americans wrestled with issues of power abroad. Much of the point, in this work as in others, is to show how such wrestling permeated U.S. culture and to consider the many permutations such wrestling took. The conversations to which I attend were part of a larger discourse but a discourse made up of particular conversations. My attention to missionary conversations' echo of Wilsonianism's paradoxical logic explores how that logic was reified in the warp and woof of a magazine's debates about missionary funding, in a denomination's battles about the relationship between Christian and American freedom, and in academic considerations about how best to aid people whose land was threatened by big business and government dams. This is a missing piece in a larger story of Americans grappling with the notion of their country's exceptionalism and the reality of its power.[24]

chapter one

PROTESTANT MAINLINE
❊ ❊ ❊

In 1984 a small war of words broke out in the United Methodist Church (UMC). *Newscope*, a weekly denominational newsletter, treated readers to accusations and counteraccusations of blasphemy, violence, and misrepresentation. The fight featured old combatants: members of Good News, a theologically conservative reform movement within the UMC, and the General Board of Global Ministries (GBGM), the official agency responsible for missions. For seventeen years, Good News had bewailed the board's "liberal" mission policy, particularly its support for liberation theology, a theological movement Good News believed substituted Marxism for the Christian gospel. By 1984 the conservatives had lost patience with the board. In January, people associated with Good News announced that they had created the Mission Society for United Methodists, an alternative agency supported by United Methodists but not officially affiliated with the denomination.

The announcement brought out sharp disagreement regarding the missionary task. In October 1984 *Newscope* reported that, while Bishop Roy I. Sano, president of the GBGM's World Division, called the board to "a regained appreciation of evangelism," long a Good News demand, he remained committed to liberation theology. According to *Newscope*, the bishop claimed that "the Holy Spirit is at work in liberation movements," and, therefore "attacks on liberation efforts are acts of blasphemy."[1] Three weeks later, *Newscope* reported Good News executive and new mission agency supporter James V. Heidinger's reply. He claimed that the bishop had accused conservatives of "helping the world's oppressors do their dirty business." Moreover, the liberation movements the bishop lauded were "nearly all" violent, and thus the bishop was calling for a "baptizing of violent revolution."[2] Sano, predictably, rejected Heidinger's characterization and the debate ended without resolution.

In some ways, the fight could be characterized as making a mountain out of a small missionary molehill. Like many so-called mainline denominations, the UMC had significantly scaled back its overseas missionaries after the 1960s.[3] In 1953 mainliners constituted over half of the North American career missionary force. By 1985 only 11.5 percent of career missionaries came from the mainline.[4] Some mainline denominations left missions altogether or retrenched so thoroughly that their overseas work all but disappeared.[5] In the case of the UMC, declining numbers of missionary personnel played a part in the fight because Good News folk contended that a dearth of missionaries indicated a weak commitment to spreading the Christian message. The fight, however, was not merely about numbers.

Sano and Heidinger's disagreement about the missionary task was also a disagreement about the effects of U.S. Cold War policy and Wilsonian logic on people abroad. They disagreed on what constituted freedom, how it related to the Christian gospel, and whether the United States basically retarded or advanced its spread. Their fight had a long history and was part of a larger postwar mainline story. After World War II, significant mainline institutions such as the Methodist Church and the *Christian Century* presented mainline Protestantism and its missionaries as part of a U.S. vanguard bringing freedom and peace to a weary world. As the postwar era gave way to the Cold War, however, many mainline leaders contended that their vision of freedom, not to mention the freedom people abroad wanted, did not necessarily align with what the United States seemed intent on spreading. In the 1960s particularly, mainline writers and denominational officials described the missionary task as counteracting the effects of American policy. Some people within the mainline, such as those affiliated with Good News, asserted that their denominations had moved beyond a healthy differentiation between the Kingdom of God and any particular nation and had joined the wrong side of the Cold War.

As the mainline's assessment of the United States' role in the world changed, so too did its public conversations about missionaries. More mundane factors such as denominational politics also altered how mainliners described what the world needed from their workers overseas. Yet one thing remained consistent. As mainline groups publicly debated the effects of America's Wilsonian logic on the world, they also embodied it. Mainliners both took up the cause of freedom (variously defined) for people abroad and asserted, implicitly and otherwise, that they knew what that freedom should look like.

1945–1959: Protecting Mainline Influence Abroad

"A troopship carrying one of the most remarkable companies of passengers ever to sail the seas in modern times should be well on its way across the Pacific when these lines are read," proclaimed a 1946 *Christian Century* editorial.[6] The remarkable company consisted not of diplomats or politicians but of four hundred missionaries to Asia. A maritime strike in San Francisco had delayed the "epochal expedition." When the strike ended, thousands of citizens joined the mayor at the opera house for a farewell celebration. Publisher Henry Luce traveled across the country to attend the festivities and gave an address in which he called the expedition "a living expression of faith in a world steeped in cynicism, of hope in a society floundering in despair, of love in a civilization sick of hatred." The *Century* editor applauded Luce's words: "He was right."[7] A longer article a few pages later was, if possible, even more laudatory. The author reported that the farewell featured a choir singing "Lead On, O King Eternal," "The Son of God Goes Forth to War," and the Hallelujah Chorus and that "the audience rose and sang as the 'Four Hundred' marched behind white-robed ushers carrying the flags of the church and of the United States down two aisles."[8] The article reported that the celebration chairman called the journey "the most significant event for American Protestant Christianity that has occurred in the twentieth century."[9] After years of war and dislocation, missionaries could return to Asia.

The articles' ebullient tones and the opera house pageantry

celebrated more than evangelists going to the Far East. The parade behind ecclesial and national flags and the address by a magazine mogul signaled that the missionaries were part of a national story. Americans, not only missionaries, remained players on the global stage. Before World War II, Americans had disagreed about how, or whether, the United States should participate in world problems. President Woodrow Wilson's vision of an American-led world order had died when the United States refused to enter the League of Nations. Isolationist impulses had stymied President Franklin Roosevelt's attempts to help the Allied powers before Pearl Harbor. But during World War II, Americans came to a new consensus: the United States should lead the world, not only through example but through participation. Five years before celebrating in San Francisco, Henry Luce, himself the child of missionaries to China, proclaimed the twentieth century the "American Century." In an editorial in his own *Life* magazine, Luce opined that Americans had "to accept wholeheartedly our duty and our opportunity as the most powerful and vital nation in the world and in consequence to exert upon the world the full impact of our influence, for such purposes as we see fit and by such means as we see fit."[10] Public opinion polls consistently showed support for an active U.S. role in the postwar world and, in the immediate aftermath of the war, American power and responsibility became the new normal. A 16 August 1945 *New York Times* editorial declared that the United States "stands before the world today not only as the mightiest of all nations but also as the principal representative of democracy."[11] A year later, another editorial commended American activity after the war: "We have assumed world-wide responsibility for the future; we have offered to surrender control of our atomic explosive if other nations will meet us halfway; we are working as hard as we can for the kind of settlement that will produce a just and lasting peace."[12] As historian John Fousek has shown, postwar responsibility to the world was not yet couched in Cold War terms. The mission was not yet Communist containment but, in Fousek's view, "to feed the starving and rebuild the world economy, to provide moral leadership in the name of American democratic values to a world that had clearly lost its bearings, and to ensure that the peace would be lasting."[13] According to Fousek, this sense of obligation was rooted in a long-standing American belief that its democratic values were really universal values. As the strongest nation standing after the war, the United States boasted the strength and the duty to shape the world.

Mainline Protestants echoed the call to responsibility. That assertion took multiple forms. *Together*, the Methodist magazine for families, heralded the Christian family as "the hope of the world." Methodists proclaimed the white, middle-class nuclear family the foundation for civilization in the nuclear age—and their publications carried the heartwarming stories and Rockwellesque pictures to prove it.[14] Other mainline outlets took a more academic view of the Protestant task. In a thirteen-article series titled, "Can Protestantism Win America?," *Christian Century* editor C. C. Morrison outlined the strengths, weaknesses, and obligations of American Protestantism. He ended the series by emphasizing the peril of the postwar moment: "Both America and Protestantism are now caught in a vast world convulsion. Civilization is in a state of collapse. The old stabilities are dissolving before our eyes. A new world is being born."[15] He argued that only an ecumenical Protestantism (as opposed to a denominationally obsessed one) could meet the exigencies of the hour. His last sentences signaled his commitment to ecumenism and his appraisal of the church's rightful role in the world: "Only such [an ecumenical church] can win America to the Christian faith. And only upon this faith can an enduring civilization be built, in America, and throughout the whole wide world."[16]

Morrison's assertion—much like the two flags leading the San Francisco missionary parade—yoked Christianity and the United States. More specifically, Morrison claimed a particular version of Christianity, ecumenical Protestantism or his version of mainline Protestantism, vital to the health of the United States. His assertion was not a postwar phenomenon. Throughout the early twentieth century, mainline Protestants assumed custodianship for the nation. Their leaders boasted access to politicians and policy makers, who themselves often belonged to mainline churches. Men (and they were almost all men) such as John Foster Dulles moved between leadership on mainline organizations like the Federal Council of Churches Commission to Study the Bases of a Just and Durable Peace and national leadership, in his case secretary of state under President Eisenhower. Former missionary to China John Leighton Stuart was named ambassador to China under President Truman. In the late 1940s, the mainline's most prominent theologian, Reinhold Niebuhr, appeared on the cover of *Time* magazine and met regularly with State Department officials who appreciated his position that acting responsibly in an unjust world sometimes demanded the choice between lesser evils.[17]

References to missionaries in mainline literature in the late 1940s echoed the calls to world building under mainline American leadership. The Methodist *World Outlook* introduced readers to Dr. Barney Morgan and his wife Caroline McAfee Morgan, serving in the Dominican Republic, and noted approvingly that they had "taken the lead in the evangelical, social, and cultural life of the republic."[18] Their leadership was not self-serving but allowed them to be alert "to everyday needs of the people, material and spiritual."[19] Stories of missionary heroism during World War II suggested that missionaries had the personal mettle and the world concern necessary to remake the world. The *Century* ran Olive I. Hodges's account of her time in a Japanese internment camp. Although the government had warned her to leave, she decided to stay: "I believed I was engaged in essential work and that my opportunities for doing that work had never been greater. That 'essential work' was teaching the fatherhood of God and hence the brotherhood of man."[20] Her experience in the camp had not embittered her. On her final day of imprisonment, former Japanese colleagues had visited, and their goodness "gives me courage to believe that even yet we can find a way for all the decent people of the world to live in peace and security."[21] Such an advance guard made a better future seem possible.

Unfolding events, however, cast a shadow over America's bright optimism. Visions of a new world united in peace gave way to the reality of a bipolar world, with the United States and the

Soviet Union both vying for dominance. Rhetoric of one world committed to peace and rebuilding gave way to dualities—the free world versus communism; democracy versus totalitarianism— and the language of cooperation was replaced by the policy of containment. First articulated by diplomat George Kennan, containment was premised on the conviction that the United States and the Soviet Union espoused incompatible values. According to historian William Inboden, Kennan argued that "because the USSR could not be appeased, nor defeated by anything less than a catastrophic global war . . . the United States instead should 'contain' the USSR by applying calculated pressure at strategic points, while waiting patiently for the Soviet system to collapse internally from the burden of its own internal contradictions and dysfunctions."[22] The policy, adopted by President Truman and followed by his successors, underwrote such varied activities as the Marshall Plan's aid to rebuild Europe in the 1940s, the Korean War in the 1950s, and sanctions against Cuba in the 1960s. Political and military leaders also believed that containment demanded increased military spending. Only a military capable of winning a war against the Soviet Union, so the logic went, would not have to fight one.[23]

Yet for the United States the emerging Cold War was not simply a matter of building bombs and developing policy. It was an ideological and spiritual conflict. Its success, so Americans were told by politicians, magazine editors, and clergy, depended on the commitment of everyday citizens. Americans in the 1950s received messages from many venues that winning the conflict of the nuclear age depended on the health of the nuclear family. Strong marriages that appropriately contained sexual energy would keep citizens morally fit enough to withstand the wiles of communism.[24] Religion too was part of the United States' arsenal against communism. Although leaders such as President Truman, President Eisenhower, and Secretary of State Dulles certainly saw the Soviet Union as a geopolitical threat, they described that threat in religious terms. They cast the conflict as one between those nations that believed in God and those committed to atheistic materialism. As Inboden notes, "differences over political structures and economic systems and even national interests, though important in their own right, paled in comparison with the prospect of a world ruled by evil, a world devoid of spiritual values, a world without God. If ever there was a cause to fight, this was it."[25] Political leaders saw religious groups as allies in the cause.

But not all the potential allies saw the Cold War world in the same terms. *Century* writers were a case in point. While the editorial board of the *Century* opposed communism and ran articles that noted communist's hostility toward religion, they also resisted what they saw as the United States' increased militarization and what they believed to be its unnecessarily hard-line positions. Early Cold War editorials campaigned against the split into two worlds and the growing reliance on military strength to keep the peace. America, one editorial claimed, seemed intent on creating an empire.[26] The *Century* countered by suggesting that the churches should put their moral energy behind creating a strong world federal order.[27] These sentiments reflected positions long held by the *Century*, which had championed international law outlawing war in the 1920s and had opposed entry into World War II. Its editors disliked military solutions and supported international organizations such as the United Nations. Rhetoric that divided the world neatly into good and evil camps and policies that seemed to undermine the possibility of cooperation between the United States and the communist bloc, cooperation they believed essential in preventing World War III, held little appeal for *Century* writers.

The *Century*'s stance—one that writer George Shepherd approvingly called moralist—has been construed by contemporaries and scholars alike as a logical outgrowth of political and theological liberalism, specifically liberalism's optimistic analysis of human capability. Theologian Reinhold Niebuhr, whose realist position assumed sin's intractability and the frequent need to choose between lesser evils in the realm of international affairs, had characterized such idealists in a 1944 book as "children of light." The term was not a compliment. These children were concerned with a higher morality but proved politically naïve. They could not counter the "children of darkness" such as Hitler or, in the postwar world, Stalin. Subsequent scholars have echoed Niebuhr's assessment. While the description and analysis have merit, they offer an incomplete picture of the moralist *Century*'s description of the world in the 1950s. The missionary conversations in the *Century* imbedded concern about policy vis-à-vis the communist bloc in a much larger concern about maintaining mainline—particularly the *Century*'s kind of mainline—influence in the world. Downplaying the communist threat was, then, not simply an outgrowth of theological liberalism. It also grew out of an analysis of what most threatened worldwide mainline influence. Mainline leadership represented by the *Century* was desperately concerned that its ability to lead would fall victim to the "world revolution" of which communism was only a parasitic part.[28]

Fear that postwar changes would end in the loss of mainline influence stemmed from one major source: China. After its 1949 takeover, the communist government of China expelled all foreign missionaries. The blow was devastating. The Protestant mainline took great pride in its work in China. It was the major mission field of the early twentieth century—the crown jewel of the movement with symbolic significance both inside and outside the church.[29] In 1947 the *World Outlook* celebrated "100 Years in China." Its tone was ebullient: "China is well on the way to becoming a Christian nation—as Christian, at least, as we are."[30] As the missionaries marching in the San Francisco Opera House showed, the turmoil of the 1930s and 1940s had given way to a glorious return to China at the end of World War II. Yet the return lasted only a few years. Communists, led by Mao Zedong, took control of China, expelled the missionaries, and closed the nation. Who bore responsibility for losing China became a major question in America—a question that also bespoke U.S. presumption about what was its to lose.

Century writers shared their country's question (and presumption) although they were somewhat divided on the culprit. Edward J. Meeman applauded missionaries for their critical self-reflection after the communist takeover and laid the blame on the laypeople who "have not backed [the missionaries] up by creating a Christian society back home—Christian in politics, Christian in business and Christian in its arts and amusements—of which they could be the advance guard and foreign representative."[31] Other writers, including the editors, pointed their fingers at missionaries. In June 1951 a *Century* editorial queried, "What Have We Learned from China?" After the editors chastised Chinese Christian leaders for their support of the revolution (the editors were not yet prepared to rethink the assumption that Christians elsewhere should do what the editors thought they should), they turned on missionaries. "What happened to bring about this situation," they asked. "Was there a touch of imperialism in our mission organizations? Did the mission boards regard the Chinese churches and leaders as first-class citizens of the Kingdom of God or as colonial subjects of the sending denominations?"[32] A 1952 editorial, "Where Have the China Missionaries Gone?," worried that the "missionary methods which were in vogue in China before the debacle" had been taken elsewhere when former China missionaries were reassigned.[33] Although some writers exonerated missionaries, most *Century* articles claimed that missionaries bore responsibility for the communist takeover and their own expulsion.

Blame led to a warning and a prescription. The warning was that other places could go the way of China. A 1954 editorial retrospect noted that mission work in India faced "almost as dubious a future as in China."[34] Africa and other parts of Asia were on the cusp of revolution as well.[35] The prescription was embracing nationalism abroad. For *Century* writers, China proved that the awakening world would not abide colonial relationships—or missionary facsimiles thereof. A 1953 *Century* editorial proclaimed that to avoid expulsion in Africa "the Christian enterprise must pay whatever price is involved to free itself from seeming to be— and frequently being—a part of the historically doomed colonial order."[36] What missionaries had failed to do in China—disavow superiority, share power, align themselves with national aspirations—they had to do in the rest of the world.

The warnings and the proposals told much about how the

moralist mainline understood and described its role in the Cold War world. Although the *Century* writers disapproved of U.S. tactics toward communism, they were hardly "soft" in their appraisal of the communist threat. Communism was a real danger, a threat to both Christianity and democracy. When writers listed "challenges" to missions, communism routinely came up, along with Islam (for which the *Century* also boasted little affection). Communists manipulated noble human aspirations for freedom and maliciously used poor socioeconomic conditions for their own end. But anticommunism was not the focus. *Century* writers asserted that their contribution to stymieing communist advance lay in championing nationalist aspirations and demonstrating that those aspirations could best be achieved through democracy and noncommunist (although not laissez-faire) economic systems.

In their discussions about missionaries, *Century* writers made a further claim: their version of Protestantism underwrote the ideas that would best combat communism. Writers routinely cited Christianity as a source, albeit an underappreciated one, for the very nationalist aspirations that were making life difficult for missionaries. George W. Shepherd, writing in 1957, claimed that "Christian missionaries, preaching the gospel of brotherly love and equality, first awakened the souls of the Asian and African peoples to the possibilities of a new society in which the dignity of every man would be recognized." According to Shepherd, "the greatest achievement of the early missionaries was that they sowed the seeds of this new age."[37] Claiming its message as the source of the world revolution allowed the *Century* to maintain that it should be involved in the revolution's direction—hence, James Robinson's firm conviction about the continuing role of missionaries in Africa: "No one will deny that the Christian missionary forces have an obligation to do everything in their power to influence Africa in the direction of peace, education, increased human dignity and self-respect, and to raise up African leaders who will work cooperatively within the family of nations and the democratic process, leaders with whom missionaries can work as trusting and equal partners both in spreading the gospel and in strengthening the church in Africa and the world."[38] Notably, Robinson's language affirmed both nationalism and supposed U.S. shibboleths, such as "democratic process." Mainline missionaries would serve as midwives to a world that was free on American terms.

The sense of continued relevance—not to mention the tendency to instruct others—was even more evident when writers moved from considering how missionaries should behave toward people abroad to addressing how other countries should relate to missionaries. During the 1950s, the *Century* repeatedly addressed what it perceived to be threats to religious liberty, including restrictions on Protestant missionaries, in Hindu India and Catholic Colombia and Italy. In Colombia, for example, the *Century* claimed that laws privileging the Catholic Church impeded the work of evangelists and resulted in violence. The magazine reported that fifty-one Protestant citizens had been killed since 1948, that Protestant homes and livelihoods were under attack, and that church property had been destroyed.[39] Beyond protesting such injustices, the articles asserted the universality of ideas such as religious liberty and separation of church and state, even as they claimed that Protestantism provided the grounding for them. The articles also implicitly maintained the superiority of Protestantism to other religious traditions—Hinduism and Roman Catholicism, specifically—and the necessity of continued American Protestant presence abroad.

The *Century* made its protests using both international law and universal truths. In "Will Colombia Become a Theocracy?," an editorial denouncing two Colombian constitutional amendments, one restricting Protestant activities to private homes and the other mandating that Protestant schools teach Catholic doctrine, the *Century* editors contended that the Colombian government and the Roman Catholic leaders cheering them were in danger of violating the United Nations Declaration of Human Rights. In their criticisms, the writers maintained that the system they espoused—the separation of church and state—was best for everyone. They criticized Colombian officials for wrongly supposing that a religious monopoly was the best way to ensure "political and social stability." An "alternative system, which separates church and state and grants to all liberty under law, is the only system which conforms to the desire of the people for freedom and in the long run can alone promise order with justice."[40] The *Century* editors knew what "the people" desired, namely, the system of religious liberty that they and their missionaries championed.

While appeals to international law and universal rights suggested that "all people" agreed on notions such as religious liberty and separation of church and state, the *Century*'s treatment of Roman Catholicism and Hinduism implicitly questioned whether all traditions could support them. While the editors made some overtures to Catholicism, avowing respect for individual Catholics, for instance, and suggesting that the National Catholic Welfare Conference should be part of a team to investigate the Colombian situation, it viewed the Roman Catholic Church's commitment to religious liberty as suspect. A 1952 editorial about restrictions on fundamentalist missionaries in Italy stipulated that the missionaries should obey Italian law. Yet "at the same time . . . Protestants everywhere should spread knowledge of what 'religious liberty' in a predominantly Catholic country really is."[41] That the *Century* believed the Vatican might have theocratic ambitions became evident in a 1953 editorial about Colombia that averred "any government which is as subservient to a church as this should be required to appear before the General Assembly of the United Nations and prove whether it is really a sovereign state or a theocratic dependency of Rome."[42] Hinduism also presented problems for the proper understanding of universal values such as religious liberty. A 1954 editorial claimed, disapprovingly, that government restrictions on evangelizing imposed "the Hindu conception of the nature of man" on everyone in India. "This conception," according to the *Century*, "is that man is bound to his family and society in an endless and inescapable sequence of incarnations. Conversions break the sequence, so are against the nature of the universe."[43] For the *Century*, however, it was Hindu anthropology that moved against the grain of the universe, proving that some traditions were more hospitable to universal values than others.

American Protestantism turned out to be quite hospitable. Remember C. C. Morrison's 1946 claim that Protestantism was the necessary foundation for world civilization. Similar statements appeared in the 1950s. In 1953, as McCarthyism swept the nation, the *Century* ran an editorial applauding a statement by the General Council of the Presbyterian Church, U.S.A., that called on the U.S. government and citizens to distinguish between dissent and treason, to abjure lying as an acceptable tactic in the fight against communism, and to recognize limitations on a nation's ability to ensure its own security. The editors quoted approvingly from the council's statement: "Attacks are being made upon citizens of integrity and social passion which are utterly alien to our democratic traditions. They are particularly alien to the Protestant religious tradition which has been a main source of the freedoms which the people of the United States enjoy."[44] These same freedoms, rooted in Protestantism, were what the *Century* affirmed as universal and believed should span the globe.

Castigating missionaries for their superior tone in China, distancing itself from hard-line foreign policy, and championing nationalism all while chiding foreign governments for not embracing ecumenical Protestantism's universal values might appear inconsistent for the *Century*. So too might its chastened tone when rehashing the China debacle alongside its continued assertion of the mainline's own importance. Whether consistent or not, it was all part of a coherent package. Although more conservative Christians often doubted it, the moralist mainline did believe in a God who ordered the world. That order, whether accepted by everyone or not, was universal because it was God's. Protestants, according to their self-understanding, did not invent ideas such as religious liberty. They simply recognized the way God wanted the world to work. Thus, the moralist mainline believed that its presence in the world was integral to purportedly universal values such as democratic process and religious liberty, values written into international documents such as the Universal Declaration of Human Rights. It believed it could rightly use these values to criticize countries threatening the presence of missionaries and, hence, the presence of those people who would help shape a world hospitable to universal values and mainline presence. Owing to events in China, it recognized in communism a threat to its influence in the world. Yet, also owing to China, it came to believe that the best route to maintaining influence was not a hard-line attitude toward communist countries, as other Cold Warriors might assume, but attention to the just desires for independence and freedom around the world. Again, maintaining its influence was a crucial concern: Protestant beliefs undergirded the desire for independence, and continuing mainline presence could help direct those desires in noncommunist, non-hypernationalist directions.

The *Century*'s discussion about missionaries in the 1950s, then, conveyed a dual message: the world deserved freedom (from communism, from colonialism, and from paternalism), and ecumenical Protestantism was necessary to the proper understanding of that freedom. Within the confines of that message, *Century* writers were trying to figure out how their missionaries could represent the best of the American Protestant tradition, the one that was on the side of the world revolution. During the next decade, that conversation would appear in denominational venues. It would also shift as the continuing permutations of the Cold War increased criticisms of U.S. power, although not mainliners' conviction that they knew what the world needed.

The 1960s and 1970s:
Encouraging Laity to Join the Revolution

Denominational mission language in the Methodist Church caught up with the *Century*'s world revolution during the mid-1960s. In the early 1960s, denominational materials depicted traditional missionaries, white men and women serving abroad performing traditional missionary tasks involving teaching, agriculture, and medicine, as suited to the world's needs. By the early 1970s, missionary discussions demonstrated a conviction that serving the world demanded fighting against the various forms of oppression for which U.S. policy bore some culpability. This change was evident in Methodist study guides and magazines. It was also recorded on mission education filmstrips.

In the early 1960s, filmstrips were still affirming conventional North American missionaries. *Missionary to Chile*, a production of the Methodist Board of Missions, followed agricultural worker Stan Moore to his first assignment.[45] The film began by emphasizing that missionaries were Americans sent overseas. Early frames showed Stan looking out the plane window as the narrator said, "Stan Moore, watch the earth go by. Every minute, miles."[46] Once Stan arrived in Chile, he met other overseas workers. All, like Stan, were white men. Their various tasks were portrayed as answering Chile's needs. The English College at which some missionaries worked produced "eager students—a generation of Protestant Chileans, active in their nation and in their church."[47] The mission treasurer Stan met in Chile enumerated the problems facing the nation—poor standards of living, inflation, and the lure of communism. He named more workers as part of the solution: "We've got to expand our mission to South America. Chile can use all the missionaries our church in North America can send."[48] *Missions at Work*, a filmstrip produced by the Evangelical United Brethren, one of the denominations that joined the Methodist Church to form the United Methodist Church in 1968, ended with a picture of two young Latin American men in pressed shirts and neatly knotted ties carrying Bibles under their arms. The narrator explained, "These young men were led to Christ through the work of our missionaries. They received their education in our mission schools. They were called to be pastors in the midst of the fellowship of Christian believers. They were trained in a theological seminary in their own country. This is missions at work in Latin America."[49] Working through education and indigenous leaders, American missionaries alleviated social ills, staved off the danger of communism, and prepared national leaders to continue the project.

Mission Is . . . , a United Methodist 1971 filmstrip, revealed a different missionary discussion. Even the old style filmstrip had been abandoned. The film promised "an audiovisual experience that is unusual in its depth," an effect achieved by using two screens and two films with the same narration.[50] The message stressed what was new as well. The film began with the narrator reciting the most traditional of all missionary mandates, the so-called Great Commission of Matthew 28:19: "Go, therefore, and make disciples of all nations, baptizing them in the name of the Father, and the Son and of the Holy Spirit."[51] Black-and-white photos of missionaries from earlier in the twentieth century filled each screen as the narrator spoke. As one frame rested on a white male missionary and a Japanese man standing in front of a trailer with "God Loves Okinawa" painted on the side, the other showed a white female missionary surrounded by black women holding babies. The narrator conceded that "there was a romance and thrill about strange people in faraway places."[52] A few frames later, the narrator acknowledged that "it was possible even to meet someone who had been helped. All very personal—and very direct."[53] But, the narrator asserted, "mission is changing, missionaries are changing."[54] The "but" placed the Stan-like missionary in an irretrievable past and announced a new breed for the future.[55]

The new missionaries did not fit the conventional stereotype. As the narrator claimed, "Mission is changing, missionaries are changing," a black woman wearing a headscarf, a button down top and a white sweater appeared on one screen. Pictured only from the waist up, it was not clear whether she was an African missionary to the United States, an African American missionary abroad, or a laywoman. The other screen featured a young white man in a clerical collar leaning back in a chair with his legs casually crossed and a phone to his ear. Pictures marking his embrace of the new age—such as Martin Luther King Jr. preaching and a man playing the electric guitar—decorated his wall. His collar marked him as a cleric, though not a traditional overseas worker. Yet in the new world, both he and the woman were missionaries.

These new workers shouldered a new task: opposition to oppressive social structures. *Mission Is . . .* asserted that "the new experience of our time is the upsetting discovery that we who are deeply compassionate in personal relationships are responsible for systems that inflict cruelty on our brothers and sisters."[56] Serving the "whole man" as Stan had done was insufficient. Changing people was not enough. Because the new world was imprisoned in systemic problems, "mission is change of society and its structures, its institutions and its life styles."[57] Although the filmstrips only said it obliquely, remaining relevant in the world demanded combating unjust systems that stemmed, in part, from U.S. policy.

The 1960s witnessed a continued U.S. commitment to democracy and anticommunism. Theoretically, the two commitments coincided in a Wilsonianism for the Cold War era. Worldwide democracy would be good for other nations and for America. It would contain communism, which was an ideological enemy, a military threat, and an economic nuisance. American intervention in other nations was, by this formula, both realist and idealist—it served U.S. values (democracy) and U.S. interests (lowering the military threat and expanding markets). Yet theory did not cross national borders well. During the 1960s, America intervened in more or less overt ways in several countries, including the Congo, the Dominican Republic, and Vietnam. While democracy might have been a stated goal of such interventions, it became apparent that the United States would settle for noncommunist stability of the authoritarian kind. The United States supported right-wing autocrats and destabilized elected leftists in order to keep communists at bay.[58]

That mainline leaders were concerned about the direction of U.S. policy was clear from the *Century*. The *Century*, long accustomed to addressing national policy, continued to do so in the 1960s. In the early part of the decade, the *Century* suggested, as it had in the 1950s, that its version of Protestantism and U.S. policy were basically compatible. In 1960 the *Century* ran an editorial on the "National Purpose and Christian Mission." "And" was the operative word. A national purpose that could also be a Christian mission would "take the language of the Constitution and universalize it. It would state our national purpose as the commitment to work for a more perfect union of nations and peoples, to establish justice and domestic tranquility in the international community, to provide for defense of the whole against aggression by any part, to promote the general welfare of mankind and to secure the blessings of liberty for this and succeeding generations."[59] When the United States used its power in the service of democracy and economic development, the *Century* applauded. President Kennedy's Alliance for Progress, a multibillion dollar aid program to Latin America that sought economic and political reforms, was another example. A 1963 editorial excused what could appear as unwanted, demeaning intervention into Latin America by the behemoth to the north. There was a difference, the editors noted, between bad intervention (dollar diplomacy, the big stick, and marine landings) and honest, beneficial intervention. Demanding substantive evidence of "a radical restructuring of Latin American economies" was the latter.[60] When America exercised its power in the best interests of others, an interest the *Century* not incidentally believed it could discern, all was well.

As the 1960s wore on, the *Century* saw little evidence that the United States was acting in the best interests of others or in the interest of freedom. After Belgium granted the Congo independence in 1960, for example, the United States backed pro-Western, anticommunist politicians rather than reformist leaders such as the first prime minister, Patrice Lumumba. *Century* writers portrayed the United States as injuring the cause of freedom and reform. One article, "The Fire *This* Time," riffed on James Baldwin's recently published *The Fire Next Time*, itself borrowed from a spiritual celebrating God's intervention on behalf of the oppressed. In addition to the refrain affirming that "Pharaoh's army got drowned," one version of the song asserted that "God gave Moses the rainbow sign. No more water, the fire next time." Like Baldwin's book, the article put current events in the context of the West's long-standing racism. "The recent Congo conflagration reveals the truth of this proverb," author David Wiley wrote. "Recent Congolese history is a record of evil in the guise of well meant Christian-legitimated westernization."[61] In the Congo case, the fire seemed less God's apocalyptic judgment on the oppressors and more the result of the United States' stoking of tinderbox history. Wiley claimed that after the Congo's pro-Western leader Moise Tshombe engendered popular uprising for refusing to include "radical reformers" in his coalition government, "the U.S. state department then invested itself in a Vietnam-type solution—the use of force to put down any group opposing 'our man,' even if helicopters and guns could not eliminate reported 'fanatic popular support for the rebels,' even if there were a possibility that the rebels represented a legitimate protest, even if 'our man' tied us to a heritage of death and corruption."[62] Wiley suggested that the United States needed to abandon a policy premised on its Cold War worldview and work toward a "Great Society" in a land wracked by inequality and poverty.

America interventionism in Latin America did no better. After touting President Kennedy's Alliance for Progress for intervening for all the right reasons in all the right ways, the *Century* had little positive to report about its government's activities to the South. The Dominican Republic provided an unfortunate example. In the early 1960s, longtime dictator Rafael Trujillo was assassinated. In 1962 Dominicans elected a reformist politician, Juan Bosch, as president. Although Bosch should have been an American favorite—a democrat committed to the kind of reform advocated by Kennedy's Alliance for Progress—he did not prove to be a popular president or hard enough on communism for U.S. tastes. When a military coup felled him in 1964, the United States protested weakly and then recognized the junta. In 1965 Bosch led an insurrection against the junta that augured well. Fearful that Bosch's return might end in a communist takeover, the Johnson administration intervened militarily. The *Century* warned that "the United States still has the big stick and the will to use it, but it will pay heavily every time it takes unilateral action in the western hemisphere and consults its neighbors later"[63] and called the U.S. interventionist policy "hemispheric McCarthyism."[64] Time and again, the *Century* found that the U.S. language of democracy and reform rang hollow. Its actions, bolstering dictators and undercutting reformists in the name of national security and anticommunism, spoke louder than its freedom-loving words.[65]

Vietnam hung above all other foreign policy concerns. Starting in 1964, the *Century* called for a negotiated settlement in Vietnam and opposed a "stepped-up war."[66] In 1965 the *Century* editors joined with the editors of rival mainline publication, *Christianity and Crisis*, to urge the National Council of Churches to speak out on U.S. policy around the world, particularly in Vietnam. The editors advocated a distinct Christian responsibility on foreign policy: "An American branch of the universal Christian community acts on different assumptions and different priorities from those of the state department. The N.C.C. should help its member churches to ask questions and make decisions that may be neglected by the government."[67] The revelation of the 1968 My Lai massacre signaled, to the *Century*, the emptiness of American rhetoric about freedom and democracy abroad. Although the *Century* would not place absolute blame for the massacre on any one feature of American life, it did claim that the 1960s had shown the United States' capability for wanton inhumanity. "But a society which assassinates its prophets, which permits its unredeemed cities to fester until they erupt in rioting and burning, which leads the league of nations in the violent crime rate, whose media of information and amusement are glutted with violence, and whose very clamor for law and order is a vengeful expression of soulful violence can hardly be presumed incapable of committing atrocities wherever it massively intervenes in other societies," it editorialized.[68] My Lai had unveiled some of the country's true colors.[69]

So too did revelations of the Central Intelligence Agency's designs on missionaries. In 1968 the *Century* reported *Chicago Daily News* writer James K. Batten's assertion that the CIA "for years has made systemic use of some American missionaries." While the *Century* and Batten agreed that incidences were infrequent, the *Century* editors were "appalled" at a practice that turned "the Christian evangelist into an instrument of the political interests of a superstate."[70] The issue reappeared in the mid-1970s. In a striking change from the 1950s, the *Century* saw Protestant and Catholic missionaries, particularly mainline Protestants and progressive Catholics such as those affiliated with the Maryknoll movement, as co-belligerents against the CIA's policy of seeking information from missionaries. After CIA director George H. W. Bush thwarted passage of a bill criminalizing the CIA's use of clergy at home or abroad by instituting his own reforms, the *Century* expressed remaining fears: "Great shadowy stretches remain: we have no promises from the other nine components of the U.S. intelligence community; no pledge that CIA agents will stop posing in clerical garb; and certainly no assurance that the CIA is not undermining or 'neutralizing' prophetic clergy who are working against repressive regimes smartly trained, even armed, with covert U.S. aid."[71] Not only did both Protestant and Catholic missionaries bear the fallout from revelations of the CIA's covert activities in countries such as Chile, but they also bore the burden of being suspected—with reason—of CIA involvement. That the United States would put servants of God in such an untenable position on the behalf of covert foreign policies bespoke the depths to which the nation could sink.

Methodist mission materials were not as explicit in naming the failures of U.S. foreign policy. Rather than challenging U.S. policy, mission education literature in the late 1960s and 1970s articulated how American Christians could remain involved in a world in which their country had done so much harm. The CIA's use of missionaries aside (it made only brief appearances in lay-oriented media), most of the references to America's harm abroad were oblique, but the strategies all pointed toward remaining on the forefront of the world revolution and undoing the harm created by an American interventionism that benefited the economic and political status quo. According to the filmstrips, mainline missions needed to listen to the world. A 1965 Methodist filmstrip, *Mission Perspective*, asked viewers to respond to the statement, "The world sets the agenda for the church."[72] However laypeople watching the film might have responded, the filmstrip made clear that the church should allow the world to set its agenda. In the frame preceding the question, the narrator talked about the church's tardiness in dealing with the inner-city conditions that erupted in the Los Angeles riots of 1964. The frame following talked about the horrors of war, using Korea as its example. Likewise, *Mission Is . . .* pictured marchers carrying signs reading "If Not Now, When?" and "What the World Needs Now is Love" as the narrator intoned that mission is responding to "what the times demand."[73] Poverty, racism, and war were the messages the world was sending. Anyone who wanted to remain relevant in the world would need to respond.

According to the educational materials, those who listened to the world's needs would engage in new kinds of missionary tasks at new locations. *Mission Is . . .* , for example, claimed that investing funds in poor people's business enterprises, involvement in welfare rights organizations, and helping voiceless people gain access to media so they could speak for themselves all counted as mission. It also asserted that those who would be missionaries needed to see the mission field in broader terms than had previous generations. Places working for justice, whether they were distinctively Christian or at home or abroad, were mission sites. A window sign identifying an organization's commitment to "Self-Respect, Self-Determination, Self-Defense" exemplified what it meant "to consider the needs of the poor and give them a chance to participate in decision-making."[74] A hand-made sign identifying "Strike City MFLU Local #4" was what "community groups at home or overseas that are involved in changing conditions which oppress both themselves and others" looked like.[75] By working alongside the poor and the workers, people involved in missions would participate in the world revolution on the right side, albeit not the side the U.S. government seemed to favor.

Mission language also tried to move away from the notion of American leadership. The church did not act unilaterally abroad but cooperated with leaders in other countries. One frame in *Mission Is . . .* showed a white man and a black man looking at a field. They exemplified "offering help wherever it is asked for."[76] Which man was the missionary was unclear. When the filmstrip talked about educators as missionaries, the person pictured was a black man and might have been an African American missionary.[77] He might also have been a "person in mission"—a designation for nationals serving in their own country. The featured medical person wore a sari, not a white coat.[78] Missionaries were no longer only Americans. They were members of the worldwide church serving wherever there was a need.

Perhaps most telling, when the narrator said that "mission is preaching and teaching . . . telling about the Christian faith," both screens showed sculptures of Jesus, not people preaching and teaching.[79] The filmstrip further elucidated "preaching and teaching" as offering "ourselves—our souls and bodies, deed and words."[80] To picture "offering ourselves," the screens featured two sides of a conversation between a white man and a white woman. Neither stood in a pulpit, neither held a Bible, and neither was demonstrably in charge of the exchange. They were, indeed, offering themselves—not a word from on high. In the case of preaching and teaching, the film moved beyond showing new people doing the conventional work. Preaching and teaching were reconfigured, and it was not clear from the filmstrip that their practitioners needed specialized training. They certainly were not Americans going abroad to teach other people about the gospel.

Of course, Americans did still go abroad. Many of them looked much like Stan Moore: white missionaries doing conventional missionary work. Myers Park United Methodist Church in Charlotte, North Carolina, for example, supported the Hammonds, agricultural missionaries serving in Sudan, during the 1970s. A 1970 bulletin contained a statement from medical missionary James W. Alley. Notably, however, Alley used structural language in his comments about the recent Bolivian revolution: "I happened to suddenly realize, I guess, that regardless of what type of political structure that may come to Bolivia that the Church of Jesus Christ must witness in the midst of that structure and the Mission of Reconciliation will manifest itself."[81] Moreover, during the 1960s and 1970s, Myers Park offered denominationally approved mission studies such as "People and Systems." The message apparently took. In 1970 Pam Patton, a member of a short-term mission team to the Congo, told the Commission on Mission that "all of the team members gained a much broader perspective on the 'mission' of the church, not just 'missions.'"[82] Another team member reminded the commission that the Congolese Methodist church was autonomous and had its own bishop. Some laity, at least, had imbibed a language in which the American church was part of a worldwide movement, acted in concert with that movement, and saw itself as part of a larger world structure. It was part of an attempt to undo the negative effects of its own country's actions.

In literature intended for pastors and laity, then, missions had undergone a redefinition. As the texts redefined, they separated church work from the nation's work. While the nation claimed to bring freedom, it more often propagated systems of bondage. Church folk, missionaries included, were to work toward freedom for all, which could mean undoing the nation's work. Both the nation and the mainline used the language of freedom. Mainline texts claimed, however, that it better understood what the term entailed.

Yet not all laity—or, for the matter, all pastors and missionaries—accepted the changes to mission nor the emerging definition of freedom. Some conservative Methodists believed that the new understanding of mission, one ostensibly designed to make the denomination responsive to the world's desire for economic freedom, succeeded mainly in making the denomination a partisan for totalitarianism and unwilling to address the world's true needs: political freedom and Jesus. In the 1980s, conversations about missionaries became conversations about which group of mainline Christians best defined the freedom other peopled needed. It was a discussion about who knew what was best for the world.

Evangelical Missionaries under Threat

In 1967 a group of United Methodists began publishing *Good News: A Forum for Scriptural Christianity*. As the journal's name suggested, the group (also called Good News) was concerned that much of what passed for Christianity in its denomination was not scriptural. The journal's opening article declared itself a resource for the "many Methodists [who] remain true to Jesus Christ, the eternal Son of God . . . true to the Holy Scriptures as God's inspired and inspiring Word . . . and true to Methodism's timeless proclamation of Jesus Christ incarnate, crucified, risen, and coming again."[83] Over the next decades, *Good News* would chronicle denominational leaders' perceived infidelity to Jesus Christ and the scriptures. Tales of declining membership, unbiblical teaching, and leftward drift filled its pages. According to *Good News*, much was rotten in the state of the mainline.

While it criticized many denominational agencies and leaders, the General Board of Global Ministries, the agency responsible for mission, received consistent critique. To the editors of *Good News*, the GBGM's new definition of mission evinced a new but not improved understanding of salvation, an evidence of theological drift if ever there was one. As Good News folks saw it, the GBGM was in sinful bondage to liberation theology, a theological movement born in Latin America in the 1950s. By Good News' account, liberation theology equated salvation with liberation from oppressive economic and political structures. Asbury Seminary professor David A. Seamands explained to readers that the GBGM conceived of salvation as "a state of peace and prosperity for mankind . . . finally revealed in the world itself."[84] In the board's theology, he argued, "The Kingdom of God is practically identified with social change, and the world therefore determines the agenda for mission. What the world says of itself determines policy, not what the Word of God says about the world!"[85] Besides offering an unbiblical message of salvation, liberation theology had led to a decline in missionary personnel. The new message, *Good News* claimed, gave little impetus to send evangelists to preach the gospel and precluded people who believed the old-time message from serving.

By the 1980s, the criticisms had taken on a more political cast: liberation theology was Marxism with a Christian veneer—and the veneer was thin. In 1980 *Good News* published an article by liberation theology critic and Louisiana State University political science professor René de Visme Williamson, who claimed that "the connection between the Latin American theology of liberation and Marxism is obvious. Everything is to be interpreted in terms of the class struggle; revolution is inevitable; Lenin's theory of imperialism is accepted lock, stock, and barrel."[86]

Good News emphasized the locks, stocks, and barrels. Williamson's article came with artwork: a drawing of a cache of guns. Although the blurb introducing the article declared that the theology's "more extreme exponents consider violent revolution and terrorism as legitimate tactics in the struggle to bring about social change,"[87] Williamson himself did not limit the embrace of violence to "more extreme exponents" but declared baldly that "the liberationists hold that violence is necessary."[88] Its more nuanced blurb aside, *Good News* generally described the GBGM's embrace of liberation theology as an embrace of violent revolution. And it was not a theoretical embrace. One of *Good News* complaints about the GBGM centered on donations of mission dollars to "revolutionary" groups. In a controversial 1983 article, "Missions Derailed"—so controversial that GBGM officials responded in a subsequent volume—James S. Robb outlined several, to his mind, inappropriate contributions to groups such as the African National Congress (which Robb described as "an organization working for the violent overthrow of the South African government")[89] and the Ecumenical Program for Inter-American Communication Action, which Robb claimed had produced a book "extolling one aspect or another of the Marxist-Leninist government"[90] of Grenada. According to Robb, the GBGM not only extolled an unbiblical understanding of salvation but was funding the wrong side of the Cold War.

Robb did not confine his frustration with the denomination to the pages of *Good News*. By 1983 he was working at the Institute on Religion and Democracy (IRD), a new Washington think-tank aimed at exposing and countering mainline denominations' purported leftward bent. The institute had several geneses. It was part of Reagan-era neoconservatism, itself a diffuse movement but one largely characterized by a belief that human freedom was best supported by democracy, which in turn was most compatible with a market economy. Prominent neoconservatives such as Lutheran Richard John Neuhaus and Catholic political philosopher Michael Novak helped found the IRD. Yet internal Methodist conflicts played a catalyzing role. David Jessup, a United Methodist layman, began investigating denominational contributions to non–United Methodist groups in 1980. Jessup claimed his impulse came from seeing the materials his children received at the United Methodist Church the family had recently started to attend. Critics of the IRD claimed that Jessup had deep ties to other neoconservative movements and relatively weak ties to the United Methodist Church—he started attending in 1979—and that his investigations seemed part of a strategy rather than a spontaneous response to Sunday School curriculum. Whatever the case, he produced "the Jessup Report," a chronicle of contributions to groups that Jessup believed had Marxist connections. *Good News* published the report, and it was distributed to Methodist delegates before the 1980 UMC General Conference. Not content with publicizing his findings and discontent with the denomination's apparent refusal to change course, Jessup partnered with Ed Robb, Good News board member, Methodist evangelist, and James Robb's father, to found an organization that would monitor where the UMC sent money and to promote denominational support for what they considered democratic movements. Their portfolio came to include all mainline denominations and the IRD board included both Protestants and Catholics.[91]

Thus, by the early 1980s, Methodist frustrations had produced a new player on the political landscape. *Time* magazine reported on the IRD in 1982. In 1983 CBS's *60 Minutes* and *Reader's Digest* produced reports on the National Council of Churches' support for revolutionary movements abroad. Both used the IRD as a source for their exposés, much to the disgust of others within the mainline who accused the IRD of providing a religious rationale for Ronald Reagan's interventionist foreign policy or, as critic Jim Wallis purportedly said, being "the official seminary of the Reagan Administration."[92]

Within the house of Methodism, the launch of the IRD was not enough to address conservative concerns about declining numbers of missionary personnel, the GBGM's support of liberation theology, or the denomination's perceived lack of evangelistic fervor—hence, the creation of the Mission Society for United Methodists in 1984. After the society's launch, relationships among it, Good News, and the IRD continued. Ed and James Robb held positions in both groups. Diane Knippers, *Good News* associate editor in the early 1980s, joined the IRD in 1981 and served as its president from 1992 until her death in 2005. *Good News* articles detailing the denomination's misappropriation of money relied on IRD information. Finally, in 1989, the Good News Women's Task force, the Mission Society for United Methodists, and the IRD established the Evangelical Coalition for United Methodist Women (ECUMW).

Members of all three groups wrote for the ECUMW Network page, offering *Good News* readers a perspective on missions shaped by neoconservative perspectives.

Good News, the Mission Society, and the IRD were part of a larger realignment in post–World War II religion. The importance of denominationalism declined in the last half of the twentieth century as people increasingly defined themselves by markers such as liberal or conservative rather than by identities such as Lutheran or Methodist. These new labels, claimed sociologist Robert Wuthnow, often applied both politically and theologically and united people across denominational boundaries. The realignment also had an international dimension insofar as liberals and conservatives split on whether the United States should primarily consider itself one among many nations or should emphasize its particular role in God's work in the world.[93]

The latter issue mattered. Although conservatives contended that the United States had a particular role in God's work in the world, they refused to identify it with the Kingdom of God. As Wuthnow has pointed out, even leaders of the religious Right such as Jerry Falwell backed away from declaring the United States a second Israel. The IRD document *Christianity and Democracy* denied that the United States was "chosen."[94] The discussions around the Mission Society, Good News, and the IRD show how mainline conservatives made their case for a special role for the United States while denying that it imposed unwanted systems, political or religious, on people abroad.

The strategy was linking democracy, Christianity, and freedom, thereby making them seem natural companions. Edmund Robb made the connection in a letter criticizing the *Century*'s portrayal of the IRD: "Our argument, in summary, is that totalitarian systems are forms of idolatry in which the state or party becomes sacred and absolute, while the individual human soul becomes only an appurtenance. The essence of democracy—and of Christianity—is the recognition that human systems are limited and imperfect. It follows that happiness and progress are best achieved through pluralism, experimentation, open debate and free choice."[95] Taking seriously the shared insights of Christianity and democracy would lead to a system of limited government that would, in turn, ensure individual freedom (the opposite of the human soul being subordinate to a totalitarian state). As IRD critic Peter Steinfels pointed out, linking democracy with limited government suggested that "democracy" had only one definition— a U.S.-style form of constitutional government—although it was a long contested term.[96] The given definition, however, allowed the IRD to claim that "the United States of America is the primary bearer of the democratic possibility in the world today."[97] According to IRD logic, one that echoed mainline thinking from the 1950s, the United States was not chosen so much as it was fortunate to possess both the political system conducive to all human flourishing and the power to promote it.

The same intertwining occurred in the laity-directed *Good News*, but more subtly. The inclusion of articles that criticized totalitarianism, lauded evangelism, and assumed a worldwide church naturalized the relationship among democracy, Christianity, and individual freedom. The September–October 1990 issue of *Good News*, for example, contained an article celebrating the growing number of missionaries from the Third World. A page over, the ECUMW Network page contained reviews of denominationally endorsed mission study materials.[98] Each review was negative—the study materials attacked capitalism, advocated salvation as liberation from unjust systems, and championed Marxism. Without making the case overtly, the juxtaposition of the articles indicated that conservative Americans and people abroad propounded the same Christianity, one that was compatible with democracy and capitalism and was not compatible with Marxism. Just as Christianity crossed cultural and national borders, so too should the political and economic systems with which it cohered. Linking Christianity and democracy made it seem that believers abroad who supported the spread of the faith would naturally support the spread of the political and economic systems it purportedly underwrote. Readers could rest assured that spreading Christianity and democracy was not a nationalist imposition but a globally desired expansion of human freedoms.

This logic also portrayed missionaries and their supporters as active participants in the cause of democracy and freedom. Missionaries serving in hospitals and schools, for example, served the institutions of civil society, precisely the type of institutions that ensured governments would not control every aspect of human existence. When missionaries spread the gospel, they used the nontotalitarian societies' civil freedom to liberate people from their primary bondage, sin. Evangelizing also helped create the kind of freedom-loving and civic-minded people who would naturally support democracy and freedom. Missionary supporters also participated. Their prayers and funds furthered the spread of what they knew the world needed: the gospel, freedom, and democracy, America's best exports.

The GBGM and the Reaffirmation of
Missionaries for the Sake of the World

Not all mainliners were so certain that the world wanted what they had to offer. In 1985 the *Century* published a glowing review of John Hersey's novel, *The Call*. Hersey, himself the child of mainline missionaries in China, told the story of missionary to China David Treadup. It was a story of changed goals and decreased expectations. When he first went to China in 1908, Treadup adopted the American missionary movement's hopeful slogan "The Evangelization of the World in This Generation" as his own. As Treadup saw the poverty of the peasants, he changed focus, proclaiming "For Jesus's Sake, the Abolition of Poverty in This Generation." Taken as a prisoner of war during the Japanese occupation, and despondent about the end of his life's work, he sardonically proclaimed a new goal: "Modernize the Yin Hsien Camp in This Generation." Upon the missionary expulsion and his return to the States, he accepted a position teaching machine shop in a local public school. To "Motorize the Village of Thornhill in This Generation" is all he dared hope for.[99]

Things were not quite so glum at the *Century* or at the GBGM, but the pathos rang true. Mainline membership, after cresting in the late 1960s, had steadily declined. Between 1968 and 1988, for example, the United Methodist Church lost 2 million members.

Those members who remained were giving less as a percentage of their income than they had in the 1960s. At the same time, evangelical churches were growing and the political success of the religious Right publicly challenged the mainline's ability to offer *the* Christian position on public policy.

Conversations about missionaries bore the marks of the time. United Methodist officials made overtures to dissatisfied laity, emphasizing that the denomination too was interested in expanding the missionary force and in evangelization. In the January 1984 issue of *New World Outlook*, as all the signs pointed to the launch of the new mission society, GBGM staffer Donald Struchen offered answers to two questions "many persons ask": "How many missionaries do we have?" and "Are there openings available for missionary work?"[100] In his first answer, Struchen acknowledged that between 1971 and 1981 the number of missionaries declined by half and offered a justification: "That period also witnessed momentous changes in the concept of mission and the kinds of service which the church is able to offer worldwide."[101] That justification aside, his second answer indicated the GBGM's support for missionaries. He quoted Dr. Randolph Nugent, general secretary of the GBGM, as saying, "Frankly, I don't think there is a time when you have enough missionaries. How could one have enough missionaries? — There is always more work to be done."[102] A 1996 United Methodist missions video, *Whom Shall I Send?*, reclaimed the early twentieth-century missionaries cast aside by filmstrips such as *Mission Is . . . .* As the "old" missionaries played across the screen in *Whom Shall I Send?*, the narrator intoned, "These are the faces of dedication, missionaries who have heard God's call and who have answered, dedicating their lives to mission, at home and in distant places." As the on-screen images turned to modern missionaries — black, white, Asian, male and female, the narrator connected their service to the past: "Today God still calls and the United Methodist Church answers."[103] The featured missionaries had various racial and cultural backgrounds and engaged in diverse tasks such as seminary teaching, mechanics, and church planting. The missionaries spoke about "the good news" and social justice. *Whom Shall I Send?* did not, however, picture missionaries supporting liberation movements or advocating significant systemic change.

The realities of denominational life—the need to woo supporters, the competition created by another sending agency—had influenced the GBGM's missionary stance. Occasionally GBGM materials acknowledged the role internal disagreements played. A 1988 *New World Outlook* interview with GBGM official John Stumbo introduced a new mission evangelism program. During the interview, he admitted that "we have a constituency in the church that has been concerned that the Board was not being evangelistic enough."[104]

Yet Stumbo maintained that the real reason for the new program was sensitivity to the world. His nod toward disaffected Methodists notwithstanding, he averred that "it needs to be said that the Board came to its decision out of its own desire to be responsive to the needs of the world."[105] He explained that "we have repeatedly heard comment from the churches and the church leaders overseas that if they had resources and personnel, new work could be initiated in a lot of unchurched areas."[106] The article's subtitle, "New evangelism thrust comes out of a desire to be responsive to the needs of the world," reinforced the point.

United Methodist media also implicitly suggested that the denomination was more sensitive to the world's needs than its conservative dissenters. Articles affirmed the GBGM's breadth— its ability to hold together evangelism and social issues—and its willingness to send missionaries abroad who could best serve the world regardless of theological orientation. Sidebars to Peggy Billings's 1987 "Toward a New Missionary Age" featured an agricultural missionary married to a Tongan woman, a missionary-pilot who graduated from the purportedly conservative Asbury Theological Seminary, and a female missionary-pastor with a degree from the more liberal Drew Theological School.[107] This emphasis on the board's irenic attitude contrasted with Bishop F. Herbert Skeete's portrayal of board critics as "those who seek to forge and remold the Board according to their own particular and personal ideological preference or theological agenda."[108] The board knew what the world needed and responded accordingly. Its critics based their actions on predetermined agendas.

Still, for all of its assertion of continued relevance, the United Methodist Church had lowered its expectations about what it could do in the world. It was not aiming so low as motorizing small towns, certainly. Yet it was also not leading the American vanguard abroad or proclaiming its fight against the ill effects of U.S. policy. *Century* articles too evinced different expectations. While *Century* editors continued their pronouncements on matters foreign and domestic, they also ran articles arguing that mainline influence in U.S. politics had ebbed. Losing influence, however, was not synonymous with having no role in the world. One repeat contributor to the *Century* during the 1980s and 1990s was Lamin Sanneh, a native of Africa, a Muslim convert to Christianity, a missions specialist, and professor at Harvard and then Yale. Sanneh claimed that analyses of Christian missions needed rethinking. Rather than drowning in a "Western Guilt Complex," bewailing missionary complicity in colonialism and neo-imperialism, Sanneh called readers to consider missions as "a translation movement," one that preserved indigenous languages and affirmed indigenous cultures as worthy vehicles for the gospel. In Sanneh's logic, missionaries past and present performed useful functions. Spreading the gospel did spread freedom—freedom from claims that some cultures were simply backward or primitive, and freedom to challenge homogenizing, globalizing forces. Missionaries, notably, did not necessarily effect change, nor could they dictate how people abroad would use their freedom. They offered people abroad tools necessary to work toward freedom. It was a useful function, albeit a diminished one.[109]

Conclusion

By the end of the twentieth century, mainline Protestants writing for the *Century*, occupying denominational offices, and running conservative renewal movements agreed that people abroad needed freedom and that missionaries were compatible with freedom. They disagreed regarding the definition of freedom and, particularly in the Methodist case, used mission literature to make the case for their definition. The ongoing debate in publicly accessible literature reinforced the importance of freedom (be it freedom from U.S. hegemony, from poverty, or from sin) *and* implied that people in the mainline (although not those *other* people) knew what freedom people abroad needed. The conversation asserted mainline knowledge about what was good for others, even as those claiming knowledge competed with each other.

The continued assertion of epistemic privilege subtly promoted the continued world responsibility of Protestant mainliners. Even as some mainline groups protested U.S. policy, and even as liberals and conservatives alike affirmed that Americans should not simply impose their ways on the rest of the world, the rhetoric surrounding missionaries echoed the country's Wilsonian logic. If America was not necessarily called to lead, the rhetoric (sometimes in spite of its explicit message) suggested that some Americans might be.

Obviously, many within the mainline did not want to echo their country's logic. In many cases, they did so, not because they agreed with it, but because denominational battles prodded them to assert their superior knowledge about what was good for the world or because theology seemed to demand it. Whether writing in the *Century* or working at Good News, mainline Protestants started with the presupposition that being involved in the church meant being involved in a worldwide church. The kingdom of God crossed borders. They could not retreat from the world (though some might occasionally retrench). Thus, they had to discern how they were supposed to be involved in the world. People throughout the mainline wanted to be on the right side of history and the correct side of the gospel. They championed for others the kind of freedom they believed God intended. But in literature disseminated to the public, theological discernment could sound a lot like the affirmation that some Americans knew best.

chapter two

EVANGELICALS
❊ ❊ ❊

In September 1945 the Free Methodist *Missionary Tidings* featured a poem, "The Converted Heathen Speaks." The author adopted the voice of a convert:

Out of the Stygian darkness
Of heathendom, brutish and base,
Out of the black superstition
That curses and crushes our race . . .
We have been lifted and pardoned
In answer to somebody's prayer.

Petition, according to the convert, empowered those "bringing the 'Light into the Darkness' / To souls who were sunk in despair."[1] Reports in that and subsequent issues reiterated the theme in prose. Missionaries stood in stark white contrast to woeful black superstition.

In 1989 a congregation of Free Methodists heard that they should no longer divide the world between Stygian darkness and American light. That year, longtime missionary to the Philippines Bob Cranston preached a Sunday sermon at Seattle's First Free Methodist Church. His sermon recounted the transfer of church leadership from missionaries to nationals. He assured the congregation that the transfer was no cause for concern. "Missionaries will come and go, and they will build houses and they will build churches and the missionaries will disappear," he said. "But it is wonderful to know that through the power of the Holy Spirit, the church will continue to march forward. His truth will be marching on as we give trust and confidence to the church around the world today." To those who worried that Christians abroad would stray from the gospel, Cranston responded "You don't have to worry about your doctrines and your standards and your traditions overseas. It will carry on through the power of the Holy Spirit." Indeed, if anyone should evoke doubt, it was not the church abroad. "I am not so worried about the church overseas as I am about the church in America," he remarked. Christians in the United States needed to shift their critical gaze from national leaders abroad to their own souls at home. "The question this morning, really, is not whether we can trust the Holy Spirit to work through [Filipino leaders]. Will we trust the Holy Spirit to work through our lives, my life?"[2]

The shift from "The Converted Heathen" to Bob Cranston reveals significant changes, as well as subtle continuities, in Free Methodist portrayals of the relationship between missionaries and people abroad. By the time Cranston took the pulpit at First Church, the image of missionaries as assured leaders and people abroad as needy recipients had changed. Missionaries, in Cranston's telling, needed to acknowledge capable national leadership. The same Spirit that empowered American evangelists also spoke to national pastors. The once firm lines between leaders and the led had dissolved. Yet beneath this picture lay a continuing affirmation of American Christianity's normativity. Fidelity to *your* doctrines, standards, and traditions, Cranston assured his audience, measured the health of Christianity abroad. People elsewhere deserved autonomy and support because they had demonstrated their faithfulness to what American Free Methodists understood as the true gospel.

Free Methodists were not alone in propagating this message. *Christianity Today*, the magazine of the postwar evangelical establishment, also responded to a changing world by increasingly emphasizing other believers' autonomy and capability while subtly reaffirming that American evangelicals were the arbiters of what counted as truly Christian. Multiple factors led to the change from Stygian darkness to trusted Christian. The rise of nationalism and the growth of indigenous churches were significant factors. Like people in the Protestant mainline, American evangelicals had conversations about missions and about their message that were affected by "the revolutionary world" and the critiques emerging from Christians abroad.

Thus, evangelical reflections on missionaries were part of a larger postwar story. They occurred in the context of rising nationalism, Cold War fears, and a growing global church. Moreover, evangelical assessments of missionaries added a wrinkle in the commonly told narrative about American evangelicals and the Cold War. Evangelicals are often depicted as Cold Warriors of the first order—and for good reason. Particularly in the 1950s and the 1960s, they embraced the United States' struggle against godless communism. White evangelicals remained supportive of the Vietnam War longer than the nation as a whole. The rise of the religious Right in the 1970s and its alliance with conservative and militantly anticommunist politicians such as Ronald Reagan further demonstrated the evangelical acceptance of Cold War ideology and American exceptionalism.[3]

Yet, without denying theological conservatives' affinity with Cold War rhetoric, conversations about missionaries among evangelicals in their flagship magazine as well as in a small denomination such as the Free Methodist Church demonstrated a more complicated rhetoric of engagement with the world in the last half of the twentieth century. While *Christianity Today* in the 1950s and 1960s encouraged readers to rally around the flag during the heights of the Cold War, the magazine and denominational materials increasingly recognized nationalist aspirations as legitimate. In later decades, with the decline of Cold War fear, discussions about missionaries grew even more critical of the conflation of the gospel and American culture and more concerned about how to act appropriately in places wary of Western power. In *Christianity Today* and denominational literature, these discussions granted authority to people abroad. As authority was granted, however, it was also retained. Whether in the pages of *Christianity Today* or in a Sunday morning sermon, American evangelicals were reassured that their form of Christianity, albeit a form of Christianity somewhat influenced by people abroad, was normative.

Significantly, the affirmation of American evangelicalism's normativity had more to do with a firm conviction that the Christian gospel had a static essence than it did with the belief that the United States was exceptional. The logic sounded Wilsonian, but the loyalties were not unequivocally American. Still, the structure and content of the public discussions about missionaries reinforced the authority of Americans. Christians abroad deserved freedom, but American Christians decided if they were using that freedom faithfully.

Postwar Missions, the Cold War, and a Case for American Exceptionalism

In 1943, Harold Ockenga gave his presidential address to the newly formed National Association of Evangelicals (NAE). His speech offered hope for the postwar world as well as a clear challenge to his fellow theological conservatives. "American not only will survive this war, but will emerge chastened, serious as to government, religion and morals and ready for an advance under the proper type of leadership," he claimed. That the assembled multitude represented the "proper type of leadership" was undeniable. The NAE, Ockenga explained, "is the only hopeful sign on the horizon of Christian history today. If we who are gathered here meet our responsibility this week it may well be that the oblique rays of the sun are not the rusty red of its setting but are the golden rays of its rising for a new era."[4] The dawn demanded a renewed commitment to evangelical leadership and action.

When World War II ended, the Protestant mainline was not alone in understanding itself as responsible for the world. Another group of Protestants, largely quiescent since the 1920s, had decided to reengage American culture and use what appeared to be a postwar era of American-led peace to spread its message abroad. Calling themselves neo-evangelicals, these conservative Protestants came from various theological streams. Within the new movement, the Reformed proved the most influential. Theological children of the 1920s fundamentalist-modernist controversy, they rejected the separatism that had characterized conservative Protestantism during the 1930s. Other conservative Protestants joined them, including Wesleyan-Holiness groups such as the Free Methodists. Although these groups disagreed over some theological issues, such as predestination and free will, and had participated in varying degrees in the fundamentalist-modernist conflicts, they shared enough to warrant making common cause: a high view of scripture, a focus on personal salvation through faith in Jesus Christ, a commitment to missions, and an aversion to mainline Protestantism. Together they created the National Association of Evangelicals, supported new organizations such as World Vision and InterVarsity Christian Fellowship, and, starting in the 1950s, subscribed to *Christianity Today*, evangelicalism's answer to the *Christian Century*. Through all these activities, they intended to do what they believed neither mainliners nor fundamentalists could: engage the culture while remaining faithful to the timeless gospel.[5]

The end of World War II and the American-led peace seemed to offer a golden opportunity for evangelical missions. Neither evangelicals nor fundamentalists had lost their commitment to missions in the years following the 1925 Scopes Trial. Depression and war, however, had impeded mission work. The war's end meant that money and energy could be redirected to evangelism abroad. It also provided a new generation of missionaries: young men, trained during World War II to fly airplanes and use radios, who could now take their technological know-how and, in some cases, their GI Bill–funded educations to advance the Kingdom of God abroad. As Ockenga had indicted to the NAE, evangelicals had set their sights on leadership in both the nation and the world.

In the years immediately following World War II, missionary literature offered a confident assessment of the relationship between American evangelists and people abroad. The Free Methodist *Missionary Tidings* averred that people abroad needed both the gospel and American leadership. The poem about Stygian darkness was part and parcel of a confident rhetoric. In a report about her work in Africa, Free Methodist missionary Hazel Adamson noted that evangelists abroad spread the gospel, "the one and only power which is able to change the African and free him from the bondage of centuries of sin and ignorance."[6] Missionary work appeared as an unequivocal good. Adamson, for example, told the story of Daniel, an African Christian. He had been hired as "house boy" at the mission. He converted, attended school, and became an evangelist. When he preached, "we cannot help but thank God for him. He is neat and clean even though his clothes are mended and his feet are bare. As he speaks the people listen attentively and we feel the presence of the Holy Spirit in our midst."[7] Adamson's language was also indicative of a rhetoric that could depict any culture as needy but tended to describe Africans as needier than others. Yet even cultures acknowledged as more civilized needed American leadership. Lora M. Jones translated a letter from Chinese Christians and sent it to the magazine: "Our immature but growing society needs the advice and guidance of God's workers," they wrote.[8] Both members of the self-proclaimed "immature" church in China and an African evangelist learning the importance of soap and the Holy Spirit depended on American guidance. The missionary, in turn, could present converts to home supporters, translate for them, and offer interpretations of them. The missionaries, however, did not need input or criticism from their converts.

The clear distinction between leaders (Americans) and the needy (those to whom Americans went) echoed evangelical confidence in their ability rightly to divide the world. Apart from the leader-needy divide, the cleavage between godless communists and God-fearing democrats proved fundamental. As Cold War anxiety swept the nation, evangelical Protestants rallied against the great red menace and under the banner of the American flag. Indeed, the Cold War helped evangelicals as they reasserted themselves as political players. By painting the battle between the United States and the USSR as combat between belief and atheism, conservative leaders named stakes that their country could not afford to lose—a message welcomed by political leaders who wanted support for a strong military and an uncompromising stance on issues such as the recognition of mainland China.[9] Moreover, evangelical millennial rhetoric, which had long predicted the end of the world, gained public credibility in the shadow of the bomb. Once largely viewed as hysterical, if not simply ignored, predictions of imminent destruction sounded more reasonable and became part of political rhetoric. While, as historian William Inboden notes, evangelicals (like mainliners) "failed to exercise a significant or determinative influence on the actual formation of American foreign policy," by the end of the 1950s, evangelicals could claim a place in the mainstream.[10] They took their responsibility to warn the world about the imminent threat. Evangelist Billy Graham, for example, lambasted Marxism in his 1950s revivals: "Either communism must die or Christianity must die."[11] The postwar world was a dualistic world, and evangelicals did not believe that a world divided against itself could long stand.

Although Graham named Christianity and communism as the ideological combatants, neither boasted an army. Articles in the newly formed *Christianity Today* suggested that supporting Christianity in the struggle meant supporting the United States. In the 1950s and early 1960s, the magazine published articles by politicians who contended that containing communism demanded a strong offense as well as a strong defense. Neither compromise nor calls for peace would move godless communists. A series of articles in the 13 April 1959 edition of *Christianity Today*, for example, rejected the mainline National Council of Churches' recommendation that the United States recognize mainland China. The writers, who included Walter R. S. Robertson, assistant secretary of state for Far Eastern affairs (writing, a note informed the reader, in the stead of the recently ill and admittedly busy secretary of state), and retired Lieutenant General William K. Harrison, who had served as senior UN delegate at Panmunjom and was chief of staff of the Far East Command during the Korean War, championed a strong military on strategic and theological grounds. Harrison decried the notion that humans could achieve peace. "The fact of the matter is there never has been a human way of gaining and maintaining peace," he averred. "God has given [sinful humanity] up to those moral evils which cause war among men."[12] An editorial in the same volume criticized those in the mainline that elevated any ethic, such as "peace" or the "elimination of poverty" above justice. The editors worried that "the restriction of war, the promotion of peace, is then unwittingly pursued to the advantage of unjust nations and to the disadvantage of decent nations. Unless justice is honored as the primary social concern, peace and plenty become canopies beneath which perverse powers promote their evil ends."[13] American military power, the magazine of evangelical conviction announced, was politically and theologically necessary.

So too was evangelism. The battle, after all, was not only against flesh and blood. In 1962 *Christianity Today* published an excerpt from Canadian prime minister John G. Diefenbaker's remarks to the Baptist Federation of Canada. Diefenbaker claimed that "the missionary zeal of individual Christians is the hope there is for the bringing about of a better world in time to stem the tide of that other world force which is the very opposite of everything that is Christian—the ominous and ever-threatening tide of materialism, whose political arm is International Communism."[14] The idea that equipping people spiritually would inoculate them against communist blandishments and lead them toward the paths of truth and democracy recurred. In the same issue, Methodist Bishop Gerald Kennedy claimed that the "uncommitted people," or those not yet aligned with the West or the East, primarily sought "recognition as free nations and free persons." While he acknowledged that they wanted "a better economic life for themselves and their families," they most fundamentally "are breathing the heady air of liberty."[15] Communism promised freedom through substituting one class for another. The promise, Kennedy claimed, was hollow because it merely substituted one tyrant for another. True freedom was based on the "democratic doctrine that no man is good enough to be trusted with unchecked power over another." Only that doctrine, moreover, would "ever establish a free society." The Christian gospel provided the basis for the democratic doctrine through its teaching that "all men are sinners, as the Bible makes clear, and all men are the victims of a lust for power."[16] Spreading the biblical message would show the communist vision for the illusion it was while preparing people for the (Western-style) freedom they really, if unknowingly, desired.

Strident language about communism continued in *Christianity Today* well into the 1960s, although the apocalyptic rhetoric toned down, as it did in the country as a whole. The Cold War culture of the 1950s—one marked by McCarthy, morally dualist rhetoric, and red-baiting—lost its fervor in the 1960s. People could stay on high alert only so long.[17] Yet concerns about Marxism, a tendency to marry American patriotism and anticommunism, and support for military power remained, particularly in *Christianity Today*. Editorially, the magazine supported the Vietnam War because, as David Settje has argued, the editors viewed the war as anticommunist rather than as interference in a civil war, the position taken by the *Century*.[18] In 1967 a roundtable discussion moderated by editor Carl F. H. Henry showed continuing concern about communism, *sans* predictions of world destruction, as well as the persistent belief that Western civilization, although not necessarily the present Western nations, boasted values such as law and individual dignity that offered the best foundation for every society.[19]

Yet the participants in Henry's forum also rejected "a one-and-one identification between the Western powers and Christianity."[20] Such admissions did not mitigate their anticommunism. They did, however, indicate that simple bifurcations no longer encapsulated evangelical views of the world. A more nuanced discussion of the relationship between Christianity and the United States was afoot.

Critique, Challenge, and the Limits of Evangelical Dissent in the 1950s and 1960s

In 1966 a small storm broke out in the pages of *Christianity Today*. The storm revolved an unlikely eye: evangelical missionary icon Elisabeth Howard Elliot. The daughter of a prominent fundamentalist family, her father had been editor of the nationally distributed *Sunday School Times*. After receiving her degree from Wheaton College, which many evangelicals considered their answer to Harvard, the unmarried Elisabeth went to Ecuador as a missionary. While there, she married fellow Wheaton alum Jim

Elliot, who, in 1954, was killed while trying to contact the Huaorani Indians. After her husband's death, Elliot published *Through the Gates of Splendor*, a hagiographical account of her husband's life and evangelistic work. She later returned to Ecuador with her young daughter to live and work among the Huaorani.[21]

Elliot seemed an unlikely person to challenge the missionary enterprise but some evangelicals worried that her first—and only—novel had done precisely that. *No Graven Image* recounted the story of a young, unmarried female missionary, Margaret Sparhawk, who went to Ecuador—as had a young, unmarried Elisabeth Howard before her marriage to Jim Elliot.[22] Sparhawk's striking failures as a missionary, including killing her one convert when he reacted to penicillin she administered, raised significant questions about the enterprise's tactics as well as the evangelical assumption that people knew God's will and that will demanded mission efforts. While a *New York Times* reviewer lauded Elliot for refusing easy answers to questions about Christian "motives, mission and modus vivendi" and, indeed, for offering "no answers at all,"[23] *Christianity Today* editor Harold Lindsell expressed a "haunting doubt" about Elliot's continued acceptance of evangelical certainties.[24] Lindsell's review prompted a Zondervan Publishing House vice president (not the book's publisher) to write a letter to the editor chastising Lindsell for deserting his role as a literary reviewer for the "less noble role" of judging "the personal, spiritual life of the author."[25] Elliot's brother, Thomas Howard, also wrote a letter noting that the "novel has begun to arouse a certain amount of confusion in the weeks since it appeared, and the flurry is turning into what amounts to an inquisition against Mrs. Elliot." Howard lamented that the inquisitors failed to understand "the nature of fiction" and "the nature of Christian faith," both of which he believed his sister comprehended quite well.[26]

The storm blew over, and Elisabeth Elliot remained a fixture in the evangelical universe. The small controversy, however, offered a synecdoche for evangelical reflections about missionaries during the 1950s and 1960s. From the books housed in a Free Methodist Church library to the pages of *Christianity Today*, people discussing missionaries in publicly accessible texts differentiated among what was open to critique (how American evangelicals had interacted with people abroad), what new realities evangelicals needed to confront (the changes in a postcolonial, nationalist world), and what could never change (an absolute commitment to the task of spreading the gospel abroad). In other words, it indicated what was up for grabs and what, most emphatically, was not.

During the late 1950s and the 1960s, evangelicals' participation in a Cold War consensus that confidently bifurcated the world did not fully account for their thinking about interactions with people abroad. Open hostility to communism did not prevent evangelicals from recognizing changes in the world and from encouraging appropriate responses to it—particularly on the part of their missionaries. The Free Methodist Women's Missionary Society (WMS) study theme for 1955, for example, was "The Christian Mission in a Revolutionary World," and its recommended reading was Floyd Shacklock's *This Revolutionary Faith*.[27] "Mankind is on the March," Shacklock told readers. "But really it is on the run."[28] The worldwide sprint toward a new order had accelerated after World War II. Shacklock highlighted new nations in the Middle East, the independence of India, and increasing nationalism in Africa as evidence. Shacklock also offered an admonition: "Christianity, if it proclaims its gospel in this century, must preach to peoples and nations that are on the march."[29]

Others echoed his message. In 1957 former WMS president Ella Maze Daniels told readers that the new world demanded missionaries with "a quality of adaptability never before needed."[30] They had to be eager to train nationals for leadership, be able to distinguish between the gospel and American customs, and be free of racial prejudice. John Morrison, writing in the newly launched *Christianity Today*, argued that overseas workers needed to give nationals the same kind of power in the church that they were seeking in government. Missionaries could not simply go about business as usual. Although their message of salvation had not changed, their task subtly had. Their job now required adapting to new, valid aspirations.[31]

Books commended to evangelicals argued that adapting to new aspirations entailed listening to the aspirants. Between 1964 and

1966, twenty-one First Church attendees—including the senior pastor—checked out either Ralph E. Dodge's *The Unpopular Missionary* or James A. Scherer's *Missionary, Go Home*.[32] *Christianity Today* published positive reviews of both books. The authors belonged to mainline denominations, but their books warranted evangelical attention because they affirmed the missionary movement and explained how the movement could survive the world revolution. Like evangelical authors, they counseled missionaries (and their supporters) to abandon their imperialistic attitudes, complicity with colonialism, refusal to relinquish power, and racial prejudice. They also claimed that Americans needed to abandon their position as privileged interpreters of their own missions. Dodge began his first chapter, "Colonialism," with complaints from "African youth." Those committed to the enterprise, he asserted, must attend to typical accusations, such as "Christian missionaries accommodated themselves to the psychology of the colonizers." He warned readers that, "harsh as they may be, the criticisms are made in the interest of the church. . . . Unless they are listened to, unless they are taken seriously, unless changes are made, those now making criticisms from the 'inside' will join the ranks of those 'outside'—who seek not to reform the church, but to destroy it."[33] Missionaries and their supporters had to heed other voices, admit their missteps, and learn how to work in a world where Western power and those associated with it stood under suspicion.

Christianity Today's reviews of the books acknowledged that the perception abroad that missionaries had been on the wrong side of national aspirations was grounded in reality. For those who did not read the book, reviewer P. C. Moore summarized *Missionary, Go Home*'s plot: "Scherer traces the history of missionary vices from the imperialistic mass conversions of early Christianized pagan rulers to the use of colonialism as a protective cloak for the reproduction of Western denominationalism, clericalism, and institutionalism on heathen soil."[34] H. Cornell Goerner's review of Dodge's book was likewise complimentary. Though Goerner felt that Dodge underestimated missionary popularity outside of southern Africa, he praised the "clear-eyed realism" with which

Dodge "confesses for the Church that its missionary representatives have sometimes reflected imperfect attitudes of their own cultural background and have not always been the champions of change."[35] Evangelical opinion makers recommended heeding the voices of critics at home and abroad, acknowledging the problems of Western power, and recognizing their complicity with it.

People inside the evangelical fold also redressed the conflation of the American way of life and the Christian message. Racism was a case in point. Ross Coggins, an executive in the Southern Baptist Convention, amplified Ella Maze Daniels's warning against racial prejudice. In a 1964 article, he noted that all too often missionaries went abroad with a "race problem." They then exposed their "latent prejudice" in ways that combined racism and feelings of cultural superiority: "By an imperious tone, by the tendency to pauperize nationals through a readiness to give and a reluctance to receive in return, by obvious resentment at working under national supervision, by the habitual choice of white people for social championship, by a disregard of opinions of nationals, and particularly by the God-is-an-American-and-his-skin-is-white-like-mine attitude."[36] Coggins also criticized racial segregation in the United States. Africans particularly had little use for a gospel preached by citizens of a society in which black people and white people did not sit at lunch counters together. For Coggins, the solution was clear. Some parts of the American way of life had to disappear: "I am not suggesting that we should lightly cast aside our national traditions; I am suggesting that we throw them aside with great force whenever they violate the spirit and teaching of the New Testament."[37]

While discussions about missionaries in *Christianity Today* and among Free Methodists during the 1960s emphasized repenting of colonialist attitudes and attending to the revolutionary world, they did not speak uniformly regarding what remade relationships would look like on the ground. In 1962 the Free Methodist Church established the World Free Methodist Fellowship. The fellowship provided a place for church leaders from autonomous national churches to meet and plan. Although the World Fellowship was not a missionary venture per se, it bore implications for overseas workers because recognizing national churches on an equal basis altered the position of Americans serving abroad. First Free Methodist Church pastor Robert M. Fine, in explaining the fellowship to his congregants in a newsletter, connected the fellowship and the changing world. "The Free Methodist World Fellowship is a unique organization born out of the vision of the world's tempo and also out of an awareness of the mature status of the church abroad."[38] Byron Lamson, the missionary secretary, explained his vision in a Women's Missionary Society recommended book, *To Catch the Tide*: "This [fellowship] means that missionaries will go to these [overseas] fields upon invitation of the mission churches, and will take appointment under the mission conference, work as partners and servants of the church. . . . The missionary will work in and through the national church."[39]

As Fine and Lamson were unveiling the new arrangement to Free Methodists, however, several *Christianity Today* writers were explaining why missionaries should *not* serve under the authority of national churches. Many evangelical missionaries served under the auspices of nondenominational agencies, not denominations. These organizations did not exist to spread a denominational structure that could then call American missionaries to service. They existed to focus on evangelism. *Christianity Today* contributor David B. Woodward argued, for example, that missionaries maintained a separate calling—reaching the lost—most effectively performed under the aegis of agencies committed to that one task. People such as Woodward claimed that they were not perpetuating colonialism or cultural superiority. They wanted American evangelists to remain independent from national churches, true. Their motivation sprang, however, from a sense of how ecclesial bodies functioned. With limited resources and many demands, churches had to make choices. Woodward wanted to make certain that evangelism never competed for money or workers. Evangelists working for organizations with only one task would not be downsized in favor of new pews or choir robes.[40]

Although they posited different visions for mission structures, Fine, Lamson, and Woodward claimed to be attentive to the revolutionary world, and they reinforced the primacy of evangelism.

Whether explaining why they were making changes to mission structures or why they were not, the writers acknowledged, at least implicitly, problems with past missionary structures. Fine noted the "world's tempo" as one reason for the new structure. Woodward had to explain how maintaining separate mission organizations, specifically organizations that kept missionaries accountable to Americans, not nationals, did not perpetuate the colonialist relationships of the past. But concern about the colonial past was always subordinate to concern about evangelism's future. Fine and Lamson did not, finally, justify the World Free Methodist Fellowship on the basis of its rebuttal to colonialism. They did so on the basis of its evangelistic upside. According to Lamson, with missionaries as extra hands to help, the national church could concentrate on spreading the gospel. Fine explained to his congregants that the new fellowship "provides a way by which the General Conferences in the world may through a constitutional council check upon themselves to see that the basic principles of Free Methodism are maintained."[41] In other words, the fellowship would contribute to doctrinal rigor. Although arguing a different position, Woodward too invoked evangelic efficacy as the ultimate criteria for any mission structure.

The discussion around missionary alleviation of social ills further entrenched the priority of evangelism. It also limited national critique. Several *Christianity Today* articles in the 1960s were reactions to a perceived mainline trend: the shift from direct evangelization centered on the death and resurrection of Jesus to a focus on systemic injustice and, according to one *Christianity Today* writer, farming. In August 1960 *Christianity Today* writer Sherwood Eliot Wirt surveyed "The World Mission Situation" and discovered two incongruous facts. First, the world population, particularly the non-Christian population, was exploding. Second, many Christians were abandoning the traditional call to foreign missions. Rather than saving the rapidly growing number of sinners, they were undertaking an "agonizing reappraisal to redefine 'mission' either as inter-church aid or as just about everything a church does through its total program."[42] The world situation had deteriorated to the point where "today the overseas 'heroes' are not those who strive first and foremost to bring nationals into the Kingdom of Christ's love, but social workers who teach contour farming." Wirt continued pointedly: "Not that contour farming is undesirable. But the Church of Christ seems not to have discovered a divine mandate for it until our century."[43] God commanded missionaries to harvest souls, not alfalfa.

Wirt notwithstanding, evangelicals did participate in service ministries abroad. Missionaries often built schools and hospitals as part of their work. On 14 March 1965, First Church bulletins carried a message from the general missionary secretary, Charles Kirkpatrick. He asserted that "no one can read the record of Christ's life without realizing that He identified Himself with the poor, hungry, and the sick."[44] Yet what preceded this comment was instructive. Kirkpatrick first reminded his readers that "in the teachings of Christ primary concern is given to the spiritual needs of man."[45] Kirkpatrick argued that Free Methodist work overseas could encompass the spiritual and the physical (a task easier, needless to say, if churchgoers gave generously), but he differentiated between spiritual and physical needs. Souls and bodies were related yet separable.

Although this separation did not deter evangelicals from teaching math and giving shots, the evangelical insistence on the priority of souls constrained responses to Western power. In conversations about missionaries, evangelicals could, and did, critique their complicity in colonial systems and they could, and did, repent of their own paternalistic ways. Yet a strong conviction that losing focus on direct evangelism in order to combat social injustice would constitute infidelity to their gospel limited what denominational officials or *Christianity Today* writers argued missionaries could do faithfully in countries beset by significant systemic problems. When answering the question "What Is the Missionary Message?," for example, American Baptist missionary Willard A. Scofield asserted in *Christianity Today*, "We should also gladly acknowledge that the Christian has a responsibility to bear witness to his faith as it relates to the great social issues of the day."[46] The "also" was important. Scofield began his article by criticizing a missionary training program he had attended at Drew

University—a training, as he saw it, in the mainline mode. Over and against speakers who contended that missionaries should identify where Jesus was already at work in non-Christian cultures and who asserted that Christ was active in secular movements to alleviate poverty and prejudice, Scofield claimed "the New Testament stresses that the missionary proclaims the good news of the Gospel and calls upon his hearers to repent and to accept Christ as Saviour and Lord." While such a confession transforms all of life, "there is surely a difference between this and the philosophy of missions that has the missionary concerned primarily about showing people how Christ is already at work in movements for social betterment."[47]

Scofield's piece reflected a typical 1960s stance. Proclaiming the good news could have social implications, but the gospel was not focused on addressing systemic injustice and entrenched Western power. Evangelical missionary texts commended service when it was personal or local, focused on immediate need rather than structural ill. As one editorial explained, "Teaching men how to raise their standards of living and how to develop technologically is neither an imperative nor a primary task of the Church. But caring for the hungry and the cold is no matter of choice or deliberation."[48] Where they redressed problems of colonialism, both *Christianity Today* and the Free Methodists focused on missionary attitudes and organizational structures. In their public conversations about missionaries, they acknowledged larger problems, problems associated with global systems from which their own country benefited, but their gospel commitment did not demand challenging these problems as mainline literature increasingly did. The conversation established that winning souls, the primary goal, demanded evangelical self-criticism but not criticism of their nation.

No Graven Image hit bookstores amid these evangelical reconsiderations and reaffirmations. It was not the first surprising publication from Elliot. In 1962, after spending several years living among the Huaorani people after her husband's death, she published *The Savage My Kinsman*. The largely pictorial piece foreshadowed themes in *No Graven Image*, such as the inadequacy of evangelical distinctions between "needy" heathens and "saved" Christians. As historian Kathryn Long has argued, the book recast the Huaorani image. No longer the savage "Auca" of 1954, they were smiling, laughing people, living in an Edenic paradise. Elliot's young daughter and a Huaorani were photographed naked and apparently unashamed, albeit also from behind. For those with eyes to see, the book undermined simple divisions between the saved and damned, the civilized and the uncivilized.[49]

No Graven Image went deeper and further. Throughout the book, Elliot questioned evangelical mores and beliefs. The book's protagonist, Margaret Sparhawk, was a single female missionary. That, in itself, was an apt reflection of the mission force. Almost since the time single women were allowed to go to the mission field alone, women had constituted well over half of evangelists abroad. Many of those women were single.[50] Yet Sparhawk's astute observations unmasked gender politics on the field. While at a conference with other missionaries, Sparhawk found herself uncomfortable with her male colleagues' easy confidence. As her male colleagues spoke, she recognized their language as one that had issued "from a thousand pulpits . . . each of them the dais of like men, men who with a notable facility and sameness of phrasing could present what was called the missionary challenge."[51] In their confident assessment of their call, they treated the women who had answered the missionary challenge—many of whom Sparhawk describes as desperately in need of pastoral care or at least human compassion—as ciphers, refusing to look them in the eye.

The juxtaposition between the male vision of success and the female experience of failure recurred. During her time in Ecuador, Margaret hosts a male visitor from the states, a man who comes, camera-around-neck, ready to take pictures of needy natives to show the folk at home. As he searches for pictures that will tell the story he has decided must be true, Margaret questions choosing "the pictures which show the poverty and primitiveness of the Indian, the successes of the missionary."[52] She privately contends that neither she nor her confident visitor "was in a position to assess accurately either the Indians' need (who could say that they were worse off than New Yorkers, for example?) or my own success (who but God knew which were the victories, which the defeats?)."[53] Her inability to know needs or name successes becomes apparent as she tries to subvert her American impulses and identify with the Indians. A good product of 1960s' rethinking, she trades her Western garb for Quichua clothes. Rather than teaching the Quichua Spanish, she tries to develop a written language for them. Both decisions draw protests. Rosa, a young Quichua woman, questions Margaret's change of clothing and asks if she has thrown away her "nice clothes." When Margaret responds that she has not and that she might wear them the next time she goes to the city, Rosa responds: "Thinking to yourself, 'Today I am white'?" Margaret recognizes the apt rebuke: "Yes. Rosa saw what it would be. A fake Indian one day, a white the next. There was hope notwithstanding that this measure might open some doors. But it did not prove to be so."[54] Likewise, Margaret's desire to preserve a traditional language through writing engenders rebuke. Spanish, not Quichua, her native friends tell her, is the language of their children's future.

Elliot's critiques of missionary attitudes and tactics stayed within the bounds of acceptable 1960s criticisms. Problems with missionary colonialism were well rehearsed and tendencies toward missionary superiority well known. Fictionalizing such problems was evangelically permissible. Her analysis of gender dynamics was unusual but seemed to attract little attention.

Where Elliot garnered significant criticism was in her fundamental challenge to the human ability to know God's will. At the beginning of the book, Margaret wants to believe the confident messages of success her male colleagues particularly repeat. Yet she finds herself increasingly drawn to Lynn Anderson, a missionary doctor. To Margaret's insistence that Anderson must have seen "spectacular cures" and good results that "justify" the hard times, Anderson replies "It is hopeless to try to weigh up the good, the bad, the futile, and the merely harmless, and hope that there will be enough of the good—in medical work, enough unequivocal cures—to justify all the rest." When Margaret asks what does justify the rest, Anderson claims "Jesus told us to do what is true. I think the truth needs no justification, no defense."[55]

Yet by the end of the book, even doing what is true has fallen under suspicion. Margaret's first convert and closest friend, Pedro, develops an infection which Margaret treats with penicillin. Pedro reacts to the medication and dies. His death precipitates an outburst from the grieving missionary: "O ineffable, sardonic God who toys with our sacrifices and smashes to earth the humble, hopeful altars we have built for a place to put Your name! Do You mock me? Why did You let him die? Why did You let me kill him? O God! I came to bring him life—*Your* life—and I destroyed him in Your name."[56] After Pedro's death, Margaret comes to two related conclusions. First, she cannot discern which of her actions are "useful" and "useless." She cannot read off of the apparent success or failure of any activity what God wanted. Second, even in the face of an inscrutable God whose ways cannot be known, she must continue to act. Margaret ends the book as a missionary, but everything else—her faith, God's will, her call, God's provision—is literally up in the air. The last scene leaves Margaret looking skyward, watching as "a condor circled, looking down on the tops of the frosted peaks, on the lakes and the serene valley."[57] Elliot does not say whether her young protagonist is relaxing in the knowledge that an omniscient God can see what she cannot or if she feels like an unimportant speck on a much bespeckled earth.

By throwing God's will into question, Elliot transgressed the limits of acceptable evangelical dissent. God, evangelical texts had declared throughout the 1960s, desired evangelization. Humans could know that and act on it. *Christianity Today* editor Harold Lindsell suggested that Margaret's final solution of worship without certainty was an "acceptable" response in the face of a sovereign God. Still, he doubted "whether the author has settled for that answer."[58] Perhaps Lindsell recognized that calling for the worship of an inscrutable God was not exactly a robust affirmation of the missionary task and was trying to say so kindly. Missiologist Peter Wagner, a frequent *Christianity Today* contributor, was more direct in the criticisms he made of the book in the *Evan-*

gelical Missions Quarterly. He claimed that Elliot risked erecting a new graven image, "a God who has failed to inform men of how He will act," in place of the old graven image, "the God who is expected to act according to our preconceived notions, based on our traditions rather than biblical exegesis."[59] Her brother countered all comers in his letter to *Christianity Today*'s editor with the explanation that Elliot offered not an "attack on faith" but a "massive protest against the misplacement of faith in circumstances, and the redirection of it toward God."[60] While his reading was plausible, it missed the fundamental concern with knowledge of God's will. Although *Christianity Today* itself had embodied the fidelity of questioning aspects of the missionary movement, its authors made clear that the questions were in service of the certain conviction that God wanted the world evangelized. Neither Sparhawk nor Elliot denied that conviction, but neither definitively affirmed that they believed it either. What little Elliot said in her own defense—"I must protest that the *book is a novel*"—did not absolve her.[61] That God desired evangelism was not a question to be left up in the air.

Elisabeth Elliot's challenge soon faded. *No Graven Image* was her only novel. After its publication, she turned her attention to the proper relationship between husbands and wives and premarital chastity.[62] The 1960s, for Elliot at least, were over. Changes wrought in discussions about missionaries were not.

The 1970s and Beyond: Renegotiating and Reinstantiating American Evangelical Control

As Margaret Sparhawk takes the overconfident, camera-bearing Mr. Harvey on tour around Ecuador in *No Graven Images*, she imagines the slideshow he will present to his home congregation: picture after picture of needy Ecuadorians, all dependent on missionary care and American financial support. Such presentations were supposed to prod consciences and open wallets.

In 1989 Free Methodist missionary Bob Cranston took a different approach when preaching at First Free Methodist Church. In place of the pathetic pictures, he offered a description of a Spirit-led, Filipino church. Cranston took his text from Acts 15, in which the apostle Peter advocated equal footing for Jews and Gentiles in the early church. Cranston told the congregation: "The question Peter spoke to that day is will you trust the Holy Spirit. Will you trust the Holy Spirit to work through the Gentiles even as he has worked through us? We face that same question as we look to a dynamic, growing church around the world. Will we trust their leadership to carry on? Missionaries will come and go, and they will build houses and they will build churches and the missionaries will disappear. But it is wonderful to know that through the power of the Holy Spirit, the church will continue to march forward. His truth will be marching on as we give trust and confidence to the church around the world today."[63]

Not that Cranston always found it easy to trust Filipino believers. He told the congregation about a ministers' conference he had attended. When only one person offered a prayer at the end of the evening service, Cranston feared the gathering lacked the proper spirit. In the midst of unprayerful silence, a Filipino pastor finally called for the closing hymn. As she did so, Cranston thought, "Somebody should just give these people an opportunity to come and act upon what has been said." He told the congregation at First Church, "In the old days, maybe that somebody would have been me. I would have felt as a leader and as a pioneer, and as a partner and a parent, I would have needed to be up there but now I said, 'no, the church, somehow the Holy Spirit has to work through the church.' So I stayed still." And to Cranston's relief, the Filipino pastor stopped the hymn and said, "God has been speaking tonight. We have heard his truth and I think there are many in this auditorium who need to act upon that truth." Cranston reported that "I watched as they came from all over the congregation. Lined up all across the front and into the first seats. I thought, Bob, you don't have to worry. You see, the Holy Spirit can work through the national church, it is working through the dynamic of the national church, and the church will continue to carry on." Ever the evangelist, Cranston threw the message into the lap of his American congregation. "The question this morning, really, is not whether we can trust the Holy Spirit to work through [Filipino leaders]. Will we trust the Holy Spirit to work through our lives, my life?"[64]

Cranston's sermon was a change from both "The Converted Heathen" and Elliot's camera-bearing Mr. Harvey. He claimed that Americans should support missions not because people abroad were so needy but because they could be independent. His sermon highlighted competent Filipino leadership and leveled distinctions between American evangelists and national Christians. He challenged the congregation's sense of spiritual superiority by claiming that "I am not so worried about the church overseas as I am about the church in America" and asking whether they were as receptive to the Spirit as a Filipino pastor.

Yet as Cranston challenged the Americans in his audience, he also restored power to them. Their praxis might be lax, but their standards were sound. He suggested that the Spirit would work in ways American Christians would recognize. And while it is probable that Cranston invested them with such authoritative judgment owing to their *Christian* identification and not their *American* citizenship, the fact remained that the people who knew how the Spirit should act were Christians who also happened to be Americans.

Cranston's sermon reflected conversations about missionaries in both *Christianity Today* and in Free Methodist publications during the 1970s, 1980s, and 1990s. Throughout the last three decades of the twentieth century, these evangelicals' reflections on American missionaries repeatedly touched on the internationalization of the church and new power relationships. They also reaffirmed a gospel message that had been challenged but not undone. Taken together, the conversations and the topics undermined a simplistic equation between American Christianity and power abroad even as the two remained in a complicated yet close relationship.

Easy identification of the gospel with American culture came under attack in the 1970s. Onetime missionary to the Philippines Miriam Adeney questioned the Western tendency to look down on cultures without a "Christian heritage." In a 1974 *Christianity Today* article she wrote "the superiority of Western culture was hardly apparent to Africans in the holds of slave ships. Or to the Australian aborigines for whom white settlers scattered poisoned meat around. Or to the Tasmanians, against whom the whites enjoyed regular open hunting season."[65] She claimed that an interest in missions should stimulate American believers to seek "solid contextual information about how our brothers live," and she urged readers to remember that "every culture is the lifeway of people made in the image of God, regardless of their standard of living." Even though, as she pointed out, King David did not believe in democracy, Noah was probably illiterate, and the virgin Mary had no indoor plumbing, "their lives were as valid as ours."[66] The next year, a report on a missions consultation noted that J. Herbert Kane, chair of Trinity Evangelical Divinity School's Division of World Missions and Evangelism, told participants that "the American missionary is an ambassador for Jesus Christ, not for Uncle Sam." According to the report, Kane "emphasized that the missionary must not equate the kingdom of God with any political, economic, or social system."[67]

The theme had received an evangelical imprimatur when Billy Graham stated it at the 1974 International Congress on World Evangelization in Lausanne, Switzerland. The conference, convened by Graham and attended by 2,300 people, reaffirmed a commitment to world evangelization. Yet Graham, like Kane, also affirmed whose the gospel was. In a *Christianity Today* reprint of his plenary speech at the conference, Graham called identifying "the Gospel with any one particular political system or culture" an error and admitted "this has been my own danger." He then told delegates (and readers): "When I go to preach the Gospel, I go as an ambassador for the Kingdom of God—not America. To tie the Gospel to any political system, secular program, or society is wrong and will only serve to divert the Gospel. The Gospel transcends the goals and methods of any political system or any society, however good it may be."[68] The statement ratified at the conference, and reprinted in the magazine, concurred. Under the "Evangelism and Culture" section, the Lausanne Covenant read "The gospel does not presuppose the superiority of any culture to another, but evaluates all cultures according to its own criteria of truth and righteousness, and insists on moral absolutes in every culture. Missions have all too frequently exported with the gospel an alien culture, and churches have sometimes been in bondage to culture rather than to Scripture." Missionaries had a difficult task: "Christ's evangelists must humbly seek to empty themselves of all but their personal authenticity in order to become the servants of others, and churches must seek to transform and enrich culture, all for the glory of God."[69]

Evangelical critiques of the conflation of the gospel with Western or, more precisely, American culture had resonance in the somewhat chastened 1970s. Although the Cold War was by no means over, the kind of clarity that came with fallout shelters had diminished. The Vietnam War, moreover, had undermined both American and evangelical confidence. By 1969, former *Christianity Today* editor Carl F. H. Henry had taken the position that, though the Vietnam War had been justified, the conduct of the war and the mood of the nation meant that after Richard Nixon's election "the only course left was to disengage American troops as swiftly as possible, while maintaining hope that other sanctions and pressures might depress North Viet Nam's voracious appetite."[70] In October 1970 *Christianity Today* republished an editorial that had first appeared in the *Los Angeles Times* written by a self-professed "liberal Protestant" about the mainline United Church of Christ's resolution calling for a cease-fire and withdrawal of troops.[71] Although the writer agreed with the UCC position, he argued that churches should not wed God to any political position be it dove or hawk. Five years later, the magazine published point and counterpoint articles on whether Christians should ever go to war. The publication of both sides of the debate bespoke allowable division within the evangelical community. That even the writer defending Christian participation in just wars admitted that the United States' long involvement in Vietnam might have been "unwise or unnecessary" revealed a sobered view of U.S. military intervention abroad.[72]

Failure in Vietnam, problems at home, and criticisms from abroad prodded *Christianity Today* writers to sort through what, if any, values the United States could rightly export. The result was complicated. In 1976 John Warwick Montgomery noted that "just as American evangelicals appear passive about expressing their convictions in the domestic marketplace of ideas, so the country in general seems more and more reticent to export its national values beyond its own boundaries." Given a history of "Promised Land mythology" that justified "carrying the big stick" and "extending our economic tentacles around the globe," the reticence was understandable.[73] Yet he did maintain that freedom was worth exporting, not because it was an American value as such but because it was part of a higher moral law to which all nations were subject.[74] Carl Henry echoed his thinking. The nation's bicentennial offered the opportunity to reflect on the "crisis over patriotism."[75] Henry noted an ongoing American mission in the world related to the notion that "God has universally bestowed inalienable human rights and the government is both divinely limited and responsible."[76] Henry did not assume that the United States in the 1970s embodied its best ideals—indeed, he declared that "the Declaration of Independence and the Constitution, even the national anthem and the Gettysburg Address, can be potently and critically turned against the present American experience"— but he still asserted that "the vision of America's distinctive mission in the world can be carried forward without the misconception that the United States is the carrier of an international salvation-history."[77] Both Henry and Montgomery contended that some American values remained universally applicable. Yet they also conceded serious problems with U.S. behavior at home and abroad.

According to *Christianity Today* articles, wars without victory and presidents needing pardons had engendered evangelical humility about the American mission and the identification of the gospel with that mission. They were not, however, the lone reasons. Missionary success was another. As the congregation and covenant at Lausanne indicated, evangelical Christianity had become a worldwide movement. The reports out of the Lausanne Conference came from African, Asian, and Latin American delegates as well as from Americans and Europeans. Western Christians did not speak for all Christians and conferences like Lausanne recognized that reality. Admittedly, such an international spread would have been apparent only to people who read all the reports—assuredly a minority of evangelicals. Yet the trend toward acknowledging the authority of Christians abroad appeared in articles that lay people would read. Twenty-eight years after "The Converted Heathen Speaks," the Free Methodist *Tidings* published an interview with missionary Gerald Bates. The interviewer asked Bates if missionaries were becoming obsolete. Although he believed that "there will always be a place for cross-cultural persons who contribute special skills and insights to the church in a milieu not their own," he began his answer by saying, "in the first place, a missionary should not be answering this question."[78] When asked how overseas workers fit into the African church, he appealed to others' authority: "We are members of the body, parts of a team—not indispensable but still important to the work—or at least our African brothers tell me so."[79] In 1975 *Christianity Today* published a two-part interview with Dr. Byang H. Kato, general secretary of the Association of Evangelicals of Africa and Madagascar. The interviewer asked Kato about recent calls for a moratorium on missions issued by some African church leaders and echoed by some American mainline leaders. Kato, as the interviewer no doubt expected, affirmed the validity of missions and called a moratorium unbiblical. He also said that, "unfortunately, a superior attitude does perhaps come through in some missionaries. The call for moratorium also serves notice that we Africans have come of age; we want people to realize that we want colleagues, not masters."[80] Appealing to the authority of Christians abroad suggested that American believers were no longer privileged interpreters of their own work and that any pretensions to remaining so would hurt the evangelical cause.

Christianity Today and Free Methodist discussions in the 1970s not only sought approval from international believers for U.S. evangelistic endeavors. They revealed to readers that international Christians were claiming the missionary enterprise—for many evangelicals, the *sine qua non* of the movement—for themselves. Missions supporters had long celebrated converted foreigners who returned to their countries as evangelists. Writers in the nineteenth century publicized the aspirations of the Hawaiian Henry Obookiah—who intended to return to his people—and the work of Ko Tha Byu, Karen evangelists in Burma.[81] In 1947 the congregation at First Church was invited to hear "Mr. and Mrs. Akichika, converted Japanese who are soon to return to Japan as missionaries," speak at an evening service.[82]

In the 1970s Christians abroad were shown not only evangelizing their own nations but ministering cross-culturally. In a 1972 *Christianity Today* article, William Shenk told readers that the "world-embracing" vision of the younger churches "suggests that a new perspective on the Church and its mission is demanded. We who have grown accustomed to controlling the initiative and resources must visualize and put into practice new ways of conducting ourselves."[83] Christians abroad agreed—sometimes pointedly. A report on an Asian missions gathering in 1974 quoted Harvey T. Co Chien, the general secretary of the InterVarsity Christian Fellowship of the Philippines: "Missions are no longer the monopoly of Western Christians." That the West could once claim such a monopoly was at least partly the fault of missionaries "who had not adequately encouraged and challenged Asian Christians to spread the Gospel abroad."[84] Yet the monopoly was over. Indeed, international Christians increasingly turned toward the United States as a mission field itself. Aminiasi Qalo, a Fijian serving in Papua New Guinea, wrote that "it is time for the Western world to accept people from other countries, not only to migrate, but to come as Third World missionaries to aid in evangelizing non-Christians. Many Western countries once labeled 'Christian' now live in modern paganism."[85] The United States needed evangelization and international Christians would help by coming to preach a gospel they claimed as their own.

The content of that gospel, however, had not undergone significant change as church demographics shifted. Even as the prominence of the "younger" churches destabilized old power relationships, the inclusion of international voices in missionary discussions reified as gospel a message long promulgated by American evangelicals.

Take Latin American theologian René Padilla. A participant at

Lausanne and a frequent *Christianity Today* contributor, Padilla chided American evangelicals for continued imperialism. In 1974 he criticized both Catholic and evangelical responses to the military coup against democratically elected leftist Chilean president Salvador Allende. Padilla noted that according to "common opinion," the coup "would have never taken place aside from the encouragement of the U.S. State Department."[86] He noted with chagrin that evangelicals—both national and missionary alike—quickly voiced support for the new regime. He acknowledged that lack of information about the junta's cruelty might have explained the acquiescence but also wondered if evangelical support was due to "political views leading them to overlook crimes that they would not have overlooked under the Marxist government." He ended his article by asking "will Christians ever learn not to try to enlist God under the political banner of their preference?"[87] A 1975 article, "Peru: Evangelicals under Attack," detailed "a wave of accusations against evangelical Christians" stemming from reports that "certain missionary agencies of American origin are being used by the Central Intelligence Agency to undermine the Peruvian government's revolutionary program."[88] Wycliffe Bible Translators received the fiercest attacks. While Padilla did call the specific accusations "distorted," he also contended that the attacks seemed plausible owing to an apparent lack of interest in the economic and political well-being of people abroad.[89]

Padilla related his critiques of imperialism to an anemic gospel. Evangelical Christians, he contended, were susceptible to the charge that they were stooges for American economic imperialism because of their "lopsided emphasis on the *preaching* of the Gospel, to the neglect of works of love." He called "the divorce between faith and works" a "denial of biblical teaching." Padilla continued: "It is high time for evangelicals to recognize that good works are not optional but are an essential aspect of the Christian mission."[90] It was a theme he had sounded two years earlier in a review of new books on missions titled "What Is the Gospel?" In the review Padilla applauded mainline theologians who called for a reassessment of the gospel in ways that undermined remaining notions of Western cultural superiority and held together the personal and social dimensions of salvation. He criticized evangelical church growth guru Donald McGavran's call to make church growth missionaries' primary focus. Padilla saw McGavran's emphasis on numeric expansion as an overreaction to "secularist" claims that the Church should primarily work toward economic and social improvement. Padilla countered, "The most urgent need of our 'fantastically growing churches' in Latin America, for instance, is to become less concerned with their own (numerical) aggrandizement and more concerned with the application of the Gospel to practical life."[91] Neither the gospel as simply verbal proclamation nor the easy assumption that changed hearts would eventually lead to changed societies sufficed, Padilla told readers.

Padilla was not a lone voice in the evangelical wilderness. Others shared his concerns. The twelve thousand students who attended InterVarsity Christian Fellowship's 1970 Urbana Missions Conference, for example, heard similar messages. Many of the speakers were white American evangelicals but not all. Argentine theologian Samuel Escobar, four years later a Lausanne delegate, delivered an address on "Social Concern and World Evangelism." He criticized the "middle-class captivity" of the evangelical church and "the fact that the most ardent defenders of evangelism have become at the same time so suspicious of social concern as to create the idea that one excludes the other."[92] African American evangelist Tom Skinner admonished, "Any gospel that talks about delivering to man a personal Savior who will free him from the personal bondage of sin and grant him eternal life and does not at the same time speak to the issues of enslavement, the issue of injustice, the issue of inequality—any gospel that does not want to go where people are hungry and poverty-stricken and set them free in the name of Jesus Christ—is not the gospel."[93] Some of the speeches appeared in the volume, *Christ the Liberator*, which Donald McGavran reviewed positively in *Christianity Today*. McGavran apparently did not hear what was said at Urbana as a critique of his work, although he would have been hard pressed to take Padilla's comments as anything else.[94] Whether or not they agreed, *Christianity Today* readers encountered voices not traditionally heard in missionary discussions question evangelical renditions of the gospel.

The questioning, however, had limits and, indeed, helped to reify American evangelical boundaries. People from abroad could, and did, challenge how well American evangelicals held together social concern and evangelism. They could, and did, challenge the notion that the two were separable. Yet they did not redefine the essential evangelical meaning of salvation. Indeed, if they appeared in *Christianity Today*, they affirmed it. Padilla, for example, criticized Latin American liberation theology. He focused on the most famous Latin American liberation theologian, Gustavo Gutiérrez. According to Padilla, Gutiérrez believed Christianity "is at present taking shape in the praxis of small groups of Christians involved in the fight for a new and free society." Moreover, he claimed that Gutiérrez's theology "is essentially the reflection upon this praxis within a concrete historical situation."[95] Padilla's assessment of Gutiérrez—"What he says is a far cry from biblical Christianity"—reaffirmed essential evangelical beliefs. By elevating revolutionary praxis above biblical authority and equating a new social structure with God's salvation, Gutiérrez offered Marxist ideology in the place of "the Gospel of Christ."[96] Padilla concluded his review with his standard warnings to American evangelicals—do not conflate the gospel and conservative ideologies, do not ignore the actual circumstances in which people live. Still, he clearly embedded the warnings in an evangelical framework. Evangelicals were correct in criticizing liberationist theology. Evangelical theology, properly understood, was sound. Padilla sought not to redefine but to make evangelicals the best versions of themselves.

Having international believers such as Padilla challenge but essentially reaffirm these beliefs suggested that the best version of the gospel already familiar to American evangelicals transcended national boundaries. The presence of international believers at conferences and in *Christianity Today*'s pages instantiated evangelicalism as an international movement. It was also useful to have people from abroad who could respond to radical critiques from other non-Western Christians. An American missionary rejecting the idea of a missionary moratorium could be construed as a Western unwillingness to relinquish control. Byang H. Kato, a Nigerian, declaring a moratorium unbiblical, undercut charges that missions were necessarily imperialistic, even if he did claim that some missionaries were so in practice. Evangelicals from abroad affirmed that one could separate the true gospel wheat from American cultural chaff.

Yet even as international evangelicals affirmed a gospel that was not American, they participated in a complex renegotiation and reaffirmation of American power. On one hand, Christians abroad really did gain a greater prominence in the American evangelical world. When Free Methodist missionary Carol Watson sent her 1989 newsletter to First Church supporters, she highlighted the work of her Rwandan colleague, District Superintendent Mark Rugamba.[97] In December 1991 missionaries Jerry and Wanda Rusher were interviewed during a Sunday morning service at First Church. They had served at a hospital in Haiti but left because of unrest. Jerry told the congregation that "there are three Haitian doctors who are continuing to work there and a large staff supporting them and they want to make it go and they are really putting themselves into it."[98] Christians abroad, Americans were told, were not just bona fide Christians but real leaders.

On the other hand, Americans retained editorial approval of the messages from abroad. *Christianity Today* chose what to print. Watson portrayed her co-worker to the folk at home. And international Christians certainly did not automatically receive positions of epistemic privilege. Jerry Rusher explained to First Church that "we've been really hoping" that the Haitians would take ownership of the hospital and that the missionary evacuation made that possible. He reported that "we had to prepare the Haitian staff to carry on without the missionaries there and it was a time of transition and we feel that it really, the Haitians really responded to this challenge and they wanted to make it go."[99] Even as the Haitians were acknowledged as leaders, the missionaries remained those with a vision for the future (Haitian ownership of the hospital) and those in possession of necessary knowledge (how to make the hospital run). Likewise, *Christianity Today* lauded the participation of people such as Samuel Escobar at Lausanne but was also quick to point out that other Third World delegates disagreed with his harsh criticisms of missionaries.[100] A year after Lausanne, Peter Wagner subtly suggested that René Padilla's admonition to emphasize training disciples more than converting lots of people demonstrated the conference's tendency to stress Christian nurture "so strongly . . . that it gained precedence over winning lost men and women to the Christian faith."[101] The main articles about Lausanne came from Americans such as Billy Graham and Wagner, who were more positive on direct evangelization and less hostile to U.S. power abroad than the two Latin American theologians.

Thus, although the inclusion of international evangelicals in missionary discussions allowed U.S. evangelicals to show that they had remade power relationships, this inclusion did not give all participants an equal share in shaping the conversation nor did it bestow on all participants equal credibility. Moreover, the presence of new voices in the missionary discussion served American evangelicalism's ends. In a world concerned with neo-imperialism and Western domination, including voices from abroad demonstrated that evangelical boundaries were not between the West and the rest even as those voices solidified the theological boundaries American evangelicals had long carefully patrolled.

This reading suggests neither that the Americans were insincere in including people from abroad nor that international evangelicals were dupes of Western Christians. New institutions such as Lausanne and new organizations such as the World Free Methodist Fellowship showed ongoing commitments to new relationships. People like René Padilla finally concurred with American evangelicals about the central message of the gospel because they believed that it was true. The import lies not in either hypocrisy or naïveté. Rather, it lies in how conversations about missionaries evinced and reinforced American evangelicals' ways of interacting with a postcolonial world. Responses to nationalism and criticisms of U.S. racism resulted in a separation of the gospel and Western culture. American evangelicalism no longer had power simply because it was American. Yet the structure of the conversation about new power relationships, missionary tactics, and the evangelists' message allowed evangelicals who happened to be Americans to retain final edit. As the conversations granted people abroad autonomy and even power within worldwide evangelicalism, they simultaneously reinscribed U.S. evangelicals' power.[102] They, ultimately, both granted that people abroad deserved freedom and decided who was using it well.

Conclusion

The evangelical conversation about missionaries in the 1970s continued until the end of the century. A similar set of topics was repeated; similar dynamics reappeared. The gospel was not simply American. U.S. workers had to do a better job of watching their authoritarian tendencies. Missionaries needed to relate faith and works without losing the essential gospel. In an article about missions after the demise of the Soviet Union, for example, *Christianity Today* reported that many Americans had rushed in, stepping on the toes of the Russian Orthodox Church, which was not pleased to learn that evangelicals considered its members insufficiently converted. Notably, other American evangelicals criticized their overenthusiastic brethren, chiding their lack of sensitivity.[103] A few years later, Samuel Escobar wrote about missions in the fast-approaching twenty-first century, reiterating long-standing arguments against Christians' separating the world on the same basis as their nation (rather than a division between communist and noncommunist, Escobar was now worried about one between Western and Muslim) and reaffirming the biblical gospel.[104]

Although Escobar obviously felt he was part of a stagnating conversation, reflections about missionaries reveal significant changes in evangelical interaction with the rest of the world over the second half of the twentieth century. American evangelicals did respond to nationalism and the growing global church in the 1950s and 1960s. Though unwilling to mount the kinds of protest of U.S. power that mainliners did, they rethought how their own structures and behaviors mimicked bad relations abroad. In the

1970s particularly, they divorced the gospel from American culture—or, at the very least, learned that they needed to do so—and separated missions from America's global political and economic reach.

Such separation could not guarantee a *Christianity Today* position on foreign policy (nor a Free Methodist or an evangelical position). Wars and rumors of wars brought out both the doves and the hawks in the 1980s and 1990s. Evangelical publications could still maintain that American values such as democracy and freedom were good, even if they were not tantamount to the gospel. The separation did, however, create room for critique. In 1999, for example, Ajith Fernando, national director of Youth for Christ in Sri Lanka, wrote in *Christianity Today* that "ever since the Gulf War, I have had the nagging feeling that recent Western military efforts may be doing more harm than good."[105] He argued that Western military efforts, seemingly backed by many Western Christians, aroused suspicions of colonialism. He lamented pictures of his "hero" Billy Graham talking with President George Bush on the day the first Gulf War began. War made missionary work harder, he argued. Once again, an evangelical from abroad challenged U.S. action abroad and asked believers in America to put their loyalty to the gospel ahead of their loyalty to their country.[106]

Fernando's article demonstrated the distinction between evangelical embrace of a Wilsonian foreign policy and an evangelical use of a Wilsonian logic in public discussions. Criticizing how the United States acted abroad was evangelically permissible. Although Billy Graham had met with George Bush during the Gulf War, the revered evangelist had contributed to the separation between American policy and the kingdom of God. While some evangelicals might bind their country and their God more closely than did Graham or *Christianity Today* writers, discussions about missionaries in the magazine and in denominations such as the Free Methodists revealed that dissent on matters national was evangelically permissible—and, indeed, those discussions had helped to render it so. Dissent on matters theological remained less permissible. While acknowledging that the United

States did not always serve the cause of world freedom, evangelicals maintained that their version of the gospel did. Fernando was evidence. He was a viable voice within *Christianity Today* because he was proof that people abroad could faithfully direct their own ministries and lead their own churches. The proof was not that he agreed politically with the American president but that he agreed with the American bellwether of evangelical belief, Billy Graham. Fernando could be trusted because he stayed within the theological boundaries American evangelicals set. For evangelicals, it was an intractable tension and one they reproduced in public conversations. They could champion freedom for people abroad but would not give up custodianship of the gospel message they believed would save the world.

chapter three

ANTHROPOLOGY

In 1988 Jonathan Benthall could not explain why missionaries were at the American Anthropological Association's (AAA) annual meeting. Benthall, the editor of *Anthropology Today*, had "dropped into" an informal session titled "Christian Anthropologists" expecting to hear about scholarship at Catholic universities. Instead he found Protestant evangelical "missionaries and missiologists from the Summer Institute of Linguistics [SIL] and similar groups."[1] Benthall was surprised by the parochial character of the conversation—he surmised by their absence that Catholics "were not considered a subset of Christian" by the attendees. While he conceded that SIL had produced one significant name in anthropology, linguist Kenneth Pike, on the whole he believed that the session demonstrated anthropology's tolerance: "Presumably [SIL] is allowed space and time at the AAA meeting as a minority interest within anthropology, and that is to the AAA's credit."[2] Benthall thought it good of anthropologists to let missionaries join the conversation.

At the AAA's 1994 meeting, missionaries helped plan a session. Benthall began his review of the AAA with a report on a "Missionaries and Human Rights," a session organized by SIL member and ecological anthropologist Thomas Headland. The discussion between anthropologists and evangelists proved "more serious and mature than at other such events."[3] The session explored the contributions of evangelists to human rights and Benthall looked forward to cooperation. He thought that "this admirably organized AAA session advanced the debate between anthropologists and missionaries."[4] He did, however, offer a caveat. Those missionaries who persisted in absolutist views—and he knew both Catholics and Protestants who fit the description—would not enhance dialogue. Not all missionaries were welcome.

Both Benthall's changed appraisal of missionaries and his caveat warrant examination. First, the change. It might appear that between 1988 and 1994, anthropologists suddenly realized that they could make common cause with missionaries to fight human rights abuses. Appearances, however, are famously deceiving. Beneath an apparently sudden change lay a long, complicated history. Missionaries did not appear on the anthropological horizon in 1988. Bronislaw Malinowski, one of the fathers of modern fieldwork, had distrusted missionaries as early as 1914. His diaries, published posthumously in 1967, revealed his contempt for the British evangelists (and his patronization of native peoples) in the Trobriand Islands: "Mentally I collect arguments against missions and ponder a really effective anti-mission campaign. The arguments: these people destroy the natives' joy in life; they destroy their psychological *raison d'être*. And what they give in return is completely beyond the savages. They struggle consistently and ruthlessly against everything old and create new needs, both material and moral. No question but that they do harm."[5] In the 1950s, Isaac Schapera, a prominent British anthropologist, derided evangelists, although not so acrimoniously in public as had Malinowski in private. In a 1956 lecture (reprinted in 1958 and in 1960), he noted that although the Tswana people of South Africa remembered some evangelists "with gratitude and affection,"[6] he believed Christian changes to Tswana life "fundamental" and "widespread" and destructive: "I doubt if 'creative' is a . . . suitable term for a process that, however much of a blessing it may have been to some individuals, has left the great majority of the people either indifferent to religion of any kind or insincere about the one they profess."[7]

Benthall's early antagonism, then, had roots in his guild's many criticisms of missionaries, criticisms that for much of the twentieth century largely occurred behind the scenes. His eventual willingness to make common cause with some missionaries was also rooted in criticism. In this chapter, I argue that in the last three decades of the twentieth century, anthropologists' critiques of missionary, and their own, complicity with colonialism and neo-colonialism opened the guild to conversation with evangelists. Anthropologists who criticized evangelists for their involvement in the spread of Western (particularly U.S.) power abroad came, in some cases, to engage missionaries who themselves had qualms about their role in the world. Moreover, as scholars acknowledged their field's own compromised past and objectifying practices, they ceded some of the moral high ground and began to describe missionaries as subjects of study rather than objects of criticism, as parts of communities rather than interlopers, as possible allies rather than absolute enemies.

Still, Benthall's caveat mattered. Even as some anthropologists became willing to talk with and to work with missionaries in an effort to free people abroad from the corrosive effects of Western, particularly U.S., power, they still asserted their superior knowledge about what people abroad needed. In many cases, their assertion rested on firm ground such as training and research. It stemmed from real concern about the threats the United States' political and economic policies posed to vulnerable peoples. Still, it repeated patterns that scholars criticized, and it became part of a larger Wilsonian conversation. As scholars criticized the effects of the American Century on indigenous people, and challenged evangelists who they often saw as tools for U.S. interests, they positioned themselves as arbiters of what was right for the rest of the world.

Claude Stipe, *Current Anthropology*, and the Debate in a Nutshell

It is not easy to date the beginning of anthropologists' self-conscious reflection on their missionary relationship. David Spain admitted that "as anthropologists we *talk* a lot about missionaries, but we seldom *write* about them."[8] Conversations in the halls of academic conferences are lost to history, but naming a key moment in anthropologists' public reflections is possible. In 1980 *Current Anthropology* published an article by Claude Stipe, an anthropologist at Marquette University. The article, "Anthropologists versus Missionaries: The Role of Presuppositions," engendered four years of debate in the journal.⁹ The discussion between Stipe and his respondents encapsulated anthropologists' concerns about missionary behavior as well as their own self-critique. It also helpfully demonstrates the discussion's thoughtful highs and spiteful lows.

The debate started politely. As the title suggests, Stipe contended that many anthropologists operated with at least one of two presuppositions: "That primitive cultures are characterized by an organic unity and that religious beliefs are essentially meaningless."¹⁰ Either belief could lead to antimissionary attitudes. Anthropologists who adhered to "organic unity" believed that changing anything within a culture—religion especially—altered everything. Change instigated by uninvited outsiders was particularly harmful. Organic unity alone, however, could not account for the general dislike of evangelists. The second presupposition could. "I suspect," Stipe wrote, "that, in at least some instances, the antipathy of anthropologists toward missionaries lies in the fact that missionaries take seriously and teach other people religious beliefs which the anthropologists have personally rejected."¹¹ Disaffected believers found it hard to like, or treat with respect, those who propagated discarded beliefs.

The immediate response was largely positive. *Current Anthropology* followed Stipe's article with brief rebuttals. Many of the respondents thanked Stipe for bringing up an important and understudied topic. Most agreed that their field had a widespread and not completely justified aversion to missionaries—although many were also quick to show their own fair-mindedness by telling good stories about evangelists. Jean Guiart and Lucy Mair, for example, reminded readers that some missionaries blunted the worst edges of oppressive regimes. Other noted the help anthropologists received from missionaries, such as translation assistance and hospitality in the field. Of course, asserting that missionaries had some good qualities did not preclude acknowledging bad ones. Robert Taylor, for instance, wrote that "Christian missionary efforts have often been plagued by ethnocentrism, insensitivity, and ignorance of cultural values and processes."¹² Other scholars described missionaries as culturally naïve—unaware of their own ethnocentricity—although possibly educable. Yet, overall, the scholars affirmed Stipe's conclusion that missionaries deserved better than they had received at the hands of anthropologists.

Stipe's explanation for the antimissionary bias won fewer fans. The field, some respondents argued, had largely moved beyond organic unity. The meaninglessness of religious beliefs also proved unpopular. Anthropologists posed alternatives, ranging from secularized graduate training to embarrassment about reliance on missionaries in the field to discomfort regarding similarities with evangelists. To counteract such unscientific prejudice, they called for introspection, controls for bias, and ethnographies of missions. Whatever the sins of missionaries, scholars could not justify unexamined predispositions.

The next set of comments pushed anthropologists' self-criticism even further. In 1982 the Venezuelan anthropologist H. Dieter Heinen chided colleagues for ignoring the comments of Martin Mluanda, one of the original respondents and "the only one to advance a decidedly Third World point of view."[13] Following Mluanda, Heinen chastised both Western anthropologists and missionaries because both "have exploited their superior ethnic and class affiliations to impose themselves on indigenous peoples around the world."[14] Missionaries did so when they made indigenous people accept "Western cultural baggage" along with Christianity, and anthropologists did so when they made Western epistemology normative. Fortunately, some anthropologists and missionaries were beginning to treat indigenous cultures respectfully. Actually, Heinen thought the evangelists were doing better than the scholars. In any case, indigenous self-determination meant that "fundamentalists" in both the anthropological and the missionary camps would soon be "sent packing by indigenous peoples who see religious and scientific paternalism as the extension of political colonialism that it is."[15] For Heinen, being Western—and colonialist—trumped the differences between anthropologists and missionaries.

The debate could be heated, particularly when the conversation turned to anthropologists who found favorable comparisons between themselves and evangelists ridiculous. Bernard Delfendahl asserted that the "essential" difference between missionaries and anthropologists lay not in some high-minded presuppositions but in attitude. "The missionary," he wrote, "goes out to teach mankind, the anthropologist to learn *from* them."[16] Missionaries could be Marxists, capitalists, or even of the oft-overlooked vegetarian variety—although Delfendahl focused on Christians. Whatever the dogma, missionaries viewed their way of thinking as superior. Although Delfendahl admitted hostility toward colonial administrators, traders, and technicians as well, he did note that missionaries alone sought "to bring into the superior fold the *inner selves* of men."[17]

Another scholar, Harry Feldman, offered an epistemological view of the relationship. Christian dogma "insists that at some point one must abandon reason and rely entirely upon faith."[18] It only made sense that "fieldworkers, as scientists and rationalists, necessarily find this doctrine obnoxious."[19] Feldman saw no hope of reconciling this difference but thought individual evangelists and scholars might be able to get along better. He also thought that the discussion about the relationship between missionaries and anthropologists led to a more significant question: how anthropologists should affect the communities in which they participate. He ended his reply to Stipe by raising questions about anthropologists' responsibilities toward native peoples—questions, one assumed, that could be answered in good, rational, and scientific ways.

The unfolding debate glossed over Feldman's final question. Rather, he and Stipe engaged in a rather acrimonious dialogue about faith and reason that soon devolved into a discussion about one controversial organization: Wycliffe Bible Translators (WBT). Stipe disagreed with Feldman's juxtaposition of Christians and scientists, and of rationality and faith. As evidence that Christian missionaries could also be good scientists, Stipe pointed to the work of the Summer Institute of Linguistics (SIL), Wycliffe's scholarly arm. As the name indicates, WBT was a Protestant missionary organization specializing in Bible translation. Often SIL supplied indigenous peoples the first written version of their language. SIL also published academic work on the new alphabets. Stipe reminded Feldman that peer-reviewed journals published SIL articles. Missionaries could be scholars too.[20]

Feldman found Stipe's SIL reference unconvincing. He argued that the group's linguistic work was a poorly executed guise for evangelistic commitments and cited a 1981 essay collection critical of Wycliffe, *Is God an American?* Math helped too. If SIL members had published, as Stipe asserted, 17 articles between 1975 and 1979 in the *International Journal of American Linguistics* (*IJAL*) and if, as SIL claimed, it had 1,372 members, "the average length of time required for one SIL member to publish one brief data paper, without considering quality, in *IJAL* is 404 years."[21] Wycliffe, moreover, was a best-case scenario: "Other missions are on the whole even less productive than the SIL."[22] At best, missionaries were very unproductive scientists. More likely, it seemed, they were not scientists at all, but people who perpetuated an unhealthy reliance upon irrational faith.

Predictably, Stipe disagreed. He quickly abandoned the esoteric dialogue about faith and reason and professed himself "disappointed" with "Feldman's gratuitous statement" that SIL used its linguistic activities as a smokescreen for evangelism. "Disappointment," however, did not do justice to Stipe's feelings about the book Feldman referenced, *Is God an American?* According to Stipe, the book demonstrated that anthropologists brought their antimissionary prejudices to the field with them. He found the book full of unfounded "innuendo" about links among SIL, the Central Intelligence Agency, and the local U.S. Embassy. The authors, he claimed, used assertion rather than argument and resorted to "character assassination" and "admittedly unsupportable charges."[23]

The debate about SIL brought anthropologist David Stoll into the fray. Stoll had contributed to *Is God an American?* and had published his own monograph on Wycliffe.[24] Stoll rebutted Stipe's defense of SIL by claiming that Wycliffe used its power advantage to press its evangelistic agenda. It also played a part in larger imperialistic programs "such as the colonization of the Amazon."[25] Stoll averred that anthropologists had a duty to expose this program before it was too late.

The *Current Anthropology* debate ended without a conclusion. It revealed much over the course of four years about the relationship between anthropologists and missionaries. Beneath the arguments, diatribes, and accusations lay hints of a messy history. The charges and countercharges were old. Certainly some anthropologists continued to feel that missionaries harmed indigenous cultures. Strikingly, however, few seemed content with Stipe's original explanation involving organic unity. Their criticisms of missionaries revolved around a cluster of issues that included ethnocentrism, deceit, and neocolonialism. In other words, the anthropologists claimed that their concerns related less to their discipline's theoretical models than they did to global realities. The problem with missionaries was not that they changed cultures but that they did so for the worse. Scholars felt entitled to hold missionaries accountable for their role in the expansion of Western political and economic power, for supporting right-wing dictators, and for preparing people for the destruction of their lands.

The *Current Anthropology* debate, however, contained another undertone. Some anthropologists were eager to reevaluate the old missionary image—but not out of love for missionaries. As good scholars, anthropologists could not justify stereotypes and prejudice. Moreover, reflection upon missionaries caused some anthropologists to suggest that they too were guilty of ethnocentrism and colonialist attitudes. Such an admission did not lead anthropologists to abandon the field, of course, but it did prod them to reconsider their stance vis-à-vis people abroad and, eventually, to grant some missionaries ally status in a common fight to aid vulnerable peoples.

Anthropologists' Critique of Missionaries and the Conversations That Ensued

The *Current Anthropology* debate demonstrated that not all anthropologists agreed on the exact nature of missionary sins. Stipe's original organic unity proposal received little support. A host of other ideas gained little traction. Yet where the discussion ended was telling. The final critiques centered on a specific missionary organization's relationship with the U.S. government. The problem was not organic unity or epistemological differences. It was complicity with expansionist, oppressive power.

Still, Stipe's original suggestion was neither completely wrong nor unimportant. What he called organic unity (and what was more commonly known as structural functionalism) had contributed to the antimissionary sentiment among earlier generations of anthropologists. Exploring the changes in anthropology over the years shows why missionaries were unpopular and why the charge of colonial complicity—not, by any account, a insignificant critique—actually made conversations between scholars and evangelists more possible than it might have been earlier.

Until the 1950s, American and British anthropology occupied different trajectories. They had their own genealogies and theoretical positions. Scholars on different sides of the Atlantic found it difficult to talk. But on both sides of the ocean, theoretical models developed that made little room for missionaries. For early work on missionaries, the British school proved more important. Missionaries appeared on the radar earlier for British anthropologists than they did for American scholars. Like Malinowski and Schapera, many British scholars performed fieldwork in British colonies and encountered British missionaries. For purposes of this chapter, the specific characterization of these missionaries is not terribly important. The theoretical framework—one that eventually had some influence on the other side of the ocean—is. Structural functionalism, the technical name for what Stipe called organic unity, held the field in Britain. The term was apt, if not melodious. Structural functionalists such as Malinowski focused on the structures of society (such as kinship) and the functions they served. According to Stanley Barrett, the model proved congenial for ethnographers because they only had to "identify patterns of action and belief, and specify their functions."[26] Ease came with a price, however. "Structural functionalism downplayed conflict and almost ignored social change."[27]

When they found change, structural functionalists did not like it. As Stipe had argued, if all aspects of society had interrelated purposes, change was not beneficial. And as Daniel T. Hughes noted, "Functionalism is teleological insofar as it assumes that the purpose of a society is to preserve itself in equilibrium and that the function of any part of that system is to maintain the system in relative equilibrium."[28] Missionaries, the great evangelists of change, altered functioning societies and threw them out of balance.

American anthropologists came equipped with their own theoretical perspective. The father of the American school, Franz Boas, bequeathed cultural relativism to his scholarly descendants. In a reaction against evolutionary understandings of culture—the sense that one culture is more civilized or simply better than another—Boas advocated historical particularism. Each culture followed its own particular trajectory and could not be judged against (or by) any other. As Thomas Hylland Eriksen and Finn Sivert Nielsen note, cultural relativism can be either a methodological or a moral principle. "To Boas," they concede, "this would no doubt seem to be hair-splitting. Method and morality were for him two sides of the same coin."[29] For anthropologists influenced by Boas, then, the notion that some beliefs possessed greater merit than others went against the grain, particularly when those ideas tended to go in only one direction: Western to non-Western.

By one reading, cultural relativism could lead where structural functionalism did, namely, to a discussion-precluding criticism of missionaries. Evangelists, particularly those who sought conversions, seemed to claim that their beliefs possessed greater merit than those of the people to whom they preached. Scholars committed to cultural relativism could simply describe the missionary project as fundamentally flawed. Yet cultural relativists were not complete relativists. Indeed, they could hardly be so: thoroughgoing cultural relativism could also undercut anthropologists' judgments of *missionary* culture. Rather than abandon all judgment, many of those who took missionaries to task in the 1970s and 1980s seemed to share anthropologist Clifford R. Barnett's perspective: "The principle of cultural relativity does not seem to excuse us from exercising judgment about the function, meaning or utility of a given practice. Rather, it is a warning that this judgment must be made in terms of the cultural context in which it is embedded."[30] Or, as one scholar said in his reply to Stipe, he would not withhold all judgment "in a world that I must share with Jonestown, Cambodia, and Three Mile Island."[31] Scholars believed they could fairly evaluate missionary activities by moving beyond analyses of evangelists' effects on internal community dynamics, by placing proselytizing activities in broader social and political contexts, and by analyzing how missionaries aided, abetted, and challenged what anthropologists (among other scholars) saw as the United States' expansionist power.

A version of cultural relativism that brought the growing political and economic power of the United States into play did not, at first glance, bode well for missionaries. Indeed, as some anthropologists began taking this broad view in the 1970s, they reached a highly critical conclusion: missionaries embodied the worst traits of America abroad. Missionary messages, associations, and activities did more than throw cultures out of balance—they threatened their very existence. The most vociferous condemnations of missionaries emerged from anthropologists concerned with indigenous rights. Two groups, Survival International, founded in Great Britain in 1969, and Cultural Survival, founded in the United States in 1972, brought together scholars and activists in various disciplines to advocate for native peoples. Anthropologists did not constitute the total membership of either organization, but they played significant roles. David Maybury-Lewis, an anthropology professor at Harvard, founded Cultural Survival. The groups sounded the alarm of genocide, the annihilation of peoples, and ethnocide, the destruction of cultures. They argued that several factors contributed to cultural extinction—bad governments, environmental decay, big businesses, and, of course, missionaries.

A grand salvo, if not the first one, appeared in *Current Anthropology* in 1973. "The Declaration of Barbados: For the Liberation of the Indians" resulted from a 1971 symposium cosponsored by the Programme to Combat Racism, the World Council of Churches, and the University of Bern. Signed by eleven social anthropologists working in Latin America, it bewailed the "colonial situation" of Indians and the "repeated acts of aggression directed against aboriginal groups and cultures."[32] The signatories identified three major groups with responsibilities toward the Indians: the state, anthropologists, and religious missions. The section on missions was the longest and the most radical. Evangelization was "ethnocentric" and a "component of the colonialist ideology."[33] Missionaries drew ire for their characterization of Indian culture as pagan, their focus on otherworldly salvation, and their imperialist grab of indigenous land and labor. Given missionary crimes, the declaration avowed "we conclude that the suspension of all missionary activity is the most appropriate policy on behalf of both Indian society as well as the moral integrity of the churches involved."[34] That missionaries would go home immediately seemed unlikely, however, so the declaration also outlined ten necessary changes in missionary behavior. These included assuming "a position of true respect for Indian culture, ending the long and shameful history of despotism and intolerance characteristic of missionary work, which rarely manifests sensitivity to aboriginal religious sentiments and values," and abandoning "those blackmail procedures implicit in the offering of goods and services to Indian society in return for total submission."[35] If evangelists did not change "they, too, must be held responsible by default for crimes of ethnocide and connivance with genocide."[36]

According to these anthropologists, missionaries served the imperialist program. It was not a new claim, but indigenous rights groups gave it new force. While some scholars, most notably the historian Arthur Schlesinger Jr., called missionaries "cultural imperialists"—a strong charge, but one that at least absolved missionaries of economic and political imperialism—anthropologists connected evangelists to U.S. neo-imperialism of the 1970s and 1980s.[37] In this depiction, missionaries served the economic, political, and cultural interests of the United States' new-style empire, an empire that allowed the United States to claim its position as leader of the free world even as it worked against what many scholars saw as the kind of progressive reforms that would break people out of economic prisons. Missionaries carried the banner for a foreign policy that lauded democracy but supported rightwing dictatorships and for an economic policy that demanded open markets so that transnational corporations could freely extract precious resources and undercut local markets. Evangelists' work, these scholars claimed, intentionally and unintentionally, gave the United States more power over people abroad. For anthropologists concerned with indigenous rights, the most egregious cases were found in Latin America and involved evangelical American missionaries—particularly the Bible translators.

Thus, the round between David Stoll and Claude Stipe in *Current Anthropology* was part of a larger bout. In the early 1980s, Stoll had a hand in two published critiques of WBT and SIL. In 1981 he contributed a chapter to Søren Hvalkof and Peter Aaby's volume *Is God an American?*[38] He produced his own study of the translators in 1982's *Fishers of Men or Founders of Empire?*[39] Survival International and Cultural Survival, respectively, published the books. The works focused on the connection among missions, colonialism, and ethnocide. For these anthropologists, the 1970s and 1980s were a perfect storm: conservatives in the White House, a politically powerful religious Right arising in America, and repressive regimes in Latin America. They watched oil companies move into native lands and saw political progressives overthrown. According to the anthropologists, the Bible translators did more than add poison to this mix. They sold it door-to-door as living water. Stoll and his colleagues had a message of their own to deliver: Christian organizations were toxic.

WBT-SIL came under scrutiny for a number of reasons. It was the largest missions organization in the world and, according to Hvalkof and Aaby, "probably the largest single institution to concern itself with the plight of indigenous peoples." Moreover, "SIL's method of operation deserves anthropological scrutiny because through its use of the native language and creation of an indigenous elite it represents a modernized form of cultural imperialism."[40] SIL appeared as the wave of the future. Owing to its size, its methods would dictate how a significant number of people, mainly Americans, interacted with people abroad. It was also a representative of the larger evangelical missionary force, a force that had overtaken the mainline movement by the time indigenous rights groups organized. Stoll and company might have been more comfortable with the practices and politics of mainline Protestants and progressive Catholics overseas but, because their concern was with the groups impacting the largest number of indigenous communities, they focused on evangelicals.

Moreover, SIL's organizational structure brought it into close contact with governments and suggested how thoroughly American evangelicalism was intertwined with (right-leaning) political power brokers. The authors claimed that WBT-SIL's dual identity— the Summer Institute of Linguistics in its relationship with governments and Wycliffe Bible Translators in its missionizing and fundraising modes—showed the immoral depths to which evangelicals would sink for government influence. To the anthropologists, their "dual identity" was a false identity. As SIL, the organization emphasized its linguistic function and received contracts for educational work from Latin American governments. Yet, as WBT, the organization sought to convert indigenous peoples and indoctrinate them in "fundamentalist" Protestantism. The anthropologists found it difficult to stomach the hypocrisy. Stoll wrote: "In fear of God and financial solvency, it has therefore come to pass that one organization has two different purposes. Various contradictory rationales have been proposed to support this position. Eunice Pike described herself as a member of Wycliffe when she translated the Bible, a member of the Summer Institute when she studied a language, and a member of both when she taught people how to read. John Beekman explained that he and his colleagues were officially in Mexico as scientific investigators, but that as individuals each was committed to indigenous church-building principles and translation of the Word."[41] Although Stoll found the duplicity of Christian missionaries disturbing on principle, he was not primarily concerned with what the duplicity indicated about the evangelists' (or linguists') morals. He was most concerned with the government-approved access to indigenous people the organization's dual identity allowed. As educators, SIL workers received government contracts to establish schools. These contracts perfectly positioned SIL to further WBT's goal of conversion and to serve American interests abroad.[42]

Anthropologists did not agree on exactly how SIL served these interests. Some authors in *Is God an American?* claimed that the missionaries knowingly worked with the U.S. military and CIA. Luis A. Pereira repeated a story—one that the editors of the volume noted lacked substantiation—about a missionary helping the U.S. Marines and the Peruvian army locate the Mayorunas Indians so that they could be driven from their mineral-rich land.[43] Stoll, on the other hand, believed that Wycliffe tried to "keep its distance from intelligence gathering and official violence."[44] Indeed, CIA charges lacked solid corroboration and, thus, demonstrated more about anthropologists' fears than SIL's activities. Yet the fears were real. The anthropologists believed that, in countless ways, conservative evangelicals rendered vulnerable cultures defenseless in the face of powerful governments and avaricious corporations.

The authors offered a particular interpretation of evangelical Christianity and missionary demographics to make their case. Scott S. Robinson (a Declaration of Barbados signer) characterized Wycliffe's message as "a mitigating and revelatory brand of faith, born of nineteenth century social frustrations, and bent upon changing the world through mass religious conversion. . . . It is ideologically opposed to confronting the issues of social injustice and capitalist exploitation."[45] Also troubling was the number of missionaries who hailed from the conservative American heartland. Bernard Arcand noted that "I have never heard of a SIL missionary coming from Harlem or Cambridge, Massachusetts."[46] Quite obviously, for Robinson and Arcand, these representatives of the silent majority associated capitalism with godliness and anything that did not smack of Adam Smith with communism. Partisans of the reflexively anticommunist Right, they did not pack land reform, indigenous self-determination, and noncooperation with transnational companies in their mental luggage.

According to the anthropologists, SIL brought unhappy alternatives disguised as real options. SIL doctrine insisted that the Indians make a "choice" between being saved and being damned. While the missionaries defended their activities as providing options, the anthropologists believed they reduced them. Stoll described the situation from the perspective of a Colombian village elder: "What does SIL's alternative belief system mean to this man? Judging from the Wycliffe Statement of Doctrine and previous Gospel victories: 1) he has the opportunity to become a genuine Christian with a personal relationship to Jesus Christ; 2) he has no proper alternative except to watch his people divided into two ideological camps, his own tradition debilitated or destroyed."[47] Saved and damned were not a buffet of alternatives. Moreover, the in or out character of SIL's Christianity split already vulnerable communities. It weakened internal cohesion precisely when native peoples most needed a united front. The choice was also stacked because SIL had power and government contracts on its side. SIL's purportedly nonsectarian schools taught fundamentalist doctrine, and its language centers indoctrinated American evangelicalism in its language informants. Heads Wycliffe won; tails indigenous people lost.

Submission to the inevitable effects of civilization further freighted the salvation option. According to the anthropologists, WBT-SIL taught that Christianity demanded respect for government authority and belief in economic individualism. Whereas the missionaries (at least according to the anthropologists) claimed that they were helping native peoples adapt to inevitable change, the scholars contended that they were robbing the Indians of the ability to do anything but passively submit to their own marginalization and possibly their own extinction. Everyone agreed that change was coming. Big business and new settlers were not going to leave Indian lands alone. The anthropologists, however, wanted indigenous peoples to have the wherewithal to engage encroaching civilization on their own terms. If that seemed a little optimistic in the face of governments with bombs and companies with oil drills, the anthropologists believed more was possible than SIL offered. The organization was too apt to help large corporations. Some anthropologists concentrated more on sins of omission— not doing all the good for native peoples that SIL could. Others focused on sins of commission—SIL's Ecuadorian branch aiding oil exploration in "Waorani [sic]" lands by securing a "reserve" for the people, for example.[48] In the end, WBT weakened tribes by imposing a divisive choice and then preparing the divided people to accept their subordinate position in the capitalist world order. A message, the anthropologists suggested, that was Good News only if God were indeed an American.

Ameliorating voices accompanied the critiques. A few cited examples of missionary aid. Thomas R. Moore even went so far as to claim that the Indians might be better off when the missionaries were present than they were when they left—at least the missionaries served as useful advocates.[49] Stoll's book noted growing diversity within SIL's ranks. He claimed that the organization's policies frustrated some of the missionaries. He pointed to missionary Bob Tripp as an example—but one who also proved his larger point. When an oil company destroyed Amarakaeri fruit trees to make room for a longer airstrip, Tripp alerted SIL authorities. The organization replied, "Keep it cool Bob." According to Stoll, "SIL was absolutely dependent on the state . . . it could not afford to confront the government or its contractors."[50] The organization's dual identity, its reliance on repressive governments, its attachment to capitalist expansion, and its commitment to individualism rendered it impotent. Or, as another anthropologist put it, "never has an ounce of penicillin cost a people so much."[51]

Other anthropologists embraced the volumes' descriptions. Reviews of *Fishers of Men* named it the authoritative account of WBT-SIL.[52] Although reviews noted the uneven nature of the essays in *Is God an American?* (a standard academic critique of edited volumes), they agreed that the authors made the central point: regardless of the missionaries' intent, Wycliffe's God served American interests.[53] Journals such as *Cultural Survival Quarterly* and *North American Congress for Latin America* echoed the concerns. They tied conservative missionaries with Republican politics at home and oppressive regimes abroad. The kind of cultural change evangelicals brought would not benefit native peoples. Certainly anthropologists did not limit their criticisms to missionaries. Bad governments and big business also received anthropologists' ire. Yet missions were part of a potent mix that threatened indigenous life.

The charges against missionaries in the Declaration of Barbados and the WBT-SIL exposés seemed to offer little hope for conversation between anthropologists and missionaries. Accusations of complicity with neocolonialism were certainly as damning as the charges that conversion changed (supposedly) static cultures. Yet the neocolonialist accusation did provide both room and reason to engage in dialogue. Although it was not possible for missionaries to convert without changing elements of a culture, it was thinkable that they might be active without serving U.S. interests. Indeed, as we have seen, since the 1950s, American evangelicals—the group most under anthropological suspicion—had become increasingly aware of their tendency to conflate the Kingdom of God and the United States. Rising nationalism and the growth of the church abroad had catalyzed a reevaluation and changes in tactics. Recall that at the 1974 Lausanne Conference, called by no less a luminary than Billy Graham, evangelicals worldwide had agreed that "the gospel does not presuppose the superiority of any culture to another, but evaluates all cultures according to its own criteria of truth and righteousness, and insists on moral absolutes in every culture. Missions have all too frequently exported with the gospel an alien culture, and churches have sometimes been in bondage to culture rather than to Scripture."[54] Graham himself reinforced the point, noting in his plenary address to the conference that he had been guilty of confusing loyalty to his country and loyalty to the gospel.[55]

Thus, neither the accusation that missions could serve national interests nor the idea that such service was a problem was news to the missionary community. Some missionary partisans claimed that the work of scholars like Stoll helpfully showed further room for improvement. Some conceded problems in their enterprise and publicly portrayed Stoll's critiques particularly as legitimate spurs to greater reform. Charles R. Taber, professor of World Mission at Emmanuel School of Religion, wrote in the *International Bulletin of Missionary Research* that, "as far as I can see, [Stoll's] analysis stands even if one discounts, as I do, Stoll's rejection of evangelism for conversion. It is to be hoped that SIL and the rest of us will learn the lesson of the dangers of allying the gospel with any form of worldly power, which always has its own agenda (which are [sic] seldom compatible with the gospel)."[56] David M.

Howard, whose sister Elisabeth Elliot had served among one of the tribes featured in *Fishers of Men*, reviewed the book for *Missiology* and verified some aspects of Stoll's account: "I know for a fact from firsthand and intimate contact with the Auca story that much of what Stoll presents is accurate, albeit presented through his filters."[57] Howard warned readers that they should not accept all of Stoll's assertions without further investigation but conceded that "if the accusations are correct, we dare not ignore them." Should they prove false, "we must either ignore them or attempt to find out why we project such an image."[58]

Reviewers who took a dimmer view of anthropologists' criticisms still reiterated Howard's final point: anthropologists might treat missionaries unfairly but, as the missionary William Kornfield's wrote in *Evangelical Missions Quarterly*, "if we are interpreted as being something very different from what we perceive ourselves as being or doing, then reassessment of the situation should be made, along with appropriate measures."[59] Kornfield detailed "appropriate measures" such as reevaluating the use of technology and of missionary compounds and ascertaining whether missionaries were preparing "tribal people" to become "capable of defending themselves in the face of exploitation from the outside world."[60] He also stipulated that indigenous people "must be free to choose or reject those elements from Western civilization that will best fit their needs and enable them to cope more effectively."[61] These evangelicals implicitly admitted that they could learn from people outside their fold—indeed, that they needed the perspective. Boundaries clearly delineating acceptable from unacceptable conversation partners served neither people abroad nor the missionary community.

Yet the missionaries had little intention of reevaluating their basic assessment of what people abroad needed. Neither did their anthropological conversation partners. In 1986 David Stoll took to the pages of the journal *Missiology* to tell evangelists what he thought they needed to do. His article "What Should Wycliffe Do?" used findings from two dissertations completed at the evangelical Fuller Theological Seminary by SIL insiders to offer critiques of the organization and to suggest an alternative: retrenchment. Reducing the number of linguists could, Stoll assured readers, enable Wycliffe to accomplish more effectively its original mission of Bible translation while being less complicit with Western power.[62] R. Daniel Shaw, a former member of SIL and a faculty member at Fuller Theological Seminary's School of World Mission responded to Stoll's article, noting that Stoll's previous anti-Wycliffe writings made Shaw wary of the anthropologist's proposal. Overall, "Stoll challenges Wycliffe's right to exist and assumes their work to be of minimal value."[63] Certainly Stoll's suggestion that retrenchment would help Wycliffe fit his own agenda quite nicely. No one should have been surprised. Whether writing an exposé of a missionary organization, conversing with missiologists, or promoting retrenchment, Stoll relied on his assessment of what would be good for Latin Americans, an assessment that involved economic and political reform. That assessment explained his criticisms in *Is God an American?* as well as some positive words about SIL in his 1990 book *Is Latin America Turning Protestant?* He noted that "although SIL can be criticized on many scores much of the leadership of current native rights organizations in the Peruvian Amazon come out of its schools."[64] He also differentiated between missionary groups ready to cooperate with the U.S. government in its attempts to wield power (such as those he linked to Iran-Contra figure Oliver North) and those that, while conservative politically and theologically, did not want to be tools of empire. The former he condemned, and the latter he was willing to praise, at least a little. The criticism and the commendation depended on the missionaries' contribution to Latin American freedom, as Stoll defined it. Like the missionaries who remained adamant that their gospel engendered universal freedom, the anthropologist contended that he knew what the world needed.

Anthropologists' Self-Criticism and Missionary Dialogue

During the same period—the 1970s, 1980s, and 1990s—that anthropologists increasingly focused on issues of neocolonialism and complicity with U.S. power when criticizing missionaries, they were also rethinking their own colonial tendencies. Reflections on their field's genesis, on scholars' involvement with the CIA, and on missionaries themselves all provided scholars with an opportunity for self-assessment. Some did not like what they found. This self-assessment, like missionary criticisms, opened opportunities for dialogue. While missionaries did not find themselves suddenly beloved by scholars, they did become anthropological subjects (rather than simply being obtrusive interlopers in indigenous communities) and, in some cases, possible allies in the fight for indigenous rights.

Anthropologists' public discussions about missionaries in the last decades of the twentieth century occurred in a scholarly milieu troubled by the guild's own colonial background. As Kathleen Gough wrote in a 1968 *Current Anthropology* article, "Anthropology is a child of Western imperialism. . . . it came into its own in the last decades of the 19th and the early 20th centuries. This was the period in which the Western nations were making their final push to bring practically the whole pre-industrial non-Western world under their political and economic control."[65] The sentiment was reiterated—and expanded upon—in works such as Diane Lewis's 1973 bluntly titled "Anthropology and Colonialism" and an edited collection that appeared the same year, *Anthropology and the Colonial Encounter*. In addition to its genesis, anthropology's present commitments were also under scrutiny. The ivory tower could not protect scholars from the decidedly murky reality of the world. In the United States in the 1960s and 1970s, that murkiness was named anticommunism and Vietnam. Anthropologists knew that missionaries were not the only Americans living abroad whom the government saw as potential allies in the fight against communism. As anthropologists began to think about their relationship with missionaries, the field was still dealing with revelations of projects Camelot and AGILE. Both were government-funded anti-insurgency studies that employed anthropologists, among other social scientists. Camelot focused on Latin America, particularly Chile; AGILE centered on Thailand. While some academics defended participation in such research, others denounced it as at least a threat to academic independence if not complicity in American neo-imperialism.[66] Gerald

Berreman, a University of California professor, made it into the *New York Times* when he refused funding that included Pentagon money for research in India. He also noted that revelations regarding anthropologists' involvement with the government made it necessary to assure Indian officials that "he was not an operative of the Central Intelligence Agency."[67] Berreman later took part in a *Current Anthropology* debate about the social responsibilities of anthropologists.[68] Although the scholars differed in their sentiments, many agreed that anthropologists had been guilty of aiding imperialism and needed to stop.

As anthropologists reflected on their colonial genesis and contemporary commitments, they advocated new subjects for study: Westerners. A field that made subjects of non-Western people alone raised ethical issues. The time had come to turn the anthropological gaze homeward or, in the words of Laura Nader, "study up."[69] The reasoning was both pragmatic and principled. Exotic others were disappearing or being acculturated. Moreover, foreign scholars were claiming the right to study themselves. Thus, a call to study new anthropological subjects made sense. Those subjects could be in new fields, like the American suburbs, or could be the overlooked Westerners in the old fields. It was time to study colonial administrators, settlers, and, of course, missionaries.

British anthropologist T. O. Beidelman was on the front end of the new scholarly trend. His 1974 article "Social Theory and the Study of Christian Missions in Africa" bemoaned the dearth of missionary studies. He noted that, even with the current attention to modern societies, "anthropologists tend to neglect those groups nearest themselves."[70] When they study their own societies, they focus "on various sub-cultures with attention towards ethnic minorities and deviant groups" and when they study abroad they attend to "nation-building and development."[71] Their blind spot was particularly a problem in missionary situations: "Anthropologists may have spoken about studying total societies, but they did not seem to consider their compatriots as subjects for wonder and analysis. In the studies of Christianity in Africa, consideration was mainly in terms of the relations of the convert to his traditional society, to the process of social change, or sometimes to the development of native separatist churches. It never included missionaries who had made the conversions or described everyday affairs at the mission station, clinic, or school."[72]

Beidelman answered his own call by publishing *Colonial Evangelism* in 1982. Almost a decade later, renowned scholars Jean and John Comaroff began publishing their two-volume work *Of Revelation and Revolution: The Dialectics of Modernity on the Southern African Frontier*. The book examined interactions among the South African Tswana and British nonconformist missionaries. Like Beidelman, the Comaroffs connected their decision to study missionaries to criticisms about their field. They explained that they were offering "an anthropology *of* the colonial encounter" on "the assumption that, if the discipline has, in the past, been an instrument of a colonizing culture, there is no reason why, in the present, it cannot serve as an instrument of liberation."[73] Making missionaries anthropological subjects allowed them to reveal "the structures and processes by which some people come to dominate others," thereby working against whatever role in colonization their field must own.[74]

Since the Comaroffs claimed that studying missionaries allowed them to analyze processes of domination, they clearly did not think that making evangelists subjects of study equaled endorsing the enterprise. Beidelman agreed. *Colonial Evangelism* and *Of Revelation and Revolution* were thoroughgoing critiques. According to Beidelman, "Christian missions represent the most naïve and ethnocentric, and therefore the most thorough-going, facet of colonial life."[75] Unlike administrators and settlers who sought "limited ends," missionaries "invariably aimed at overall changes in the beliefs and actions of native peoples, at colonization of heart and mind as well as body."[76] The Comaroffs' criticism went even further. They described the evangelists' mission as a "quest to refurnish the mundane."[77] Although purportedly religious, the missionaries wanted to reform all aspects of life to fit their Protestant and, in the Comaroffs' Marxist view, therefore capitalist vision. Indeed, the Comaroffs argued that early British industrial capitalism and Protestant political economy were integral to each other.[78] While not always on board with the political aspects of colonialism, the missionaries served the cause of empire by encouraging a "revolution in habits" that brought the Tswana into the market.[79] By championing European dress, wage labor, and new agricultural practices (among other things), the missionaries helped "to remake people by redefining the taken-for-granted surfaces of their everyday worlds," a key part of colonization.[80] According to Beidelman and the Comaroffs, conservative American evangelicals were not the first servants of government power. Regardless of nationality, all missions led to uneven exchanges that benefited the already mighty and bound the comparatively powerless.

Obviously, not all ethnographies of missions contained positive portrayals. Yet some did portray evangelists positively, or at least neutrally. The year 1978 saw the publication of *Mission, Church, and Sect in Oceania*. The volume combined thoughtful analyses of the evangelist-anthropologists relationship and ethnographic essays about missionary activity. For example, James D. Nason analyzed Congregationalist evangelists in the Solomon Islands. While admitting their ethnocentrism, he denied that their impact was "inherently dysfunctional." Contact with the Western world changed the islands. The missionaries contributed "a religious doctrine that did not inherently change social organization but instead provided an ameliorative symbolic context within which changes could be undertaken without massive interpersonal disruptions within the community."[81] In 1980, Renato Rosaldo published *Ilongot Headhunting, 1883–1974*, a study of the practice among a once-remote tribe in the Philippines. In the introduction, Rosaldo thanked the local New Tribes missionaries for cooperating with his research. He also described New Tribes' role in cultural change, particularly in changing assessments of headhunting, without rancor. He did not treat the missionaries as interlopers. Rather, he explored how different Ilongot responded to the evangelists and to the changes they, as well as others, effected.[82]

The ethnography of missions also led some scholars to enlist missionaries as allies, however begrudgingly at first. Anthropologist Allyn Stearman intended her 1987 work *No Longer Nomads* as a revisiting of the Sirionó peoples first studied in Allan Holm-berg's 1969 *Nomads of the Long Bow*. She worked in the village of Ibiato and found, to her dismay, that she could not ignore its character as a fundamentalist Protestant mission. She had to ac-count for its survival when other tribal towns—non-Protestant, nonmission towns—had disappeared. In spite of unfriendly inter-actions with other evangelists, she realized "I would have to at-tempt to study the missionary presence as dispassionately and objectively as I would my primary subjects, the Sirionó."[83] In a 1989 work on the Yuquí tribe, Stearman once again considered the role missionaries played in cultural survival, albeit still somewhat grudgingly. Six years later, however, Stearman joined forces with the New Tribes missionaries to stop a development project threat-ening the Yuquí. According to a 1995 *Christianity Today* article, Stearman testified that "if the New Tribes people had not inter-vened, the Yuquí would have been overwhelmed."[84] She com-mended the mission for using its role in the community and its power as a U.S. organization well.

Stearman's commendation demonstrated how changes in the anthropological guild redounded upon missionaries. Anthro-pologists' critique of their own colonial past and their tendency to divide the world into studiable "others" and unstudiable Western-ers eventuated in making missionaries subjects. As subjects, mis-sionaries might still find themselves criticized—T. O. Beidelman and the Comaroffs were proof—but they also found themselves taken seriously as elements of indigenous communities. In some cases, their designation as community members allowed anthro-pologists to view them as well-placed potential allies in the fight against the worst effects of expansionist Western power.

Stearman's work also showcased the dynamics of anthropolo-gists' approval. Her studies had included missionaries *and* cri-tiques of them. In her book on the Yuquí, she acknowledged that New Tribes protected the Yuquí, while disagreeing with its gospel and fearing that the organization was unprepared and unwilling to aid the Yuquí in ways she thought necessary. She ended the book with an assertion: "The New Tribes missionaries accepted the responsibility of bringing the Yuquí into the modern world and so they must also confront the long-term consequences of this action. The Yuquí have a right to survive as a people, and that right is now entrusted to the mission."[85] When she joined forces with the mission six years later, she applauded the missionaries for, in essence, doing what she had recommended. They were worthy partners because they agreed to her terms.

Thus, while the ethnography of missionaries allowed anthropologists to treat evangelists as subjects and eventuated in some positive assessments, anthropologists did not abandon their own role as experts. They maintained their academic privilege, namely, offering different interpretations to missionary encounters from what either missionaries or indigenous people might offer. On one hand, this tendency was what being an academic entailed. The failure to analyze missionary encounters critically (which was different from being negative about all missionary encounters) was, simply, poor scholarship. In 1991, for example, Kenelm Burridge published *In the Way: A Study of Christian Missionary Endeavours*. An enlargement of his chapter from *Mission, Church, and Sect in Oceania*, it put missionary practices "within a context framed by their Christianity and varieties of community organization."[86] Burridge tried, in other words, to explain missionaries in their own terms. Reviewers were not kind. Mary Taylor Huber found Burridge's argument "hermetic" and T. O. Beidelman, who complained about the prose he had to wade through to figure out the argument, found the book analytically wanting.[87] Good scholarship meant studying missionaries as subjects, not buying into their moral universe.

Still, anthropologists' status as experts possessed another valence. It could also be read as an assertion that anthropologists knew indigenous people better than they knew themselves. In his generally positive review of the Comaroffs' work, for example, the historian Paul Landau noted that they exercised interpretive power over Tswana actions, articulating which actions indicated conscious resistance to missionaries, which indicated no resistance, and, their central interest, which indicated an unconscious resistance. In asserting that they were conscious of what the Tswana were not, Landau claimed that the Comaroffs "ignore a certain amount of deliberate Tswana expression and grant a proportionately greater amount of authority to themselves as authors."[88] Authorial privilege was not a problem for the Comaroffs alone. Anthropologist Joel Robbins contended that the Comaroffs, like other anthropologists, held notions about how change occurs (slowly) and what religious belief entailed (agreement with propositional truth) that prevented them from taking seriously indigenous people's reports of a sudden, conversionary change or a Christian commitment that demonstrated itself more clearly in a general pattern of life than in absolute agreement with doctrine.[89] Where indigenous accounts of religious experience varied from scholarly standards of religious conversion, scholars trusted their own standards.

Granted, the stakes in academics seeing themselves as experts on others—even when the academics were wrong—might not have seemed very high. (A famous quotation, probably misattributed to Henry Kissinger, holds that in the academy the fights are so vicious precisely because the stakes are so small.) There were stakes nonetheless. Many anthropologists had agendas beyond tenure and promotion. They wanted their work to contribute to political and economic liberation (à la Stoll and the Comaroffs), and they used their expertise to address immediate problems, such as land loss (à la Stearman). How they viewed the realities of people abroad helped to determine their actions and whom they would partner with. Their descriptions of people abroad were also promulgated in textbooks and college classrooms, shaping how nonanthropologists viewed people abroad. If the average college freshman did not wade through *Of Revelation and Revolution*, she might still learn that Latin Americans were converting to forms of Protestant Christianity harmful to their own interests or that American interpretations of African religion proved more determinative to scholarly appraisals than the experience of Africans themselves.

Moreover, anthropologists boasted influence outside Anthropology 101. They have long been implicated in foreign policy. As John Borneman has argued, anthropologists create ideas about the "Other"—who the Other is, whether the Other can be assimilated—that bear on U.S. activity abroad. Borneman notes that "a conceptual framework or model," precisely what anthropologists develop, "is a perceptual orientation for political action."[90] To take one example, "during the Vietnam War, anthropological models of humanness were very much congruent with, if not themselves employed as, the conceptual tools that enabled an envisioning of the Vietnamese as radical cultural Others, yet domesticable, in transition much like American Indians, and integrable into the institutions of electoral democracy and free market capitalism."[91] The newest academic tomes did not necessarily lay open on State Department desks, but scholarly ideas about people abroad could influence how policy makers saw the world.

Scholars such as Stoll, Stearman, and the Comaroffs would have been well aware of this reality. They worked in the decades following the publication of Edward Said's landmark book, *Orientalism*, in which he argued that representations of the Middle East served the imperial program of the nineteenth and twentieth centuries. They worked in a field increasingly conscious of its own neo-imperialist background. All sought to challenge Western power. Yet, they could not fully escape the problems of their own authorial privilege. Like the Orientalists who, Said conceded, were at the time unwittingly used by the empire, modern anthropologists unwittingly echoed a familiar theme: they were the arbiters of what constituted freedom for people elsewhere.[92]

Conclusion

At the end of the twentieth century, many anthropologists believed that what people abroad needed was autonomy from U.S. power. Scholars criticized missionaries insofar as they believed that they impeded such autonomy and worked with them insofar as they thought they would contribute to it. The anthropologists' position was understandable. They had seen the ill effects of Westernization on indigenous communities and wanted to use their expertise to protect vulnerable people.

Yet in their public work, anthropologists also repeated patterns they protested. The United States justified its power in the world by claiming that it was spreading freedom abroad—and that it was the ultimate arbiter of what constituted true freedom. Anthropologists, in turn, argued that they were contributing to indigenous autonomy abroad—and that they knew what that autonomy demanded. The point is not that anthropologists were abnormally blinded to their own ironies or uniquely hypocritical. As we have seen, they could be self-reflective and were no more hypocritical than other Americans struggling with their country's power. Rather, anthropologists' conversations about missionaries show that, if politics is the art of the possible, history is, in part, the study of what was possible. For many thoughtful men and women in the American Century, leaving the world to contend against U.S. power alone was not possible. Acting without using the privileges that came with expertise and with citizenship in a superpower was also impossible. People who both rejected the notion of the United States as a redeemer nation and would not wash their hands of the world had to share in the American paradox.

chapter four

GENDER
※ ※ ※

In 1950 the *Christian Century* reported that female self-interest was impeding an important development in missions. The *Century* was excited about joint efforts between the Foreign Missions Conference (FMC) and the National Council of Churches (NCC)—a movement toward organizational merger. Women, however, were blocking the road to cooperation. They demanded a "cosecretarial arrangement" in the new organization in which a man and a woman would share leadership duties. The *Century* described the demand as "a resurgence of the 'feminist' movement" and lamented that movement adherents "often seem to put its demands ahead of the best interests of the Kingdom."[1] Women would have been as well served by a single-secretary system as men, the article implied. They boasted no need for a separate voice.

Although the *Century* writers seemed baffled by women's demand for equal representation in the new organization, they should not have been surprised. Women's fight for power in missions was long-standing. In the late nineteenth century, women began organizing separate mission societies. They raised and dispersed funds, sponsored female workers abroad, and elucidated their own missions theory. By the end of the nineteenth century, women constituted the majority of missionaries abroad *and* were the backbone of missionary support at home. Notwithstanding their accomplishments, the women's boards had to wage an oft-losing battle to remain separate in the twentieth century. Male-dominated mission boards and denominational agencies mounted several arguments against women's organizations. Some focused on capability—claiming women could not handle money, for example—while others focused on the damage successful women's groups did to the larger male-run cause by, among other things, taking money away from the official, denominational boards. According to historian Dana Robert, however, no argument proved so compelling as the one men made in the early part of the twentieth century: efficiency. With efficiency as the stated good, many denominations forced women's groups to merge with the official boards or significantly limited women's work. As denominations eliminated women's boards, members of the growing faith missions movement avoided the trouble of future dismantling by setting themselves up under male control from the beginning. Thus, by the end of World War II, most autonomous women's boards were a thing of the past. The few that survived underwent merger in the 1950s (e.g., the Woman's American Baptist Foreign Missionary Society) or saw their power severely truncated (the story of Methodist women).[2]

The history of women's missionary boards, like the *Century*'s complaint about women's intransigence regarding the proposed FMC-NCC reorganization, could be read as an internecine ecclesial dispute with little importance outside the world of church councils and denominational politics. The disputes, however, involved more than denominational restructuring. They showed a persistent concern that the church speak authoritatively on issues with global implications as well as a usually implicit belief on the part of men that such an authoritative voice would be masculine. The *Century*'s response to the cosecretarial proposal was part of the Protestant mainline's postwar world-shaping project. *Century* writers had several reasons for believing that combining the FMC and NCC would serve the mainline's leadership agenda. Melding the foreign and the national would integrate the church's work abroad with the rest of its mission. It would also model the kind of institutional unity that the *Century* had long championed as necessary for Christian witness and influence. Rather than diluting Christian influence with a plethora of institutions, one organization would study and speak to the central issues of the day. While the *Century* did not claim that the spokesperson for the new organization had to be male, it did assert that two entities dominated by men most properly spoke to such issues. Women, although long involved in missions in greater numbers than men, contributed nothing to the discussion that warranted making certain that their distinct voices were heard.[3] By denying women's relevance to the discussion and by naming entities led by men as capable of speaking for men and women (a claim not made for the women's organizations), the *Century* reinforced the relationship between masculinity and authority, particularly authority in matters international.

The *Century*'s association of men with political power was embedded in a specific historical context—the United States' postwar ascension to world leadership. It was also an association that long preceded the 1950s and extended beyond it. This chapter explores the relationship among conversations about missionaries, gender, and U.S. power in the postwar decades, attending to both the continuous association between masculinity and power and the historically specific ways that association was manifested.

Previous chapters have argued that in their postwar discussions about missionaries, mainline Protestants, evangelical Protestants, and scholars expressed concerns about how their country exercised power in the world. For differing reasons and in differing ways, they criticized aspects of U.S. economic and military intervention around the world. Yet, in various ways and again for various reasons, they echoed the Wilsonian logic with which the United States justified those interventions. This chapter investigates another way in which Americans simultaneously challenged their country's power abroad: gender. Conversations about missionaries were gendered as were international politics. I argue that these conversations reified understandings of gender that underwrote U.S. power abroad—even when the conversations were critical of U.S. power. In other words, conversations about missionaries were gendered and that gendering often worked against the conversations' explicit critiques.

Unlike previous chapters, which concentrated on missionary discussions within one group, this chapter looks more broadly across U.S. culture. Rather than an exhaustive chronological survey, I focus on key moments and telling discussions. I turn first to ecclesial discussions in the 1950s and show how the portrayal of female missionaries allowed the mainline, itself increasingly critical of U.S. policy, to appear on board with the American project of world responsibility after World War II. I then focus on the discussion in popular culture and use two novels, one from the 1960s and another from the late 1990s, to explore how works that criticized the United States could reify the logic of U.S. power. These three episodes demonstrate that while constructions of gender, evaluations of U.S. activities, and assessments of missionaries all changed throughout the second half of the twentieth century, the public association of power and masculinity—an association that served U.S. power—continued.

Female Missionaries and Mainline Responsibility

One year after the *Century* complained about women impeding the work of the united Division of Foreign Missions, the Methodist *World Outlook* profiled a woman in leadership, Dr. Esther Shoemaker, superintendent of a hospital in India. The writer, Eunice Strickland, recounted Shoemaker's accomplishments but first established the good doctor's feminine credentials. "It was on the platform at a session of the Board of Missions and Church Extension of The Methodist Church that I saw her first—a demure little lady, sitting 'among the doctors.' The graceful black-and-white Indian sari which she wore added to her look of femininity."[4] The accompanying photograph highlighted Shoemaker's feminine appeal. Rather than showing her at work as either a physician or a hospital administrator, the picture was a headshot of a pleasant-looking American woman, with nicely coiffed hair and sensible glasses. Her sari marked her as a missionary but did nothing to emphasize that Shoemaker spent her days overseeing both men and women.

Apparently *Century* writers were not the only ones worried about missions becoming aligned with the feminist movement. While some of the women writing for the *Outlook* might have sided with the cosecretarial arrangement the *Century* abhorred and may have wanted to keep independent authority for the Methodist women's missionary organization, they also wanted to portray their female missionaries as proper women even as those missionaries challenged conventional notions of gender. The problem was not new. Female missionaries had long implicitly challenged conventional notions of gender. Since the beginning of the movement, some women had engaged in activities deemed "unfeminine" at home. During a time when women rarely preached in America, Sarah Boardman Judson, Deborah Wade, and Calista Vinton, nineteenth-century missionaries to Burma, worked as itinerant evangelists.[5] In the late nineteenth century, overseas work provided single women especially with vocational opportunities and personal autonomy not available in the States. Yet depictions of female missionaries attempted to soften their unconventional edges. Biographies of itinerating women either argued that the women were not, in fact, preaching or emphasized the ladylike manner in which the missionary performed her unladylike vocation. Single female missionaries in China portrayed themselves as "good" daughters and "genteel" ladies to their supporters.[6] For these women, presenting themselves in a manner palatable to folk at home demanded negotiating between realities on the field and expectations in the States.

Although the need to appear womanly remained constant through the decades, the circumstances of the postwar years altered the stakes and the strategies. After World War II, the United States underwent one of its periodic "crises" of masculinity. The Great Depression and the war had both contributed to new economic roles for men and women. As men lost jobs during the Depression, many women contributed to or, in some cases, earned the family income by working outside the home, albeit in "women's jobs." When the Depression gave way to war, even more women entered the workforce, now in jobs traditionally performed by men. Rather than viewing these new economic relationships as permanent and potentially positive, however, most Americans believed that the entry of women in the workforce— particularly married women—was an unfortunate aberration. The end of the war brought calls for a return to what many perceived as traditional gender roles: women at home and men at work. The new shape of the U.S. workforce, however, brought another concern: the emasculated organization man. Postwar jobs got men back in the workforce only to put them behind desks, working for large companies that valued conformity more than robust independence. According to cultural commentators, it was a crisis.

The crisis was not merely domestic. Postwar rhetoric tied sexual matters in homes and at home to those international. The supposed crisis in masculinity possessed grave implications for the home and the homeland. If on nothing else, foes such as liberal Arthur Schlesinger Jr. and conservative Joseph McCarthy agreed on this: manly, independent strength was needed to defeat communism abroad and prevent its spread at home. Communists would take advantage of military, political, or personal weaknesses. Anyone who did not conform to heterosexual gender norms posed a national security risk. On both the left and the right, homosexual men were described as indulging in unnatural desires and operating in secret, tendencies that made them vulnerable to the socially disordering message of Marxism and its clandestine method of operation. The lavender threat paved the way for the red menace. Women operating outside of their proper roles also presented a political problem because they created psychologically weak children, especially boys. Psychologists decried "Momism," a coddling, overprotective mothering that produced dependent, immature men—not the kind of men equal to the task of keeping the free world free. According to experts in the 1940s and 1950s, for their own good, for the good of their boys, and for the good of their country, women needed to be "contained" by strong men. If properly contained, they would rear children able to defend freedom. They would also provide sexual outlets for husbands who would then not need to indulge the kinds of perversions that would then make them vulnerable to communist wiles. Creating nuclear families in which a strong father exercised authority over a domestically contained mother and freedom-ready children was seen as crucial in the United States' victory in the nuclear age.[7]

Making single, female missionaries with M.D.s who ran hospitals congenial participants in the U.S. project of leading the world and stemming the communist advance entailed highlighting various ways such apparently uncontained women fit with the program. Emphasizing their femininity was one route. Eunice Shoe-maker was demur in her sari. In 1961 Dr. Lalla Iverson, a single medical missionary wrote an article for the Methodist magazine *Together* about "the special compensations and opportunities of life without a family."[8] Iverson, the director of a medical organization in India, allowed that single persons could find satisfaction in jobs, hobbies, and nonmarital relationships. Still, she remained committed, in principle, to the pattern of 1950s domesticity: "I would not choose this pattern [of singleness] in preference to the normal functions of a woman, provided these were based on a foundation of real love. But it is my pattern, and not an unrealistic substitute."[9] The depictions indicated that single, female missionaries performing professional jobs abroad were not undermining the 1950s reassertions of traditional gender norms.[10]

The results of female missionaries' work also mitigated their challenges to prevailing gender norms. Their lives, albeit unconventional, enabled women abroad to become like middle-class, Protestant, American women. Joe and Dorothy Davis, Methodists serving in the Central Congo, explained to readers in 1953 the importance of training young girls. "Graduates who have been taught in the Girl's Home make good wives, and help their husbands in their work," they assured supporters. "They realize the significance and sacredness of marriage, they have learned sewing, housewifery, gardening and the three R's."[11] A 1948 *Outlook* article tied the elevation of women's status in Portuguese East Africa with the attainment of domestic skill. The article's artwork made clear the need for elevation. The caption above a picture of smiling African women read: "At the moment they do not seem at all depressed by the not-very-high status of women."[12] Missionaries addressed the problem through mission schools like Canaan, "a practical sort of model or practice home where the students are free to work out their own salvation in the way of budgeting, menus, and original ideas for daily living."[13] Though neither the Apostle Paul nor John Wesley had described menu planning as a way of working out salvation, Methodist missionaries believed it a necessary component in becoming a proper Christian woman.

Because proper gender roles were correlated with democratic politics, making American gender prescriptions normative throughout the world served the anticommunist cause. In another 1948 article, writer Dorothy McConnell described the work of American missionaries among Burmese women. The article seamlessly wove together American leadership, Christian womanhood, and democracy. McConnell recounted meeting a group of Burmese women in a missionary's home. Now that the end of war allowed missionaries to return to Asia, the Burmese women eagerly sought the American's advice on a range of issues. Specifically, the women sought help in establishing a Woman's Society of Christian Service, guidance in conducting their private devotions, and wisdom on preparing themselves to be citizens in an independent, democratic country. That Burmese women wanted the missionaries' assistance, and that their areas of interest were similar to those of Methodist women in America, signaled that their sisters in the United States need not fear that their political independence would go the way of communism.[14] A January 1954 pictorial, "Methodist Women around the World," told the same tale. The pictures portrayed women abroad teaching other women, just as missionary women had taught them. An editorial comment noted, "Differing in dress and in facial structure, there are, nevertheless, certain characteristics that are found in Methodist women everywhere."[15] Like Methodist women at home, these women studied the Bible, participated in Women's Society meetings, and read copies of World Outlook. Such familiar pictures of femininity indicated not only that women abroad had become proper women but that they were part of the Christian bloc that could withstand gender-bending communists.

The possible challenge that female missionaries presented to prevailing gender norms in the 1940s, 1950s, and early 1960s, therefore, was contained in Methodist mission publications. Moreover, acceptance of gender norms and the gendered logic of U.S. power suggested that the mainline criticism of its country during the 1950s that we saw in a previous chapter was also contained. Fundamentally, the mainline was on board with the U.S. project of world leadership. The criticisms it mounted focused on strategy and specific issues, not the assumption of world leadership. Indeed, by spreading purportedly democracy-supporting gender norms and downplaying the leadership of American missionary women, the mainline movement aligned itself with the dominant vision of U.S. power as male and ready to lead.

In later decades, people throughout America mounted more incisive critiques of U.S. power in the world. They also troubled the carefully calmed gender waters of the 1950s. During the 1960s and 1970s, the mainline more openly criticized U.S. policy. It also grew more receptive to the feminism that the *Century* dismissed in 1950. A United Methodist filmstrip that attempted to convince parishioners that the move from "foreign missions" (with all of its colonial associations) to "the mission of the church" contained an explanation of systemic evil. Ice cream, the soothing female voice narrating the filmstrips intoned, provided one example. Against the picture of an ice cream cone, the narrator noted that "we buy chocolate with the sugar to sweeten it and wonder what the price will be tomorrow but do we ever think about the perpetual poverty of the workers who harvest the cocoa nuts that make our chocolate?"[16] Bad systems served Americans well but kept others in poverty. Thirty-nine frames later, the narrator lauded the work of the Women's Division. "Women, you know . . . or do you know all our strengths?"[17] As the narrator suggested that women possessed heretofore unrecognized capabilities, the filmstrip featured a number of women picketing a New York grocery store with signs such as "Gristedes sells scab grapes."[18] No longer "contained" housewives who unthinkingly participated in unjust economic systems, these women protested exploitative businesses, simultaneously challenging the gender order and the powerful systems it underwrote.

Mounting criticisms notwithstanding, however, U.S. and male power continued to reinforce each other. People troubled by the former often implicitly reified the latter, which, owing to the long-established relationship between power and masculinity, ultimately reinforced both.

Missions, Gender, and Power in
At Play in the Fields of the Lord

The relationship among gender, missions, and American power was not only evident in ecclesial discussions; it also appeared in popular fiction. In the decades following World War II, several popular novels featuring missionaries were published. All raised questions about U.S. power, although how intertwined they believed the missionary movement was to it varied. Yet reading the novels with attention to gender demonstrates that even as the stories challenged U.S. hegemony abroad, they reified the relationship between masculinity and power upon which that hegemony rested.[19]

I use two novels to show how this reification occurred: Peter Matthiessen's 1965 novel *At Play in the Fields of the Lord* and John Grisham's 1999 best seller *The Testament*. Both question U.S. power abroad, both boast strong female characters, and both end with a man whose masculinity had been shaped into a form that could be trusted with power.

THE COLONIAL CRITIQUE

In 1959 and 1960, novelist, *Paris Review* founder, and nature writer Peter Matthiessen traveled throughout South America. His trip produced two books: the nonfiction *Cloud Forest* and the novel *At Play in the Fields of the Lord*. According to William Dowie, the latter allowed Matthiessen to explore imaginatively what he had been unable to do during his trip, specifically, spend time with one of the Amazon's most remote tribes, the Amahuacas.[20] In *At Play in the Fields of the Lord*, the Amahuacas have become the Niaruna, an Amazonian tribe whose land the local comandante wants. The comandante has at his disposal two American soldiers of fortune, Wolfie Guzman and Lewis Meriwether Moon. He holds their passports in hock and will return them once Guzman and Moon bomb the Niaruna.

Two American missionary couples are also playing in the Lord's fields. Leslie and Andy Huben are young and handsome missionaries with a successful evangelistic track record among Indians considered more civilized than the Niaruna. Owing to their performance, they are sent to the Niaruna. To assist their work with the remote tribe, their mission organization, New Fields, sends Martin and Hazel Quarrier and their young son Billy, formerly missionaries among the Sioux in South Dakota. Unlike the Hubens, the Quarriers are an "ugly couple" and Martin, though the scion of a missionary family, has achieved little success. Reasons for Leslie's apparently better record soon become clear. Converting people is Leslie's only ambition. He cares little about the means to conversion. He refuses to confront the comandante's plans to bomb the Niaruna because, as he tells an aghast Martin Quarrier, "if the Niaruna *can* be cowed a little, they will be softened up for an outreach of the Word, and this will make our—yes, *your* work too, Martin, don't look at me like that—a darn sight easier."[21] Quarrier rejects Huben's logic. He also rejects Leslie's less violent evangelistic methods, such as baiting potential converts with "cloth and beads, mirrors and ax heads."[22] Quarrier, at times in spite of himself, has some respect for Indian culture. In Huben's eyes (and sometimes his own), that makes him a poor missionary.

The main action of *At Play* occurs among the Niaruna. The missionaries establish a small mission station on the outskirts of the Niaruna forest. They are joined by some converts and some soldiers for protection. Unbeknownst to them, one of the soldiers of fortune, Lewis Moon, is living among the Niaruna. Under the influence of *ayahuasca*, a local hallucinogenic, Moon steals the plane with which he was to bomb the Niaruna, parachutes out of it, and lands in Niaruna territory. The Indians, having seen him come out of the plane and descend from the sky, believe that he is a god, Kisu. Both the mission and Moon prove disruptive to the Niaruna. The Niaruna—Moon included—debate attacking the mission. One young warrior, Aeore, unseats the older, more cautious chief Boronai owing to his greater willingness to go to war. The Niaruna's attacks on the mission prompt Leslie Huben to notify the comandante, who seizes the excuse to bomb the Niaruna village.

The interactions among the Americans, the local comandante,

the "civilized" Indians, and the "wild" Niaruna showcase problems of colonialism and Western expansion. The comandante's plan to annihilate the Niaruna so their land can be developed most explicitly portrays Western power's threat to native peoples and undeveloped lands. The missionaries oppose the comandante's plan but their work among the Indians is its own kind of strafe bombing. The mission pits Indian against Indian. When the Hubens and Quarriers go to the Niaruna, they bring with them soldiers from another tribe, the Quechua; debate over how to respond to the mission's presence divides the Niaruna; and visits to the mission expose the Niaruna to influenza, resulting in widespread death. Although the comandante and the missionaries disagree about how to treat the Niaruna, they all operate with the assumption that the Niaruna must be brought out of their isolation. The comandante wants them civilized out of their land or killed. The missionaries want them brought into the mission.

Lewis Meriwether Moon serves as evidence that the government and missionary paths intertwine and lead almost inexorably to native extinction, wherever missionaries, governments, and natives encounter each other. The son of a half-white, half-Cheyenne man and a half-white, half-Choctaw woman, Moon grew up on a Plains reservation. Missionaries "decided to make an example of him" because he "was bright, and he had a fine war record, and he was a Christian."[23] He attended the state university but was thrown out for assault and robbery before graduation. Moon's own missionary past shows that civilization and Christianization had resulted in enervation and destruction for American Indians. His complicated attitude toward Indians indicates a confused self-identity brought by the loss of cultural moorings. Until he encounters the Niaruna, "the only Indians Moon would acknowledge were the old men of his childhood who had survived the long wars with the whites on the Great Plains."[24] Yet Moon was the kind of Indian he despised. As a child he knew that "he was not like the old men, nor even like his father; he spoke American and raised the American flag at school; he wore blue jeans and looked at magazines in stores and stood around outside the movie in the town, searching his pockets as if he had real money; he did not believe in visions. Like all the children, he killed his hunger at the mission house on Sunday and afterward felt ashamed."[25]

Moon's inner conflict, born out of the clash between white and Indian cultures, takes him to the Niaruna, but his role among the Niaruna is deeply ambiguous. He has come to the Niaruna because he views them as real Indians. He lives among them and accepts one of the chief's wives as a lover. Still, he is not Niaruna. His shoeless feet are tender to the ground. He does not share the Niaruna comfort with an audience during sex. Moreover, by positioning himself as a god, he places himself above the people. His appearance delays the ambitions of Aeore, the young, aggressive warrior who is training to be a jaguar-shaman. With the god Kisu present, the shaman is unnecessary.

Moon does intend to help the Indians. Knowing that the comandante will use any attack on the mission as an excuse to annihilate the Niaruna, he cautions the tribe's leader, Boronai, against Aeore's plan to rid the jungle of missionaries. In the early days of his influence, Moon is pleased with his position and power. Reflecting on his decision to go to the jungle, he remembers that "what had not occurred to him in the beginning was how he might help the Niaruna." With time, however, "he saw that he could help protect these rivers from the white man; with any sort of leadership, the Indians could rule their wilderness indefinitely."[26] Yet, as the missionaries on the plains that Moon despised and the missionaries in South America he dislikes both discovered, even well-intentioned attempts to help (or lead) other people can go wrong. When discussing with Aeore how any eventual battle between the Niaruna and the Indians must seek to avoid significant casualties, "Aeore looked incredulous: to accept in advance the sacrifice for tactical gain of even one of their own warriors was offensive to him. . . . his reaction, which would have been typical of a Cheyenne, was a rebuke to Moon, reminding him as it did how far his long experience as a white man, as a white soldier, had removed him from the Old Ways."[27] In Moon, the difficulties anyone with any white blood would have in serving well any group of native peoples becomes painfully manifest.

Matthiessen's critique of colonialism in various forms is thorough. He shows the threat native peoples face from politicians eager for them to take their subordinate place in the Western economic order. He also demonstrates that people with more benevolent intentions—missionaries like Quarrier, for example—can unwittingly do harm. They foment dissension among native people. They misunderstand and undervalue the culture. Lewis Moon's conflicted self-identity and his own interactions with Niaruna testify to how deeply colonialist attitudes affect people and how problematic the expansion of white power (even white power that is only half white) can be.

WHAT IT MEANS TO BE A MAN

At Play in the Fields of the Lord is about colonialism. It is also about manhood. Just as Moon searches for real Indians, the book searches for authentic manhood. Various alternatives present themselves, from the *machismo* of the comandante to the European urbanity of the local priest, Father Xantes. Matthiessen's explorations of masculinity occur most prominently, however, through the three major male characters: Leslie Huben, Martin Quarrier, and Lewis Moon.

The question of manhood—What constitutes it and what type of manhood will prove beneficial for others?—is explicitly raised throughout the book. After listening to jibes about his infatuation with Andy Huben, Martin Quarrier challenges Lewis Moon to a fight saying, "Well, come outside! If you are man enough!"[28] Later, Quarrier wonders of Moon, "What sort of man was this?"[29] After his own run-in with Moon, Leslie Huben reflects that "he had gotten a kind of nervous feeling, kind of silly or *unmasculine* or something" (emphasis in the original).[30] Andy Huben shares her husband's doubts about his masculinity. She tells Martin that she had come to him with a problem because "I thought you were a man. . . . Leslie is a boy."[31]

Having invited readers to consider manhood, Matthiessen portrays one form of it as fatally flawed. Leslie Huben radiates optimistic, confident, white American manhood. He is young, successful, and handsome, already a "legend" in the mission when the book begins. A college athlete, Huben left a "lucrative job in the real-estate and insurance business to emulate St. Paul."[32] Andy was originally drawn to him because he was so different from "the mild young men in rimless glasses" she met in her father's house.[33] Leslie had seemed to her "an ideal combination of Christian decency and warm-blooded manliness."[34] He is the man next door.

As a prototypical American man, Leslie embodies a version of masculinity intimately tied to U.S. postwar power. His athletic, confident manliness was viewed as one antidote to the interrelated postwar crises of masculinity and communism. He is the strong, confident man who sees himself as the leader of his family and, concomitantly, as the leader of other people.

The connection between masculinity and U.S. power was not an artifact of the 1950s alone. John F. Kennedy, in his presidential campaign and his administration, emphasized his own elite masculinity—what historian Robert Dean calls his "aristocratic persona embodying the virtues of the stoic warrior-intellectual."[35] He surrounded himself with other elite men and claimed that his administration would reverse the course of eight years of Republican "softness" by closing the purposed missile gap with the Soviet Union and by sending vigorous, independent men to places abroad where communists were making inroads as coddled American diplomats sat securely in their embassies. While Kennedy's own version of masculinity was elite—it was the manhood of Choate and touch football at the family compound in Kennebunkport—he tied the masculine fitness of common men to U.S. strength abroad as well. As president-elect he penned an article in *Sports Illustrated*, explicitly connecting masculine and national strength: "The harsh fact of the matter is that there is also an increasingly large number of young Americans who are neglecting their bodies—whose physical fitness is not what it should be—who are getting soft. And such softness on the part of individual citizens can help to strip and destroy the vitality of a nation."[36] He called the young men of America to make their bodies fit for the defense of the United States. As Dean notes, "Kennedy subscribed to cyclical and organic theories of national power: nations grew strong in their youth and declined with age, just as men's bodies did."[37] The sign to the rest of the world that the United States was young and vigorous would come as the president stood toe to toe (and man to man) with Khrushchev and refused to blink, as the military built arms sufficient for the protection of U.S. interests worldwide, and as men around the country prepared their bodies and spirits to carry out their civic duty, bolstering democracy and defending the country against any form of communist infiltration.

By the time the all-American Leslie Huben hit the shelves in 1965, his version of masculinity had fallen under some criticism. Betty Friedan published *The Feminine Mystique* in 1963, arguing that the 1950s prescription for traditional gender roles constricted women. The foreign policy associated with confident, virile American men was also losing its luster in the hills of Vietnam. Although Matthiessen's critique did not necessarily draw from either source directly, Huben's character raised related points. The same confidence and need to assert masculinity that prodded both the Kennedy and Johnson administrations to increase involvement in Vietnam led to Huben's disaster among the Niaruna. Johnson told author Doris Kearns that he feared that if he "lost" Vietnam like Harry Truman had "lost" China, Robert Kennedy would claim that he "had betrayed John Kennedy's commitment to South Vietnam" and that "I was a coward. An unmanly man. A man without a spine."[38]

Huben too viewed success among the Niaruna as a test of leadership and proved equally unable to see the signs of coming failure. His own version of capitalist exchange—trinkets for professions of salvation—garnered only disloyal clients, more interested in the goods than the message (not unlike the right-wing dictators who took U.S. support without instituting democracy). His determination to interpret everything that happens in his mission as a sign of spiritual success makes him unsympathetic, if not inhumane. During their time at the mission, Martin Quarrier's son Billy dies. Huben insists that the sad event will lead to the conversion of the Niaruna. That pronouncement draws a stinging rebuke: "Death took my son," Quarrier responds. "But if He had, the Lord would not be welcome to my son."[39] What looked like Leslie's appropriately masculine confidence at the beginning of the novel is unveiled as callous hubris at the end. After watching her husband hide cowardice and insensibility under self-righteous religious conviction, Andy Huben aptly summarizes what has happened to him and the masculinity he represents. "Do you know something, Leslie. . . . You've shrunk."[40]

Yet Matthiessen's critique of Huben's masculinity was not a critique of masculinity altogether. Indeed, *At Play* repeatedly questions whether Leslie is a man at all. His name, Leslie, and his wife's name, Andy, are gender bending. The couple, although married for several years, have no children, an unexplained situation that leaves open the possibility that Leslie lacks virility. Andy herself calls Leslie "a boy." By suggesting that the problematic version of masculinity Leslie carries abroad is not really masculinity at all, Matthiessen allows the possibility that there is an appropriate way to be an American man in the world.

The two other most prominent men in the story, Martin Quarrier and Lewis Moon, differ from Leslie's all-American manhood. Quarrier is ugly, conflicted, and unsuccessful. Moon is disloyal, biracial, and rebellious. Both are more sympathetic than Huben. They are possible manly alternatives.

Unlike Leslie, whose character does not change over the course of the story, Martin Quarrier develops during his time in Latin America. When he arrives, he is an evangelical missionary who possesses misgivings about some evangelical missionary practices. While Leslie Huben turns a blind eye to the comandante's bombing plans and his participation in the local slave trade in order to curry favor for the mission, Martin wants to oppose both on principle. Rather than contenting himself with the Indians' assertions that they have become Christians—and rewarding those testimonies with U.S. goods—Quarrier demands evidence of conversion. By the end of the book, Quarrier no longer considers himself a missionary. After his son's death and his wife's descent into madness, he begins to doubt his calling. As the mission falls apart, he attempts to tell the Niaruna about the comandante's genocidal plans. In the process, he meets Moon and realizes that the word the missionaries have been using for Jesus, "Kisu," actually refers to the very spirit the Niaruna take Moon to be. Reflecting on his doubts and his missionary failures, Quarrier decides that he is "unqualified to be a servant of the Lord."[41] He tells Moon that he intends to return to the Niaruna but as an ethnologist. He has been, he says, "more of an ethnologist than a missionary right along."[42] Although Martin appears bookish and uncertain next to Huben, he proves thoughtful, principled, and capable of change. He is not, however, the novel's hero. Quarrier is killed by one of the supposedly civilized converts while trying to warn the Niaruna about the comandante. He sacrifices his life for the Indians yet his sacrifice accomplishes nothing. He is a man, a good man, but, ultimately, an ineffectual man.

Lewis Moon becomes a man capable of effecting change—although until the final pages of the book, he seems impotent. Moon is unable to save the Niaruna. The comandante attacks the village. Aeore leaves the Niaruna. The new chief takes those who remain away from their traditional land, a retreat that the Niaruna considered "the sign of a dying clan."[43] The book, however, does not end with the Niaruna debacle. The book ends with Moon floating eastward, alone. He floats further into the jungle, away from missionaries, government officials, and the Niaruna. During the trek, he comes to resolution about his central problem: his competing identities as white and Indian. The conflict between the two had led him to the Niaruna and, once there, had undermined his plan to become fully one of them. Should Moon ever want to do the kind of good he had envisioned, he must solve this conflict. The trip down the river accomplishes the feat. Floating in his boat, in a place where there "was no sign of man," he "felt bereft, though of what he did not know. He was neither white nor Indian, man nor animal, but some mute, naked strand of protoplasm."[44] Becoming neither white nor Indian, man nor animal could be read as an annihilation of self. For Moon, however, the loss of competing identities allows for his reconstitution as the universal man. As he continues to drift, he thinks "Am I the first man on earth; am I the last?"[45] Progenitor or survivor, Moon is now the hope of the future—he will constitute or reconstitute the human race. In the final scenes, he makes a fire "in celebration of the only man beneath the eye of Heaven."[46] Moon is the lone man under heaven and the bringer of fire. He is both Adam and Prometheus.

The novel's end is open to multiple interpretations. It is possible that Moon's new identity is predicated on his separation from all other people. Like Huck Finn, he may have decided to light out on his own, having seen civilization once before. In this scenario, Moon's masculinity would undermine the relationship between manhood and power over others. True manhood would be not just independent but isolated.

The resonances of Adam and Prometheus, however, suggest another reading. You do not start the human race or discover fire and end your days living alone. Nor do you become part of the anonymous crowd. Indeed, Moon has become precisely the kind of man who can effectively live in the world. As Richard F. Patteson has argued, the resolution of Moon's identity allows him "to return from the fields of the Lord to the field of human involvement."[47] Moon's many assets, his intelligence and his bravery, for example, will no longer be subordinated to his rage and his confusion. Now as the first man, the prototypical man, he can bridge divisions among other men. He is now a man capable of leading in a way that no other man in the novel could. He is not a partisan of any race or nation. Unlike Leslie Huben, he is intelligent and truly brave. Unlike Aeore, he is not driven by anger. Unlike Martin Quarrier, he is physically strong and confident. Unlike the missionaries in the novel, this new Prometheus brings to people something that they need, indeed, something that will make them less dependent on the wills of unpredictable gods.

In this reading, Matthiessen has crafted a manhood capable of leadership. And, make no mistake, it is *man*hood. Moon is the either the first or last *man* on earth and the only *man* beneath the eye of heaven. That "man" does not denote "human" is clear from the persistent question throughout the novel of what makes a man, a question always asked in reference to someone male. Although Andy Huben and Hazel Quarrier figure prominently in the book—Andy, particularly, is notable for her perceptive analysis of the men involved with the mission—their fates depend on the male characters' actions. Thus, after his critique of colonialism, Matthiessen reinscribes the relationship between power and masculinity. That is not to say that in the end he accepts colonialism. It is to say that he does not completely undo the gendered logic underwriting colonialism and that he leaves open the possibility that the right kind of leader the world has been looking for is an American man.

Missions, Gender, and Power in *The Testament*

In 1999 readers of John Grisham's *The Testament* met an evangelical missionary who shared many of Leslie Huben's theological convictions. Grisham's book featured Rachel Lane, a missionary serving with a nondenominational faith mission (the fictional World Tribes) in Brazil's Pantanal, the world's largest wetland. Like Huben, Lane believes in a literal heaven and a literal hell. She believes that without a confession of sin, faith in Jesus Christ as savior, and a conversion experience, people spend eternity in the latter. She feels uncomfortable with swearing but perfectly at ease asking people where they expect to spend the afterlife.

Theological affinity aside, Lane and Huben share little else. Where Huben is hubristic, culturally insensitive, and cowardly, Lane is humble, culturally aware, and courageous. She serves as a doctor among an isolated tribe. Unlike Huben, who used trinkets to woo converts, Lane cares for anyone in need without attaching strings. Although she hopes to convert the indigenous people, she respects their culture and does not equate Christianization with Americanization. Indeed, this point most differentiates Grisham's character from Matthiessen's. Leslie Huben is the paradigmatic American man abroad—he is what happens when the boy next door is exported. Rachel Lane, on the other hand, offers both implicit and explicit critiques of U.S. culture. She criticizes capitalistic practices that denude the rainforests. Heir to a multibillion dollar fortune, she rejects goods gained through U.S. corporate culture in favor of a simple life in the Pantanal. Both Rachel and

Leslie are evangelicals, but their relationship to their homeland differs greatly.

That John Grisham shared an assessment of the trouble the United States created abroad with Peter Matthiessen but differed on his evaluation of evangelical missionaries was not surprising given Grisham's oeuvre and life. *The Testament* was Grisham's eleventh novel and a greater critical success than Grisham's previous endeavor, *The Street Lawyer*. In Grisham's case, critical success did not signal a literary masterpiece but greater character development and a more variegated plot than his earlier novels boasted. The novel retained, however, one of Grisham's common themes: the deleterious effects of wealth and power. Grisham's novels typically featured a David and Goliath battle wherein David was a young, idealistic lawyer or law student fighting for the underdog against some Goliath-like representative of corporate, politically connected America. *The Testament* varied slightly in that all of the lawyers were seasoned and the true idealist (Rachel) never appeared in a courtroom. Still, the theme of wealth-induced moral corruption remained.[48]

The Testament posited a solution to this corruption: religious faith. Religion had not featured prominently in any of Grisham's previous novels, but he dismissed the notion that religion's prominence in *The Testament* signaled a newfound faith in his own life. In a *USA Today* interview published in conjunction with his book, Grisham called himself a "moderate Southern Baptist" (noting that "there's no such thing as a liberal Southern Baptist") and revealed that he had been to Brazil on short-term mission trips "six or seven times" since 1993.[49] Adding religion to the novel was an authorial challenge but not a personal stretch. Grisham explained that he wanted to take Nate, a character who has "tried power and women and booze and drugs and the fast life and all the good things that money can buy" and who has "crashed and burned four times in 10 years" and "sort of follow him on a kind of spiritual journey, his quest for a spiritual core. I was challenged by the goal of seeing if I could make such a spiritual journey work in a popular novel, in commercial fiction."[50] Grisham's public statements and his book indicated a deep respect for religious people as well as a strong sense that good missionaries, far from importing the worst aspects of Western lifestyles abroad, served well the people among whom they worked.

Yet, like *At Play in the Fields of the Lord*, *The Testament* reinforced the power structures it explicitly condemned. In telling the story of a missionary who refused a fortune and a lawyer who found God, Grisham too criticized expansive Western power even as he reified its gendered structure.

CHRISTIANITY AND A NEO-IMPERIALIST CRITIQUE

Most straightforwardly, *The Testament* celebrates the Christian faith of evangelical missionary Rachel Lane and criticizes American greed and Western expansion. The book begins with moral vacuity and greed in America. Aging billionaire Troy Phelan has called his dysfunctional family together to watch him sign the will that they presume divides his fortune among them. Before signing, he undergoes a psychiatric evaluation to prevent his heirs from challenging his final wishes on the grounds of insanity. He then signs the will and immediately commits suicide. Unbeknownst to his family (three ex-wives with six spoiled, lazy adult children among them), Phelan has another will, one that leaves his entire fortune to Rachel Lane, his secret, illegitimate daughter. He also tells his lawyer to delay the will's reading for as long as possible. As their conniving father suspected, his disinherited heirs believe themselves quite wealthy and spend wildly. By the time the real will is read, they have racked up huge debts. They then contest the will, forcing Phelan's lawyers to find the missing heir.

The Phelan family is not alone in witnessing to the morally corrosive effects of great wealth. At the beginning of the book, Nate O'Reilly, the successful litigator charged with finding Rachel, is twice divorced, estranged from his children, and just finishing his fourth stint in rehab. Nate is less reprehensible than the Phelan kin but remains another sign of the personal costs stemming from America's materially obsessed culture.

Rachel Lane, on the other hand, testifies to another way of life. A medical missionary serving in the Pantanal, she lives simply among the people. After finding her, Nate describes her lifestyle to another lawyer: "She lives alone in a hut with a thatched roof, no plumbing, no electricity, simple food and clothes, no phone or faxes, and no concern about the things she's missing."[51] Indeed, Rachel is so content with her life that she declines her inheritance. When Nate accuses her of using her vocation as way to escape real life, Rachel claims a serenity that neither Nate nor her half siblings know: "I have perfect peace, Nate. I surrendered my will to Christ many years ago, and I follow wherever He leads."[52]

Language such as "surrendering my will to Christ" indicates that Rachel is an evangelical missionary. Although Grisham never uses the designation "evangelical" for her, her rhetoric, practices, and affiliations mark her as part of the movement. She forthrightly confesses to Nate that she believes in heaven, hell, and the necessity of conversion. When he uses the word "helluva," she asks him to watch his language. When Nate decides to convert, she guides him through an evangelical conversion script in which he repeats a prayer asking for forgiveness and empowerment: "Dear God, Forgive me of my sins, and help me to forgive those who have sinned against me. Give me strength to overcome temptations, and addictions, and the trials ahead."[53] Her missionary organization, World Tribes Missions, evangelizes among the most remote people in the world—a program akin to evangelical groups such as Wycliffe Bible Translators and New Tribes Missions that are not affiliated with a denomination and focus on bringing the gospel to unreached groups. Conversionist, pious, and part of a parachurch group, Rachel is an evangelical through and through.

In *The Testament*, however, evangelical Christianity does not equal complicity with Western power. On his trip to find Rachel, Nate sees the devastation wrought by big business. Rachel confirms what he sees, explaining that the native people farm on land until it loses fertility, move to another place, and return only when the land has recovered. Development threatens their ecologically sensitive mobility. She tells Nate, "We decimate their population with bloodshed and diseases, and take away their land. Then we put them on reservations and can't understand why they're not happy about it."[54] The "we" signals that Rachel understands

Americans (like herself and Nate) to be part of the problem. Her willingness to criticize her country demonstrates that her evangelical religion has not made her sympathetic to the spread of a Western economic system. Indeed, the book suggests that faith in God can help people resist its allure. When Mr. Montgomery, one of Phelan's lawyers, first contacts World Tribes to find Rachel's whereabouts, he explains that she has inherited significant wealth. World Tribes, however, has guaranteed Rachel that no one connected with her father's family would ever learn her location. The World Tribes worker and Mr. Montgomery have the following conversation:

> "I'm sorry, Mr. Montgomery," he said without sitting. "We will not be able to help you."
> "Is she in Brazil?"
> "I'm sorry."
> "Bolivia?"
> "I'm sorry."
> "Does she even exist?"
> "I can't answer your questions."
> "Nothing?"
> "Nothing."
> "Could I speak to your boss or supervisor?"
> "Sure."
> "Where is he?"
> "In heaven."[55]

Allegiance to a God overcomes the temptations of wealth.

Rachel knows that indigenous survival demands resisting Western power. At the end of the book, Nate learns that Rachel has died from malaria. Before her death, she drafted legal documents putting her new fortune into a trust and naming Nate as the administrator. The money is to "a) to continue the work of World Tribes missionaries around the world, b) to spread the Gospel of Christ, c) to protect the rights of indigenous peoples in Brazil and South America, d) to feed the hungry, to heal the sick, shelter the homeless, and save the children."[56] Once again, evangelical faith and a critique of the economic and political forces that render so many hungry, sick, and homeless are tied.

Although reviewers did not consider *The Testament* great literature, several compared it to Joseph Conrad's critically acclaimed (and, in a postcolonial world, critically deconstructed) novel, *The Heart of Darkness*. Both involve journeys into jungles and raise questions about Western civilization. Grisham's book, however, flips Conrad's moral geography. In *Heart of Darkness*, the African interior makes a savage out of a Western, civilized man. Nate O'Reilly, on the other hand, becomes a better man by going to the Latin American interior. By living in the Pantanal, Rachel Lane distances herself from the ills of civilization: greed, self-centeredness, and their attendant broken relationships. Where Conrad's book seemed to suggest that Westerners forswear colonialism in order to protect themselves from the savagery of Africa, Grisham posits that there is great sickness in the United States from which people abroad needed protecting. Although it is possible to be good and be an American—Rachel does note on her will that she is a citizen of the United States—*The Testament* indicates that the materialist disease the United States spreads abroad is endemic to it and bad for the world.[57]

THE RIGHT KIND OF AMERICAN (MALE) POWER

Even as *The Testament* questioned American morality and U.S. power abroad, it reinforced gender conventions that underwrote that power. It was not, however, simplistically gendered. Rachel Lane was one of the most competent and clearheaded characters in the book (both characteristics traditionally gendered masculine). She was a missionary, a field dominated by women, and a medical doctor, more commonly a male job. In love at one time, she claims that God led her to end the relationship because her boyfriend did not possess the physical strength to serve in the mission field. Eschewing domestic life could render Rachel androgynous, but her physical description militates against it. She carries herself "with an easy elegance," and Nate notices that "her eyes were dark blue, almost indigo. No wrinkles, no makeup. She was forty-two years old and aging quite well, with the soft glow of one who knew little stress."[58]

Nate, for his part, does not at first glance appear to be a character offering reassurance about either male or U.S. power. Far from starting the book as a competent, rational man, he is introduced while finishing a stint in rehab. Having destroyed two marriages and his relationship with his children, he has lost control of his life. While his battle against the disinherited heirs showcases his professional acumen, the story focuses on his moral redemption. He wants to leave the competitive world of law and increasingly finds camaraderie among Christians who care little about their rung on the ladder of worldly success. The state of his soul has overtaken concerns about being a man of recognized wealth and power.

Yet Nate O'Reilly ends the book as a man of significant power, albeit of a new kind. Before her death, Rachel Lane names him as the administrator of the multibillion dollar trust she establishes to support the work of World Tribes and to protect indigenous rights. By one narrative logic, one that focuses only on the text and ignores context, Nate's appointment is a nongendered climax to a story of friendship and redemption. During his time in Brazil, Nate earned Rachel's trust. She shows that trust—and affirms the turn his life has taken—by giving him control over her fortune and responsibility for people about whom she cares deeply.

By another logic, however, one that puts *The Testament* in its historic and cultural context, a novel about a devout female missionary and a competent male lawyer reinforced the relationship between power and masculinity in both the church and politics. That relationship was under discussion among evangelicals during the last three decades of the twentieth century. The denominations and organizations that constituted evangelicalism had never spoken uniformly on gender and leadership. Some groups, particularly in the Wesleyan-Holiness tradition, granted ordination to women. Other groups reserved ordination for men. Emphasis on gender roles in marriage and society also varied throughout the movement. The 1973 Chicago Declaration of Evangelical Social Concern, signed by such luminaries as longtime *Christianity Today* editor Carl Henry, stated, "We acknowledge that we have encouraged men to prideful domination and women to irresponsible passivity. So we call both men and women to mutual submission and active discipleship."[59] During that same decade, however, other evangelicals mounted a significant critique of feminism and began building ecclesial and political coalitions around "family values." Jerry Falwell, founder of the Moral Majority, made opposition to abortion and feminism central components of his political activity. Grisham's own denomination, the Southern Baptist Convention, experienced a conservative takeover in 1979. Over the next two decades, the Southern Baptist Convention increasingly emphasized a return to "biblical" gender roles, culminating in the 1998 Baptist Faith and Message Statement that enjoined wifely submission and the 2000 version that reserved ordination for men.[60]

Gender discussions spilled over into missions as well. Those seeking greater leadership for women turned to female missionaries to make their case. In 1984 the missiologist and proponent of women's ordination Miriam Adeney wrote a *Christianity Today* article celebrating nineteenth-century missionary Mary Slessor as a role model for contemporary women. Titled, "A Woman Liberated—for What?" Adeney's article urged, "let us be strong, creative, goal-oriented women. But not only that, let us also be liberated beyond the confines of the philosophies of our day, liberated as was Mary Slessor to the Word and the Spirit."[61] Women within the missionary guild were also contesting their marginalization in a movement they numerically dominated. In 1985 former missionary Joyce Bowers decried the decline of female leadership in missions between 1920 and 1980 and lamented that "women's unique perspective on all mission issues (not just relational or home-and-family ones) is lost because neither women nor men recognize the value of women's potential contributions."[62] An article in *Christianity Today* five years earlier showed the validity of her concern. The 1980 article contained one paragraph about frustrations expressed by some women involved with the Consultation on World Evangelization (COWE). They lamented that "their sex had provided only 9 percent of COWE's 650 participants, none of the plenary speakers, and only three of [the Lausanne Committee on World Evangelization's] 50 members."[63] The program director, Saphir Athyal, simultaneously acknowledged and denied a problem. *Christianity Today* reported that, "denying discrimination," Athyal "indicated that women were represented in the miniconsulatations where the real work was done, and that every effort had been made to encourage the different regions to send women."[64] Athyal recognized a need for more women's voices but also suggested that while the movement needed women in the trenches—good soldiers were always welcome—missions did not suffer from a paucity of female leadership. Others took Athyal's opinion a step further. Elisabeth Elliot criticized women who sought greater power within missions. In the early 1990s, the Southern Baptist Convention struggled with the Women's Missionary Union over the union's decision to aid a new, moderate Baptist agency with curriculum, leading one male Baptist leader to call for women to be "hard-wired" to conservative leadership or risk losing their denominational status.[65]

The Testament did not explicitly address the gender concerns prevalent in Grisham's evangelical community—the community in which the fictional Rachel Lane would live. Lack of explicit address, however, was not gender neutral. For all of Rachel's competence and personal bravery, she fits comfortably within the gender expectations of late twentieth-century American evangelicals, including the increasingly conservative expectations of the not so moderate segments of Grisham's own denomination. Because she is not married, wifely submission is a nonissue. She is a doctor who also attended seminary, but she is not ordained. Rachel offered no challenge to what groups like the Council for Biblical Manhood and Womanhood, a parachurch group founded in the midst of evangelical debates about gender, and the 2000 Southern Baptist Faith and Message would declare: God reserves ordained ministry for men while allowing women to exercise their gifts in nonleadership roles, including missionary work. Moreover, Rachel not only operates within conservative gender expectations but makes them appear efficacious. Rachel needs neither ordination nor organizational power to serve the people of the Pantanal well. Her lack of interest in worldly matters, including power, impresses Nate. Her submission to World Tribes decisions, such as not giving her money for a new boat motor, as well as her complete confidence in God (who in Christian theology is technically neither male nor female but who is referred to with the capitalized male pronouns "He" and "Him" throughout the book) increases Nate's admiration. The efficacy of conservative gender roles within the church is further substantiated when Nate returns to the United States. Although a woman facilitated his conversion, an ordained man, Episcopal priest Father Phil, nurtures his faith by integrating him into a (male-led) congregation and teaching him to pray and read the Bible.

The Testament's gender logic also participated in the construction of a "hegemonic masculinity" for the century's last decade. Gender theorist R. W. Connell has argued that at any given time one form of masculinity (and it is always a masculinity) is "culturally exalted" above other masculinities and all femininities. He calls this form "hegemonic masculinity" and notes that, while not all people holding political or economic power are male or personally fit the hegemonic masculinity of their time, "hegemony is likely to be established only if there is some correspondence between cultural ideal and institutional power, collective if not individual."[66] In the 1990s, changes at home and abroad made a new masculinity hegemonic. Since the 1960s, feminists had been criticizing the ideal of the patriarchal father who benevolently ruled his nuclear family. People who might discount feminism were hard pressed to ignore another attack on the postwar ideal: economic reality no longer allowed the illusion of a country comprised of one-breadwinner households. The world situation also called for a new manhood. Post-Reagan and post–Cold War, the image of manhood that stood ready to stare down a longtime and purportedly equally powerful enemy no longer sufficed. Rather than one powerful enemy with many proxies, the world faced numerous threats to what the United States considered law and order. In Iraq, Kosovo, and Somalia—to name only a few—the United States decried what it declared as violations of international law. A need for order also appeared in the economic realm. With the dissolution of the Soviet Union and the growing openness to capitalism in China, the already globalized economy grew even larger. The United States, of course, wanted to increase its market share.

The hegemonic masculinity constructed amid the exigencies of the 1990s involved sensitivity, toughness, rationality, and competency. Assertive action, like that undertaken in the first Gulf War, affirmed that the (men) leading the United States no longer suffered from the emasculating "Vietnam Syndrome," an unwillingness to intervene abroad. No less an authority than President George H. W. Bush declared after the cease-fire in Iraq that "we've kicked the Vietnam Syndrome once and for all."[67] Yet after years of feminist critique, leadership also demanded some sensitivity. Before going to war, Bush had declared his intention to make the United States a "kinder, gentler nation." The invasion commander, General "Stormin'" Norman Schwarzkopf, also displayed a more sensitive side. Columnist Ellen Goodman lauded the successful general as "a man who is on speaking terms with his emotions, willing to express his fears, but not paralyzed by them. Someone who isn't afraid of violence, but doesn't like it. An Army man who calls war 'a profane thing.'"[68] He also, for good measure, enjoyed opera. The chairman of the Joint Chiefs of Staff, Colin Powell, received praise for another component of 1990s masculinity: competency. Amid speculation that he would run for president in 1996, news stories emphasized Powell's ability to get things done. Results, not bravado, made him a fit leader.[69] The same attributes were valorized in economics, another traditionally masculine domain. In a study of the *Economist*, a magazine aimed at the Anglo-American elite, Charlotte Hooper found a consistent, though not unchallenged, emphasis on a masculine ideal she calls "bourgeois-rationalist." With the global economy as the new frontier "hegemonic masculinity is being reconfigured in the image of a less formal, less patriarchal, but more technocratic masculine that has the whole globe as its playground."[70] In the age of "It's the Economy, Stupid," leading the world entailed manipulating balance sheets and creating innovative technologies.

By the end of *The Testament*, Nate O'Reilly is a vision of 1990s hegemonic masculinity. His relationship with Rachel Lane offered a means by which he, the competent male, would gain the sensitivity and compassion needed to use his power rightly in the world. Although Rachel was strong and smart enough to help Nate change, at the end of the day, her superior morality and spirituality were not enough to protect indigenous people from encroaching businesses and environmental destruction. The people needed someone who could operate well in the world, without subscribing to the values of the world. Read against a culture in which using rationality and competence compassionately to help other people was coded masculine, it was not surprising that that someone turned out in Grisham's novel to be a man.

Conclusion

Arguing that *The Testament* reflected and participated in the construction of a hegemonic masculinity is not to say that such was Grisham's intent. Nor is it to claim that *The Testament*, any more than *At Play in the Fields of the Lord*, supported U.S. policies that also reflected and participated in the construction of hegemonic masculinity. The books really did raise questions about U.S. power abroad and about the health of U.S. culture at home. The point is that the books were embedded in cultural discourses that constrained challenges. Direct attacks on aspects of U.S. power stood in tension with the probably unintentional ways the books implicitly supported the gendered logic of that power. As the mainline magazines of the 1940s and 1950s demonstrated, segments of the U.S. population that would question both the country's power and its gendered structure had, in the not-too-distant past, supported both, albeit with some caveats. The long tradition of gendering power and looking for a manhood (and a man) capable of saving the world did not die out in the sexual revolution of the 1960s. Reports of murder notwithstanding, feminists did not kill it either. Even a succession of female secretaries of state had not upended the fundamental logic of masculinized power. Getting outside of the gendered logic underwriting U.S. power was difficult, even for the critics.

CONCLUSION
❊ ❊ ❊

Some critics of U.S. power did attack its gendered logic. Barbara Kingsolver for one. In 1998 and 1999, Kingsolver's *The Poisonwood Bible* joined John Grisham's *The Testament* on best-seller lists. Her story garnered critical acclaim and a wide readership. Short-listed for the Pulitzer Prize, it received the commercially more important endorsement of Oprah's Book Club. Spurred by reviewer's acclaim and Oprah's approval, many Americans made their way through 587 pages of political allegory in which a male evangelist with a messiah complex stood in for the United States' destructive machinations in the 1960s Congo.[1]

While the novel itself rambled a bit, the book and critical reaction to it summarized the state of missionary discussions at century's end. Familiar themes—bad U.S. foreign policy, insensitive missionaries, and hubristic manhood—reappeared, as did an old quandary: could Americans who recognized the problems with their country's behavior manage not to repeat its logic?

In *The Poisonwood Bible*, Kingsolver embedded the story of the Price family in the tragedy of postcolonial Congo. The Prices, four daughters, a mother, and a domineering missionary father, Nathan, travel to the Congo just as the country gains independence from Belgium. During their time in Africa, the nationalist Patrice Lumumba is elected as prime minister. Within a couple of months, he is deposed in an U.S. sanctioned—if not U.S. orchestrated—coup d'etat and then assassinated, paving the way for thirty years of dictatorship under U.S.-backed Mobutu Sese Seko.

Kingsolver used Nathan's ethnocentric behavior in the village of Kilanga as a microcosm of U.S. interference in Africa. She was not subtle in her strategy. Kingsolver told one reviewer that she responded to criticism that her book is political allegory with "well, yes, you got it" and told another that Nathan "is our nation."[2] As the Congo undergoes political convulsions, Nathan dictatorially insists that his family and the village of Kilanga conform to his ideal of Christian civilization. He plants a garden in typical American fashion, in long, flat rows. When he finds that the African women have replanted his garden with the seeds in mounds, he replants in rows. When rain pours, ruining his rows and washing away his seeds, the African women's wisdom becomes apparent—to everyone except Nathan. His missionary tactics are as hubristic. He forces children into the local river for baptism, unwilling to heed their disinterest in conversion and their fear of the crocodiles. He thinks he speaks the language well and, week after week, ends his sermons with the phrase "Tata Jesus is bangala," which he thinks means "Jesus is good." He fails to recognize that the way he pronounces bangala means "poisonwood," thereby declaring Jesus a toxic, skin-burning plant.[3] As the political situation unravels in the Congo—thanks, in no small part, to another patriarch (Dwight D. Eisenhower) who is forcing Africa to pay the price for the Cold War—Nathan refuses to heed the advice to remove his family. At the same time, his youngest daughter, Ruth May, dies. Fearful for the fate of the rest of her daughters, his wife flees in the midst of civil strife, leaving Nathan and his poisonous gospel behind. Just as Nathan failed to see that the villagers had a lifestyle well adapted to their environment, the United States refused to recognize the integrity of the young Congolese political system. Nathan's evangelization ends in the destruction of his family and the village while the United States abets the end of Congo's young democracy all in the name of spreading freedom abroad.

In its picture of a missionary and nation with messiah complexes, *The Poisonwood Bible* echoed a common sentiment in late twentieth-century missionary conversations: people abroad have suffered from imperialist practices, religious and political, and such practices must end. That such a sentiment was widespread was evident from the steady stream of positive reviews issuing from newspapers and magazines. Even the occasional negative review of the book echoed the message. *Christianity Today*, the magazine of evangelical conviction, carried a largely negative appraisal of the book. Yet the reviewer, Tim Stafford, did not oppose critical portrayals of either missionaries or the United States on principle. Rather, he disliked Kingsolver's because she "sheds no light on the nature of single-minded, imperious missionaries. She is no better at showing how Nathan's preaching might actually work to poison African culture, or how American greed and power poisoned American politics." And then, the most telling line from Stafford, a former missionary to Africa: "Such topics beg for a novelist's insight."[4] Even evangelicals agreed that Americans, missionaries included, had done great ill in the world. The problem with *The Poisonwood Bible* was that its assessment of the problem lacked nuance.

Lack of nuance is not normally a mortal sin, but the charge demonstrated just how difficult critiquing U.S. power could be. Kingsolver, to the applause of many, clearly advocated freedom for people abroad. Yet for all her sensitivity to issues of power—one that even undid the gendered logic others had fallen into—and her thorough critique of U.S. foreign policy, Kingsolver drew criticism for how she used her own authorial privilege. Her own way of remaining involved in the world could be accused of another kind of cultural superiority. In her critique of men, missionaries, and America, some critics claimed that Kingsolver's lack of nuance when it came to her African characters pristinized African society, depriving it of the kind of deep description she bestowed on her female, American characters. In *Time* magazine John Skow noted that Price was not Kingsolver's only one-dimensional male character. "One male African teacher, in particular, is so patient and virtuous that he seems—cultural bias alert here—almost Christlike."[5] A vitriolic piece in the *New Republic* by Lee Siegel asserted that Kingsolver "does not care about Africa (I mean, intelligently and respectfully care, with a sense of its alterity and its complexity)."[6] The one-dimensional goodness of African characters demonstrated that "only her intrepid heroines, not the Africans themselves, get the burdensome dignity of moral struggle, confusion and anguish."[7] According to Siegel, Kingsolver's simplistic rendering of Africa had real consequences. Kingsolver published her book after the Rwandan genocide and the 1996–97 Congolese war. Both traced their histories back to colonial problems, but both also witnessed horrific treatment of Africans by Africans. While Kingsolver gave her readers the satisfaction of taking a moral stance on an Africa-related issue (covert operations by the CIA are bad), she failed to give them a picture of Africa that would help them sort through the morally fraught situations its people encountered. Africa was once again merely a backdrop upon which Americans could demonstrate their superiority, be it as an ethically attuned writer or as morally sensitive readers.

Comments in other reviews indicated that Kingsolver's critics, even the hyperbolic Siegel, had a point. Jan Williams Banker summarized Kingsolver's description of the African villagers: "[The book] features the exotic, disaster-prone Congolese, who never feel sorry for themselves except when children die—then they weep and howl."[8] The New York Times Book Review claimed that the "greatest character" in the novel "is collective, the Congolese, whose perfect adaption to the harshness of their lives amid drought, hunger, pests and disease is simply beautiful."[9] Such comments were meant as commendations of the book and the Congolese. Read one way, they may have indicated that Kingsolver did a worthy job of presenting another culture to a largely American audience. Yet read another, they indicated that, in the service of condemning U.S. wrongs, Kingsolver perpetuated an updated version of the noble savage myth, creating a picture of Africans that Americans could easily love. Kingsolver wanted the United States to stop harmful interference in Africa, but in making her case, she presented Africans as she imagined them and as her readers would like them. She knew them best.

Kingsolver's book and its critics reflected larger trends. By century's end, many missionary conversations betrayed discomfort with U.S. power in the world. They also demonstrated the difficulty in critiquing that power without replicating some of its patterns. As we have seen, the problem was not new, although how Americans viewed their interactions, and the interactions of their country, abroad had changed. Immediately after World War II, missionaries were seen as part of a U.S. phalanx, finally taking its rightful role as a world leader. The early years of the Cold War added urgency to that leadership. They also witnessed some criticism of how the United States chose to engage a bifurcated world. That criticism, however, did not fundamentally question the country's leadership role. The tumults of nationalism and of the 1960s changed the critique. While not everyone joined the chorus of critics at the same time—mainline and evangelical views of missions and America, for example, had different chronologies— a growing realization that people abroad wanted and deserved autonomy led to a more full-throttled challenge to missionary practice and U.S. policy. In the 1980s and 1990s, missionary conversations among disparate groups took as a given the need to respect leaders in other countries even as the conversations showed great division on how harmful the United States really was. For example, Good News United Methodists, with their links to the Institute on Religion and Democracy, maintained a much more optimistic appraisal of American action abroad than their denominational leadership. Yet Good News folk accepted the premise that Christians abroad deserved control of their own endeavors. They simply expected that, once given control, people abroad would want to replicate "the best" of U.S. society and culture. Good News Methodists believed, like many people engaged in missionary conversations, that other people would see the world their way and that their shared vision was best for everyone.

To some extent, arguing that missionary conversations revealed a Wilsonian paradox is simply to say that people have a perspective and, all things being equal, want others to share it. Mainliners, evangelicals, anthropologists—they could hardly be faulted for having a way of seeing the world. They would communicate nothing if they did not describe that way of seeing the world to others. Still, a persistent conviction that Americans knew what was best for others had real-world consequences. It influenced mission policy, church decisions, and research agendas. It concurred with—even as it challenged—Wilsonian political rhetoric that clearly celebrated U.S. leadership in the world. As the decades of the Cold War gave way to a new world order, which then gave way to the terror and confusion of the first decade of the twenty-first century, some ramifications of the continuities and changes in missionary conversations began to reveal themselves. So too did the country's continuing commitment to describing itself as what was best for the world.

Sex, Rights, and World Citizens

In the first decade of the twenty-first century, issues related to sexuality and human rights demonstrated the complexities brought by past missionary success, growing cultural sensitivity, and continuing American power. Debates about sexual orientation, specifically whether practicing gays and lesbians were participating in sinful behavior, whether they should be ordained, and whether their churches should officially recognize their unions, were a case in point. These debates roiled several mainline denominations, and they did not end at the water's edge. Christians abroad had strong opinions on human sexuality. Although Christians in Africa, Asia, and Latin America did not speak with one voice on the issue, they tended to deny the compatibility of homosexual practice with Christian discipleship. This position allowed U.S. conservatives to tout their agreement with the global church. Before the United Methodist 2008 General Conference, in which the ordination of gay and lesbian ministers was once again on the table, the *UMAction* newsletter, an IRD publication, asked, "Will the UMC learn from the experience of our fast-growing UM churches in Africa . . . which preach and live the traditional Christian Gospel?"[10] While the UMC maintained its opposition to gay and lesbian ordination and marriage, the Episcopal Church in the United States did not. Amid warnings that his election would end in schism within the worldwide Anglican Communion, American Episcopalians elected Gene Robinson, an openly practicing gay man, bishop in 2003. Some Anglicans abroad accused the American church of ignoring worldwide opinion and acting unilaterally. A few bishops in the global south did more than complain. They offered conservative Episcopalians their leadership, creating new Anglican institutions in the United States that were not under the jurisdiction of the American church.[11]

Evangelicals faced their own difficulties with Christians abroad, again over sexuality. While American evangelicals shared beliefs about the sinfulness of homosexual practice with many Christians in the global South, they did not always agree on how to handle the issue. When Christian legislators in Uganda brought forward a 2009 bill that made certain homosexual acts punishable by imprisonment or even death, prominent U.S. evangelicals criticized their efforts. Megachurch pastor Rick Warren, whose Saddleback Church boasted extensive work in Africa, opposed "the criminalization of homosexuality."[12] Charles Colson, founder of Prison Fellowship, called the punishments in the bill "horrendous."[13] Such comments prompted Ugandan churchman David Zac Niringiye to protest that "the international community is behaving like it can't trust Ugandans to come up with a law that is fair."[14]

Whether liberal or conservative, living in a global church, not to mention a global world, was fraught. When Americans opposed stances adopted by people abroad, they risked the accusation that their behavior reflected the United States' Wilsonian imperialism. Yet, in many cases, the Americans did not view themselves as acting primarily as Americans. They believed that their position stemmed from Christian conviction and understood themselves to be speaking primarily as Christians. Presiding Episcopal bishop Frank Griswold, who supported Robinson's election, acknowledged that it was painful for the global church but refused to repent for his support because "it's very difficult to apologize for an action when those who took part in it believe it was under the leading of the Holy Spirit."[15] Rick Warren defended his denunciation of the Uganda bill by saying, "As an American pastor, it is not my role to interfere with the politics of other nations, but it is my role to speak out on moral issues."[16] Colson appealed to universal human rights, something he believed was central to "the presentation of the gospel."[17] Griswold, Colson, and Warren saw themselves not as Americans telling Africans what to do, but as Christians chiding other Christians for a lapse in practice. For Christians abroad, however, Christian and American identity was not so easily parsed. By virtue of their American citizenship, pro-gay mainliners and not-that-anti-gay evangelicals were enmeshed in power relationships that colored their actions. Their positions may have been influenced by the Holy Spirit, moral repulsion, or human rights. Still, the nationality of the people making the decision was anything but incidental.

If disagreeing with international Christians risked accusations of American arrogance, agreement had its own moral ambiguity. The *UMAction* newsletter that touted the spiritual superiority of African orthodoxy over American liberalism also campaigned against a proposal that would designate that United States as a "regional conference" of the United Methodist Church, a move that would deny overseas United Methodists voting rights. *UMAction* accentuated its commitment to a globally inclusive church, calling the proposal "segregation" and quoting a United Methodist leader who asked, "Why do we not want the church around the world for decisions we think only touch U.S. hands?"[18] Yet the article indicated that more than a desire to affirm the global church underlay *UMAction*'s position. The editors reminded readers that about one out of three delegates to the upcoming General Conference would come from Africa and that "most international delegates affirm traditional Christian beliefs and reject theological liberalism."[19] The article invoked the Anglican schism over homosexuality as an example of what could transpire if American churches did not have the ameliorating influence of conservative Christians abroad. Thus, while the article made the case for including United Methodists in Africa in all United Methodist decisions on the basis of a global church and inclusivity, it also clearly supported such inclusion because the votes from abroad would favor conservative positions. It was not clear that people from abroad would receive such support if they departed from their conservative stances.

Americans outside of churches dealt with similar dilemmas— sometimes to their own surprise. In the 29 January 2006 issue of the *New York Times Magazine*, readers encountered Daniel Bergner's article on evangelical missionaries in Africa amid articles on nuclear proliferation, bird flu, and spring fashions. Bergner's article focused on Rick and Carrie Maples, African Inland Missionaries working among Kenya's Samburu people. From the outset, Bergner's piece defied easy stereotypes of white Americans imposing belief and compelling cultural change. The magazine's cover pictured Rick Maples in a blue button-down shirt and khaki cords standing shoulder-to-shoulder with a Samburu warrior. Their physical proximity and identical facial expressions—steady gazes and unsmiling mouths—suggested camaraderie and equality. Combined with the bold caption "The Post-Colonial Missionary," the picture indicated that "what in God's name American evangelicals are doing in Africa" might not be what readers expected.[20]

The Mapleses were evangelicals but not the Nathan Price-esque fire-and-brimstone, committed-to-American-greatness variety. Though Rick and Carrie wanted to convert the Samburu to Christianity, Bergner emphasized their attempts to present the gospel message in an idiom that would resonate with the Samburu: "They intend, gradually, to hold more and more Christian services not under a roof but under the acacia trees amid the manyattas. . . . And they plan to teach the lessons of the Bible not through the preaching of written verses but through an emphasis on expansive story-telling that will fit with the Samburu's oral tradition."[21] The missionaries proved patient in their witness. Rather than seeking quick conversions, they were studying the language and the people. Their commitment was long term. "For us, this is home," Rick told Bergner.[22]

Of course, problems remained in the contact of cultures. Bergner reported that, after converting the Samburu, the Mapleses hoped to "coax them to judge their traditions by the standards of the Gospel. In this way, they plan to inspire—not impose, they stressed—crucial elements of transformation in culture."[23] Such a statement could have cued a litany of imperialist crimes missionaries had committed against Africans. Certainly, transformation of other cultures had long been a major argument against overseas workers. But the article took another direction because the practice the missionaries most wanted judged by gospel standards was female circumcision.

Bergner sympathized with the missionaries' program. Rick and Carrie discussed sex "much more often and openly than I expected," he reported.[24] The missionaries believed God had created sex for pleasure and "to take away God's gift of pleasure is not right."[25] Though the Mapleses had a conservative sexual ethic—they believe intercourse biblically restricted to heterosexual marriage—and did not think women should hold the highest position of leadership in a church (African or American), Bergner argued that "amid the Sumburu culture, the Mapleses could seem to be not only Christian crusaders but also bold and progressive social reformers, champions of female emancipation and sexual fulfillment."[26] Unlike some attempts at cultural transformation—forcing Africans to dress in Western garb or forcing changes to the local economy—opposition to female circumcision proved difficult to denounce.

Thus, the missionaries' program of cultural change raised hard questions for Bergner. He admitted, "It was almost impossible, as an outsider, not to think about the state of the Samburu women the way Rick and Carrie do. It was almost impossible not to wish for transformation."[27] On the other hand, Bergner worried about the consequences of cultural change. He found it "hard to miss what the Samburu have. All across Africa, I had heard cries of desperation, cries for Western rescue. But even in a season of drought, with the threat that livestock would start to die, I heard nothing like this from the Samburu." They seemed, "as much as the people of any culture can, satisfied with their lives."[28] Given their contentment, should the missionaries interfere with any tradition, even one as abhorrent as female circumcision? Bergner found himself in an intractable paradox, torn between his desire for Samburu autonomy and his commitment to human rights, as he, an American, defined them.

Missionary Conversations in Twenty-First-Century America

Just as Bergner's article about the Mapleses appeared amid issues of war, illness, and consumption, the new century's conversations about missionaries occurred amid war, rumors of terrorism, a housing boom, and a global bust. Most specifically, the majority occurred after the terrorist attacks of September 11, 2001. Commentators at the time talked about September 11 as the day that everything changed. Although much psychically about the United States changed that day, much rhetorically did not. Familiar themes echoed in President George W. Bush's designation of the post-attack United States as "the light of the world" and his justification of the Iraq invasion as an opportunity to spread freedom and democracy.[29] And the theme was not simply the rallying cry of conservatives. In his 2009 inaugural address, President Barack Obama rejected "as false the choice between our safety and our ideals," telling Americans that "our Founding Fathers faced with perils that we can scarcely imagine, drafted a charter to assure the rule of law and the rights of man—a charter expanded by the blood of generations. Those ideals still light the world, and we will not give them up for expedience sake." He told the watching audiences, national and global, that "we are ready to lead once more."[30]

Just as in the twentieth century, missionary conversations intersected with such presidential proclamations. They occurred in the context of public policy and could not be divorced from them. How, exactly, the marriage of the two worked was not as clear. It would be too much to suggest that reflections on missionaries either caused certain stances regarding foreign policy or clearly reflected stances on foreign policy. The relationship was more complicated. Perhaps it is best to say that conversations about missionaries were one place where opinion makers explored how they thought Americans approached global issues.

Take evangelicals and the Iraq War. Before President George W. Bush ordered the invasion of Iraq, white evangelicals were some of the war's most ardent supporters.[31] *Christianity Today* editors suggested that just war criteria might fit the situation.[32] High-profile evangelicals such as the Southern Baptist Convention's Richard Land and Prison Fellowship's Charles Colson argued that war could, under certain circumstances, be the compassionate alternative. But not all evangelicals agreed.[33] Ethicists from evangelical institutions such as Fuller Theological Seminary and Wheaton College signed a statement, along with Catholic and mainline theologians, claiming, "As Christian ethicists we share a common moral presumption against a preemptive war on Iraq by the United States."[34] Clearly, an "evangelical" consensus did not exist, even at the level of leadership and opinion makers.[35]

Complex reflection did, at least in some quarters. While some churches and parishioners simply wrapped themselves in the flag, some evangelical leaders and opinion makers sorted through a number of relevant issues. They talked about just war criteria and how, or whether, it had changed in an age of global terrorism. In a 2002 *Christianity Today* roundup of opinions about a preemptive war—opinions that were, perhaps not surprisingly, all given by men—theologians and ethicists disagreed about whether the United States currently possessed sufficient cause for an attack (assuming that one was ever justified) and what sufficient cause would entail. While the Southern Baptist Convention's Richard Land harbored no doubts about the moral ends the United States hoped to achieve—removing a "really atrocious, war-crimes-committing dictator who terrorizes and enslaves his own people"—some experts suggested that "if Congress or other nations do not approve of a U.S. strike, it may be a sign that it is not the moral option."[36] The United States, for reasons principled and pragmatic, should not go it alone nor should it absolutely trust its own moral sense.

Once opinions about the justice of a preemptive strike became moot, evangelicals continued to reflect on the war. While the community at large remained supportive of the war far longer than the rest of the American public (white evangelicals also provided a bastion of support after President Bush's approval ratings fell among the general public), conversation about the war evidenced concern about how the president viewed the United States' role in the world. In May 2003 *Christianity Today* ran an article on "the moral vision that launched the Iraq War."[37] The article quoted President Bush explaining this vision as "a distinctly American internationalism that reflects the union of our values and our national interests" and cited his belief that the United States was "called" to "lead the world to peace."[38] Although Tony Carnes, the author, kept his cards close to his chest, he did cite evangelicals who worried, for reasons both political and theological, about the president's vision, noting that "some worry that Bush is confusing genuine faith with nationalist ideology" and quoting an evangelical who worried that the president's policy constituted hubris rather than moral leadership.[39] Four years later, even more doubt appeared. The September 2007 issue ran two articles questioning both policy and principles. Editor Ted Olsen reported on a meeting between the president and conservative reporters in which the president explained that spreading liberty was, for him, a theological principle. Olsen reported that at least two of the reporters present strongly objected to the president's view. One called the president "flat-out wrong" and another labeled him a "heretic."[40] The other article, an opinion piece written by Baptist ethicist David Gushee, claimed that one lesson evangelicals could take from a war he thought the United States needed to leave "honorably and soon" was that "we must become more discerning when our nation's leaders advocate a military solution." The end of the war, he claimed, should bring a time of "national (and Christian) mourning and repentance."[41]

Conversations about missionaries among evangelicals in the preceding decades did not fully explain these reflections upon the war. Indeed, the conversations were too multivocal to issue in one evangelical voice on the war. But the conversations about missionaries did provide one forum in which evangelicals, like other Americans, worked through ideas about how their fellow citizens and how their country should act in the world. They offered opportunities to distinguish between Christian conviction and U.S. ideology. They also provided forums in which issues that would reappear in discussions about foreign policy—issues like universal truths, cultural imperialism, and human rights—were discussed.

They also demonstrate why getting out of the nation's Wilsonian logic was so difficult. It is all very well to talk about letting other people do as they wish, of letting them have freedom. It is very much another thing to live in a world where people do brush up against each other (as the anthropologists found "organic unity" is a myth), where some people oppress other people (although not all people may define oppression in the same way), where people hold different beliefs about ultimate truth (or whether it exists), and where people bear witness to each other's cruelties, pains, and victories through an ever-widening array of media. As people in the United States became increasingly reflective about the world around them, their country's behavior, and their role in it, they could not simply abjure action in the world. So they made what decisions they could, what judgments they could render—and they made them in the context of a powerful country, one that they sometimes supported and sometimes railed against. In the process, they publicly described themselves, as their country did, as arbiters of what the world needed. And, more often than not, they suggested that the world needed Americans, although not necessarily America, to lead the way.

Notes

INTRODUCTION

1. Michener, *Hawaii*, author's note.

2. For a less sympathetic reading of Michener, see Hutchison, *Errand to the World*. On Hawaii in the context of American thinking about Asia, see Klein, *Cold War Orientalism*.

3. Michener, *Hawaii*, 761.

4. Ibid., 353.

5. Novels do not necessarily reflect the opinions of their authors. In *Hawaii*'s case, however, the book reiterated themes Michener took up in his nonfiction writing. See, for example, Michener, "'Aloha' for the Fiftieth State."

6. See, for example, Feldstein, *Motherhood in Black and White*, 9–11; McAlister, *Epic Encounters*, 4–8; Klein, *Cold War Orientalism*, 6–17.

7. On the United States' liberal democratic internationalist policy and its relationship to the Cold War, see Layne and Schwarz, "American Hegemony," 5. Political scientists use liberal democratic internationalism and Wilsonianism more or less interchangeably, although the former's roots precede Wilson's presidency. See, for example, Smith, *America's Mission*, 7. Walter Russell Mead explores various strands of U.S. foreign policy and tightly connects Wilsonianism with missions in *Special Providence*.

8. McDougall, *Promised Land, Crusader State*, 145.

9. Stephanson, *Manifest Destiny*, 125.

10. Christopher, "America's Leadership," 6.

11. Scholars of international relations have a lively debate about the efficacy of Wilsonianism and the extent to which it has actually guided policy. For a historiography of the debate, from a realist perspective, see Ambrosius, "Woodrow Wilson." For a celebratory appraisal of Wilsonianism, see Ninkovich, *Wilsonian Century*.

12. See, for example, Brands, *Devil We Knew*, 12–17.

13. The literature on the American missionary movement is vast, although work that focuses on the impact of the movement in the United States is not. See Bays and Wacker, "Many Faces." For overviews of the movement, see Hutchison, *Errand to the World*; Hill, "Missionary Enterprise"; Robert, *American Women in Mission*. One of the persistent questions regarding missions is their relationship to cultural imperialism. My work looks at the question of power from another angle—one I believe does more to illuminate actual

power dynamics than does the cultural imperialism debate. Nonetheless, that debate has been a significant one in the field. See, for example, J. Hunter, *Gospel of Gentility*; Schlesinger, "Missionary Enterprise"; Porter, "Cultural Imperialism"; Dunch, "Beyond Cultural Imperialism."

14. On missions to Native Americans, see especially Axtell, *Invasion Within*; Bowden, *American Indians*; Wheeler, *To Live upon Hope*.

15. Makdisi, *Artillery of Heaven*, 31. On millennialism and missions, see Rogers, "Bright and New Constellation."

16. For differing perspectives on the reasons for Anderson's policies, see Hutchison, *Errand to the World*; Harris, "Denominationalism and Democracy." On the women's missionary movement, see Robert, *American Women in Mission*; Hill, *World Their Household*; Wills, "Mapping Presbyterian Missionary Identity."

17. Beecher, *A Plea for the West*, 83–84.

18. Strong, *Our Country*; Edwards, "Forging an Ideology."

19. Dennis, *Christian Mission and Social Progress*, 47–48.

20. On the fundamentalists-modernist controversy and missions, see Lian, *Conversion of the Missionaries*; Marsden, *Fundamentalism and American Culture*; Patterson, "Loss of a Protestant Missionary Consensus"; Hill, *World Their Household*; Wacker, "Second Thoughts on the Great Commission." On the growth of faith missions, see Robert, "Crisis of Missions"; Robert, *Occupy Until I Come*.

21. Hutchison, *Between the Times*; Carpenter, *Revive Us Again*.

22. Although a small denomination in the United States (around forty thousand members), the Free Methodists have a robust missionary force and have become vastly more numerous overseas than they are at home. Thus they proved an apt place to study the dynamics between Americans and their coreligionists abroad. As a denomination, the Free Methodists are solidly within American evangelicalism. They were founding members of the National Association of Evangelicals (NAE) and members of their board of bishops have occupied chairs in the NAE's administration. Through their six church-sponsored colleges, they have a greater institutional presence in American evangelicalism than their numbers might suggest.

23. The UMC and its predecessor churches boast the greatest number of members among mainline congregations. The Methodists have also considered themselves "America's Church," so they proved particularly apropos as subjects of a study that looks at "The American Century." They, like the Free Methodists, have extensive and easily accessible archives, and boast churches like Myers Park UMC in Charlotte, North Carolina, with congregational archives.

24. Recent major works that combine cultural history with a focus on

Americans' considering their country's role in the world include McAlister, *Epic Encounters*; Kaplan, *Anarchy of Empire*; Klein, *Cold War Orientalism*; Renda, *Taking Haiti*.

CHAPTER ONE

1. "Bishop Sano Blasts New Mission Agency Pamphlet," 3.
2. "Good News Executive Exchanges Heated Remarks," 3.
3. I recognize difficulties with the term mainline. The term usually refers to seven denominations (American Baptist, Congregational/UCC, Disciples of Christ, Episcopal Church, the Evangelical Lutheran Church, the United Methodists, and the Presbyterian Church, U.S.A.) Some scholars have further subdivided the mainline into liberal or moderate categories or delineated among the churches by the height of their liturgy. Furthermore, most mainline denominations have liberal, moderate, and conservative interest groups. All of these divisions might mitigate against something called a mainline. Yet as historian Peter Williams has noted, the term "evokes a constellation of religious ideas, institutions, and movements specific enough to be very useful as an informal description." Williams, *America's Religions*, 333. Mainline denotes a social reality, namely, a group of denominations affiliated with the National Council of Churches and its predecessor bodies. For work on the mainline, see Roof and McKinney, *American Mainline Religion*; Wuthnow, *Restructuring of American Religion*; Warner, *New Wine in Old Wineskins*; Hutchison, *Between the Times*; Balmer, *Grant Us Courage*.
4. Anderson, "American Protestants," 113–14. Anderson cites statistics from Coote, "Taking Aim on 2000 A.D." See also Hill, "Missionary Enterprise," 1695.
5. See, for example, Hutchison, *Errand to the World*; Robert, "From Missions to Mission," 377; Wacker, "Waning of the Missionary Impulse."
6. "End of Strike," 1171.
7. Ibid.
8. S. Hunter, "Sea Strike Delays," 1186.
9. Ibid.
10. Luce, "American Century," 63.
11. "Problems of Peace," 17.
12. "One Year After," 20.
13. Fousek, *To Lead the Free World*, 63.
14. See Hall, *Conceiving Parenthood*.
15. C. C. Morrison, "Protestantism and the Lordship of Christ," 835.
16. Ibid.
17. On Niebuhr, see Fox, *Reinhold Niebuhr*. On Dulles, see Immerman,

John Foster Dulles; Toulouse, *Transformation of John Foster Dulles*. On the Protestant establishment, see Hutchison, *Between the Times*; Inboden, *Religion and American Foreign Policy*.

18. Kellar, "Mission United," 5.

19. Ibid., 8.

20. Hodges, "Citizen of an Enemy Country," 1005.

21. Ibid., 1006.

22. Inboden, *Religion and American Foreign Policy*, 17–18.

23. For overviews of containment, see Gaddis, *Strategies of Containment*; McDougall, *Promised Land, Crusader State*.

24. May, *Homeward Bound*, 114–34.

25. Inboden, *Religion and American Foreign Policy*, 4–5.

26. "Empire Is Justifiable," 453.

27. "United States and World Government."

28. Shepherd, "The West vs. Asia and Africa"; Niebuhr, *Children of Light*. For scholarly evaluations that echo Niebuhr, see Wald, "Religious Dimension"; Hertzke, "Assessment of the Mainline Churches"; Inboden, *Religion and American Foreign Policy*. For a view that credits the 1950s' *Century* with a more realistic approach, see Marty, "Peace and Pluralism."

29. Lian, *Conversion of the Missionaries*, 4–5; Reed, *Missionary Mind*.

30. "One Hundred Years," 5.

31. Meeman, "Christianity and Profits," 219.

32. "What Have We Learned?," 757.

33. "Where Have the China Missionaries Gone?," 1372.

34. "Retrospect," 1576.

35. J. Robinson, "Awakening Africa."

36. "Christian Outlook," 8.

37. Shepherd, "The West vs. Asia and Africa," 327.

38. J. Robinson, "Awakening Africa," 43.

39. "Protestants Petition," 1252.

40. "Will Colombia Become a Theocracy," 484–85.

41. "Protestant Freedom," 1117.

42. "Protestants Petition," 1252.

43. "India Veers Away from Religious Liberty," 485.

44. "Dissent Is Not Treason," 1318.

45. *Missionary to Chile*, Records of the Mission Education and Cultivation Department, General Board of Global Ministries, United Methodist Church Archives—General Commission on Archives and History, Madison, N.J. (hereafter UMCA).

46. Ibid., frame 4.

47. Ibid., frame 22.

48. Ibid., frame 34.

49. *Latin America: Missions at Work*, Records of the Evangelical United Brethren Church, Board of Missions, UMCA, frame 73.

50. *Mission Is . . .* , Records of United Methodist Communications, UMCA. *Leaders Guide for "Mission Is . . . ,"* Records of United Methodist Communications, UMCA.

51. *Mission Is . . .* , frame 1–2.

52. Ibid., frame 8.

53. Ibid., frames 15–16.

54. Ibid., frames 17–20.

55. The distant past was conceptually distant, not necessarily chronologically so. The picture of Dr. Limus Bittner and Okiro Oshiro in front of the "God Loves Okinawa" mobile hospital had appeared in *World Outlook* in 1954 as part of a report on the Methodist's work in Japan. See "Cause of Christ," 19.

56. *Mission Is . . .* , frame 24.

57. Ibid., frame 32.

58. See Schmitz, *United States and Right-Wing Dictatorships*; Westad, *Global Cold War*.

59. "National Purpose," 4.

60. "Honest Intervention," 731.

61. Wiley, "The Fire *This* Time," 200.

62. Ibid., 202.

63. "Blunders in Dominican Republic," 637.

64. "Hemispheric McCarthyism," 1277.

65. MacKay, "Latin America and Revolution—I"; MacKay, "Latin America and Revolution—II."

66. "Getting Out," 1583.

67. "On Foreign Policy," 863.

68. "Self-Respect after My Lai," 1569.

69. On the *Century* and Vietnam, see Toulouse, "Days of Protest"; Settje, "'Sinister' Communists."

70. "Spies," 985.

71. Larson, "Wolf in the Shepherd's Frock," 700. Concern over the CIA's use of missionaries persisted. See "C.I.A. Recruitment"; Cotter, "Spies, Strings and Missionaries."

72. *Mission Perspective*, United Methodist Communication Records, UMCA, frame 19.

73. *Mission Is . . .* , frame 39.

74. Ibid., frame 51.

75. Ibid., frames 55–56.

76. Ibid., frame 64.

77. Ibid., frame 67.

78. Ibid., frame 65.

79. Ibid., frame 85.

80. Ibid., frame 88.

81. Sunday Bulletin, 15 March 1970, Myers Park United Methodist Church Archives, Charlotte, N.C.

82. Commission on Mission Minutes, 1 September 1970, ibid.

83. "There Is Good News," 3.

84. Seamands, "Missions without Salvation," 25.

85. Ibid., 26.

86. Williamson, "Theology of Liberation," 19.

87. Ibid., 18.

88. Ibid., 25.

89. J. Robb, "Missions Derailed," 20.

90. Ibid., 22.

91. On the history of the IRD, see Tipton, *Public Pulpits*. For a history from the perspective of United Methodism's evangelical wing, see Case, *Evangelical and Methodist*, 109–33.

92. Wall, "Anticommunism Binds IRD to White House," 1115–16.

93. Wuthnow, *Restructuring of American Religion*. On the liberal-conservative divide, see also Warner, *New Wine in Old Wineskins*; Carroll et al., *Being There*.

94. Neuhaus, "Christianity and Democracy," 20–21; Wuthnow, *Restructuring of American Religion*, 247.

95. E. Robb, "Christian Scandalmongering," 27.

96. Steinfels, "Christianity and Democracy," 81.

97. Neuhaus, "Christianity and Democracy," 20.

98. "1990/91 Mission Study Books," 27; Anderson, "Who Will Evangelize."

99. Hersey, *Call*. See also Klausler, review of *The Call*.

100. Struchen, "Q&A about Missions," 44.

101. Ibid.

102. Ibid.

103. "Whom Shall I Send?," Customized General Conference Version, 1996, Records of the Mission Education and Cultivation Program Department, General Board of Global Ministries, UMCA.

104. "Interview," 22.

105. Ibid.

106. Ibid.

107. Billings, "Toward a New Missionary Age."

108. Skeete, "Embracing the Future in Mission," 6.

109. Sanneh, "Christian Missions." See also Sanneh, "Particularity, Pluralism and Commitment"; Sanneh, "Global Christianity."

CHAPTER TWO

1. "Converted Heathen Speaks," 1.

2. Tape of Service, 3 December 1989, First Free Methodist Church Archives, Seattle, Wash. (hereafter FFMCA).

3. On evangelicals and Cold War politics, see Pierard, "Billy Graham and Vietnam"; Inboden, *Religion and American Foreign Policy*; Whitfield, *Culture of the Cold War*; Lahr, *Millennial Dreams*; Crouse, "Popular Cold Warriors"; Settje, "'Sinister' Communists"; Pierard, "From Evangelical Exclusivism."

4. Quoted in Rosell, *Surprising Work of God*, 101–2.

5. Dayton, *Discovering an Evangelical Heritage*; Marsden, *Fundamentalism and American Culture*; Carpenter, *Revive Us Again*. Historians have debated about the place of the Wesleyan-Holiness movement within evangelicalism as well as the utility of the term "evangelical." See Sweeney, "Historiographical Dialectics"; Dayton, "Search for the Historical Evangelicalism"; Bassett, "Theological Identity"; Dayton, "Some Doubts"; Hart, *Deconstructing Evangelicalism*; Horton, "Is Evangelicalism Reformed or Wesleyan?"; Johnston, "American Evangelicalism"; Sweeney, "Essential Evangelicalism Dialectic." Much of this debate centers on whether Holiness theology actually fits well with the theology of the neo-evangelical movement and on how much influence Holiness and Reformed types in the movement exercised on each other. For my purposes, those questions are interesting but largely irrelevant. Theologically appropriate or not, Free Methodists aligned themselves with the neo-evangelical movement. They participated in the founding of the NAE, their colleges joined the evangelical Christian College Consortium, and their churches subscribed to *Christianity Today*.

6. Adamson, "Power of God," 220.

7. Ibid., 221.

8. "Chinese Y.P.M.S.," 20.

9. On this point, see Lahr, *Millennial Dreams*; Inboden, *Religion and American Foreign Policy*, 101.

10. Inboden, *Religion and American Foreign Policy*, 101.

11. Graham, "Satan's Religion," 41.

12. Harrison, "Search for Peace," 8–9.

13. "Peace Drive," 21.

14. Diefenbaker, "Mission to the World," 13.

15. G. Kennedy, "Defender and Invader," 10.

16. Ibid.

17. Whitfield, *Culture of the Cold War*, 205–18.

18. Settje, "'Sinister' Communists."

19. "Churchmen Look."

20. Ibid., 14.

21. Elliot, *Through Gates of Splendor*.

22. Elliot, *No Graven Image*.

23. Brody, "Books of the Times," 37.

24. Lindsell, "One Doesn't Tell God," 29.

25. Thatcher, letter to the editor, 18.

26. T. Howard, letter to the editor, 18.

27. "Mission Study Themes," 186. Recommended reading was serious business. The WMS announced study themes every year, and members received points for the number of books read.

28. Shacklock, *This Revolutionary Faith*, 15.

29. Ibid., 24.

30. Daniels, "Missionary in Today's World," 105.

31. J. Morrison, "Too Little and Too Late."

32. The statistic is more impressive than it sounds. Neither Dodge nor Scherer appeared on the Free Methodist Women's Missionary Society recommended reading list for 1964 or 1965. A book on the list written by the Free Methodist general secretary for missions was checked out by twenty-one people between 1963 and 1967. Although it is impossible to know for certain, it seems likely that a readership of about twenty people was what a missionary title could expect. It is also probably the case that those who read missionary books—particularly those not recommended by the denomination—were the people most interested in missions and the most likely shapers of opinions about them.

33. Dodge, *Unpopular Missionary*, 17.

34. P. C. Moore, "Missions Reassessed," 36.

35. Goerner, "He Is Not without Love," 26.

36. Coggins, "Missions and Prejudice," 3.

37. Ibid., 5.

38. Fine, "The World Fellowship," *Newsletter*, 27 May 1964, FFMCA.

39. Lamson, *To Catch the Tide*, 30. Note that Lamson's proposal did not forestall the possibility of going into new territory. A missionary could still go into new territory and start a church. Those churches would not be part of the fellowship until they reached autonomous status.

40. See, for example, Woodward, "Missionary Calling"; Fulton, "Are We Going out of [the Missionary] Business?"; Fulton, "Evangelism."

41. Fine, "World Fellowship."

42. Wirt, "World Mission Situation," 6.

43. Ibid.

44. First Free Methodist Church Sunday Bulletin, 14 March 1965, FFMCA.

45. Ibid.

46. Scofield, "What Is the Missionary's Message?," 16.

47. Ibid., 17.

48. "Hunger of the Masses," 25.

49. Long, "In the Modern World but Not of It."

50. On the role of single female missionaries, particularly in the nineteenth and early twentieth centuries, see Welter, "She Hath Done What She Could"; J. Hunter, *Gospel of Gentility*; Robert, *American Women in Mission*.

51. Elliot, *No Graven Image*, 110.

52. Ibid., 190.

53. Ibid.

54. Ibid., 167.

55. Ibid., 157.

56. Ibid., 237–38.

57. Ibid., 244.

58. Lindsell, "One Doesn't Tell God," 29.

59. Wagner, "A New 'Graven Image?,'" 232.

60. T. Howard, letter to the editor, 18.

61. Elliot's protest appeared at the bottom of Wagner's review: Wagner, "A New 'Graven Image?,'" 29.

62. Elliot, *Passion and Purity*; Elliot, *Let Me Be a Woman*; Elliot, *Mark of a Man*.

63. Tape of Service, 3 December 1989, FFMCA.

64. Ibid.

65. Adeney, "Do Your Own Thing," 12.

66. Ibid., 14.

67. "Guidelines for Mission," 51.

68. Graham, "Why Lausanne?," 7.

69. "Lausanne Covenant," 23. On changes in Graham's social and political positions, see Pierard, "Billy Graham and Vietnam"; Pierard, "From Evangelical Exclusivism."

70. Henry, "Nation in Trouble," 38.

71. Kucheman, "Churches and the Viet Nam Issue," 15.

72. Knight, "Can a Christian Go to War?," 6. For the counterpoint, see Augsburger, "Beating Swords."

73. Montgomery, "Should We Export the American Way?," 57.

74. Ibid., 58.

75. Henry, "Of Bicentennial Concerns," 15.

76. Ibid., 16.

77. Ibid.

78. "Dynamic People," 8.

79. Ibid.

80. Kato, "Christian Surge in Africa," 7.

81. Mason, *Karen Apostle*; Dwight, *Memoirs of Henry Obookiah*.

82. Sunday Bulletin, 16 March 1947, FFMCA.

83. Shenk, "Missions in Retrospect and Prospect," 11.

84. Steers, "Asians Consider Asia," 40.

85. Qalo, "Partnership in Missions," 21.

86. Padilla, "Church and Political Ambiguity," 41.

87. Ibid., 41–42.

88. Padilla, "Peru," 46.

89. Ibid., 46–47.

90. Ibid., 47.

91. Padilla, "What Is the Gospel?," 35.

92. Escobar, "Social Concern and World Evangelism," 104.

93. Skinner, "The U.S. Racial Crisis," 205.

94. McGavran, "Lion in Missions."

95. Padilla, "Theology of Liberation," 69.

96. Ibid.

97. "News from Carol," Spring and Summer 1989, FFMCA.

98. Tape of Service, 8 December 1991, FFMCA.

99. Ibid.

100. Plowman, "View from Lausanne."

101. Wagner, "Lausanne Twelve Months Later," 8.

102. My view of U.S. Christians' relative power aligns with Robert Wuthnow's critiques of the so-called new paradigm of world Christianity. The new paradigm, best represented by Philip Jenkins, focuses on the growth of Christianity in the global South and the end of the global North's numerical dominance. Wuthnow cautions that numbers do not tell the whole story, particularly the story of comparative power. See Wuthnow, *Boundless Faith*; Jenkins, *Next Christendom*.

103. Sidey, "An Overdose of Glasnost."

104. Escobar, "Missions' New World Order."

105. Fernando, "Bombs Away," 76.

106. Ibid., 76–77.

CHAPTER THREE

1. Benthall, "A.A.A. Annual Meeting, Phoenix," 24.
2. Ibid.
3. Benthall, "Missionaries and Human Rights," 1.
4. Ibid., 2.
5. Malinowski, *Diary in the Strict Sense of the Term*, 41.
6. Schapera, "Christianity and the Tswana," 498.
7. Ibid., 501–2.
8. Spain, review of *Colonial Evangelism*, 205.
9. Stipe, "Anthropologists versus Missionaries," 165–68.
10. Ibid., 166.
11. Ibid., 168.
12. Taylor, "Reply to Stipe," 174. Taylor's reply, like Guiart and Mair's, appeared at the end of Stipe's article.
13. Delfendahl, Heinen, and Stipe, "On Anthropologists, Missionaries, and Indigenous Peoples," 338.
14. Ibid., 339.
15. Ibid.
16. Delfendahl, "On Anthropologists vs. Missionaries," 89.
17. Ibid.
18. Stipe and Feldman, "Further Thoughts on Anthropologists and Missionaries," 298.
19. Ibid.
20. Ibid.
21. Feldman and Stipe, "More on the Antagonism," 114.
22. Ibid.
23. Ibid., 115.
24. Stoll, *Fishers of Men*; Stoll, "Words Can Be Used"; Stoll, "Higher Power."
25. Hvalkof, Stipe, and Stoll, "On the Summer Institute of Linguistics," 125.
26. Barrett, *Anthropology*, 66.
27. Ibid.
28. Hughes, "Mutual Biases," 77.
29. Eriksen and Nielsen, *History of Anthropology*, 40.
30. Barnett, "Is There a Scientific Basis?," 23.
31. Petersen, "Reply to Stipe," 173.
32. "Declaration of Barbados," 268.
33. Ibid.
34. Ibid.
35. Ibid., 268–69.

36. Ibid., 269.

37. Schlesinger, "Missionary Enterprise."

38. Hvalkof and Aaby, *Is God an American?*

39. Stoll, *Fishers of Men.*

40. Hvalkof and Aaby, "Introducing God," 14.

41. Stoll, "Words Can Be Used," 30.

42. For another perspective on WBT-SIL, one that emphasizes SIL's ability to work with left-wing governments and to separate its mission from the mission of the United States, see Svelmoe, *New Vision for Missions*; Svelmoe, "General and the Gringo."

43. Pereira, "Go Forth," 113. The editors were dubious enough about the story to include another account, one that did not mention SIL, in a footnote.

44. Stoll, *Fishers of Men*, 84.

45. S. Robinson, "Fulfilling the Mission," 41.

46. Arcand, "God Is an American," 77.

47. Stoll, "Higher Power," 70.

48. Vickers, "Jesuits and SIL," 55.

49. T. Moore, "SIL and a 'New-Found Tribe,'" 142.

50. Stoll, *Fishers of Men*, 157.

51. Arcand, "God Is an American," 82.

52. Rappaport, review of *Fishers of Men*, 442–43; Vickers, review of *Fishers of Men*, 200–1.

53. Barbira-Freedman, review of *Is God an American?*, 420–21; England, review of *Is God an American?*, 711–13; Mayer, review of *Is God an American?*, 617–19.

54. "Lausanne Covenant," 23.

55. Graham, "Why Lausanne?," 7. On Graham's changing political views, see Pierard, "Billy Graham and Vietnam," 37–51; Pierard, "From Evangelical Exclusivism," 425–46.

56. Taber, "Fishers of Men," 35.

57. Howard, "Fishers of Men," 382.

58. Ibid.

59. Kornfield, "Fishers of Men," 312.

60. Ibid., 313.

61. Ibid.

62. Stoll, "What Should Wycliffe Do?," 45.

63. Shaw, "Ethnohistory, Strategy, and Bible Translation," 47.

64. Stoll, *Is Latin America Turning Protestant?*, 330.

65. Gough, "New Proposals," 403.

66. Eder, "Peril Called Inherent," 5.

67. Lelyveld, "India Still Wary," 7.

68. Berreman, "Is Anthropology Alive?," 391–96.

69. Nader, "Up the Anthropologist," 284.

70. Beidelman, "Social Theory," 235.

71. Ibid.

72. Ibid.

73. Comaroff and Comaroff, *Of Revelation and Revolution*, 1:xiii.

74. Ibid.

75. Beidelman, *Colonial Evangelism*, 5–6.

76. Ibid.

77. Comaroff and Comaroff, *Of Revelation and Revolution*, 2:9.

78. Ibid., 2:409.

79. Ibid., 2:8.

80. Ibid., 1:313.

81. Nason, "Civilizing the Heathen," 136.

82. Rosaldo, *Ilongot Headhunting*.

83. Stearman, *No Longer Nomads*, 67.

84. Abbot, "Unearthing Civil Dialogue," 53.

85. Stearman, *Yuquí*, 150.

86. Burridge, *In the Way*, ix.

87. Huber, review of *In the Way*, 388–89; Beidelman, review of *In the Way*, 660–61.

88. Landau, "Hegemony and History," 515.

89. Robbins, "Continuity Thinking," 5–38.

90. Borneman, "American Anthropology," 667.

91. Ibid., 669.

92. Said, *Orientalism*. On Said and American anthropology, see Said, "Representing the Colonized," 205–25.

CHAPTER FOUR

1. "Rebirth Offers Opportunity," 1541.

2. For the story of the rise and fall of women's mission organizations, see Robert, *American Women in Mission*; Hill, *World Their Household*; Tucker, "Female Mission Strategists."

3. By the early decades of the twentieth century, female missionaries outnumbered male missionaries two to one. See Tucker, *Guardians of the Great Commission*.

4. Strickland, "Power of the Glad Heart," 27. As a female physician, Shoemaker was a rarity in America. By 1960, only 5 percent of medical school graduates were women. See Martin, Arnold, and Parker, "Gender and Medical Socialization," 334.

5. Robert, *American Women in Mission*; Hunt, *Bless God and Take Courage*. For a description of how female evangelists fared in America, see Brekus, *Strangers and Pilgrims*.

6. J. Hunter, *Gospel of Gentility*.

7. Cuordileone, "Politics in an Age of Anxiety"; Dean, *Imperial Brotherhood*; May, *Homeward Bound*; Cuordileone, *Manhood and American Political Culture*; Rosenberg, "'Foreign Affairs' after World War II"; Feldstein, *Motherhood in Black and White*.

8. Iverson, "For Those Who Live Alone," 30.

9. Ibid., 31.

10. During the 1950s, men married at an average age of twenty-two. For both men and women, the average age for marrying was a drop from previous decades. See Mintz and Kellogg, *Domestic Revolutions*, 178–82. For family ideology during the 1950s and 1960s, see Bendroth, *Growing up Protestant*.

11. Davis and Davis, "Call of the Central Congo," 9.

12. Watson, "Kambini's New Jerusalem," 27.

13. Ibid.

14. McConnell, "Energy and Hot Countries."

15. "Methodist Women," 27.

16. *Mission: A Christian Presence*, Records of the Mission Education and Cultivate Department, General Board of Global Ministries, UMCA, frame 31.

17. Ibid., frame 70.

18. Ibid., frame 71.

19. The novels include Michener, *Hawaii*; Elliot, *No Graven Image*; Hersey, *Call*; Mercer, *Rachel Cade*.

20. Dowie, *Peter Matthiessen*, 51–54.

21. Matthiessen, *At Play in the Fields of the Lord*, 24.

22. Ibid., 154.

23. Ibid., 26.

24. Ibid., 77–78.

25. Ibid., 89.

26. Ibid., 202.

27. Ibid., 264.

28. Ibid., 49.

29. Ibid., 65.

30. Ibid., 232.

31. Ibid., 291.

32. Ibid., 10.

33. Ibid., 229.

34. Ibid., 230.

35. Dean, *Imperial Brotherhood*, 169.

36. J. Kennedy, "Soft American," 16.

37. Dean, *Imperial Brotherhood*, 181.

38. Kearns, *Lyndon Johnson and the American Dream*, 253.

39. Matthiessen, *At Play in the Fields of the Lord*, 215.

40. Ibid., 233.

41. Ibid., 336.

42. Ibid.

43. Ibid., 332.

44. Ibid., 372.

45. Ibid., 373.

46. Ibid.

47. Patteson, "Imperialist Idea," 14.

48. For largely positive reviews, see Zoba, "The Testament"; Jones, "Grisham's Gospel"; Dyer, "In New Grisham, More Plotting"; Donahue, "Spirit Moves Grisham's 'Testament'"; Bauer, "Peretti Out-Grishams."

49. Kelly, "Brazilian 'Testament' to Faith," D8.

50. Ibid.

51. Grisham, *Testament*, 303.

52. Ibid., 244.

53. Ibid., 246.

54. Ibid., 241.

55. Ibid., 49.

56. Ibid., 430–31.

57. For reviews, see Pate, "In Grisham's Latest"; Dyer, "In New Grisham, More Plotting"; Walker, "Grisham Concocts Improved Formula." On *The Heart of Darkness*, see Achebe, "An Image of Africa."

58. Grisham, *Testament*, 224.

59. Sider, *Chicago Declaration*; Mouw, "Awakening the Evangelical Conscience."

60. On the role of gender in the rise of the religious Right, see Dowland, "Family Values"; Harding, *Book of Jerry Falwell*. On the conservative resurgence in the Southern Baptist Convention, see Hankins, *Uneasy in Babylon*.

61. Adeney, "A Woman Liberated," 30.

62. Bowers, "Women's Role," 359.

63. Douglas, "Lausanne's Extended Shadow," 44.

64. Ibid.

65. "Rein in Women's Group," 423. On this episode, see also "SBC Women's Group Asks for 'Clarification'"; "SBC Women."

66. Connell, *Masculinities*, 77.

67. Dowd, "War Introduces a Tougher Bush," 1. On the Vietnam syndrome, remasculinization, and Iraq, see Ducat, *Wimp Factor*; Niva, "Tough and Ten-

der"; Mariscal, "In the Wake of the Gulf War"; Jeffords, *The Remasculinization of America*.

68. Goodman, "New Male Model," 6.

69. Meacham, "How Colin Powell Plays the Game"; Parshall, "Powell & Schwarzkopf"; Roberts and Auster, "Colin Powell Superstar."

70. Hooper, *Manly States*, 193. See also Hooper, "Masculinist Practices and Gender Politics."

CONCLUSION

1. Kingsolver, *Poisonwood Bible*.

2. Warmbold, "'Poisonwood Bible' Preaches Wrongs," K12; Silver, "Kingsolver Writes for Social Change," G1.

3. Kingsolver, *Poisonwood Bible*, 276.

4. Stafford, "Poisonous Gospel," 90.

5. Skow, "Hearts of Darkness," 113.

6. Siegel, "Sweet and Low," 36.

7. Ibid.

8. Banker, "Mission Trip to Africa Turns Family's World Upside Down," 4.

9. "Editors' Choice," 6.

10. "United Methodist General Conference, April 23–May 2."

11. Sachs, "Anglican Disunion"; Bates, "Anglicans Warn U.S. Church"; Dart, "Gay Bishop Confirmed"; Steinmetz, "Gay Episcopal Ordination Smacks of Arrogance to World."

12. Bailey, "Intercontinental Divide," 17.

13. Ibid., 18.

14. Ibid.

15. "Episcopal Bishops Remain Defiant on Gay Bishop's Election," 14.

16. Bailey, "Intercontinental Divide," 17.

17. Ibid., 18.

18. "UM Evangelist Warns against Segregation Plan for UMC."

19. Ibid.

20. Bergner, "The Call."

21. Ibid., 43.

22. Ibid.

23. Ibid.

24. Ibid.

25. Ibid., 72.

26. Ibid.

27. Ibid., 74.

28. Ibid.

29. "President Bush's Remarks on September 11, 2002."

30. "President Barack Obama's Inaugural Address."

31. Carnes, "Disappointed but Holding," 78.

32. "Bully Culprit."

33. Hertz, "Is Attacking Iraq Moral?"; Colson, "Just War in Iraq."

34. "100 Leading Christian Ethicists Oppose Iraq War."

35. On evangelical leaders and the Iraq War, as well as evangelicals and foreign affairs during the George W. Bush administration, see den Dulk, "Evangelical 'Internationalists' and U.S. Foreign Policy during the Bush Administration"; den Dulk, "Evangelical Elites."

36. Hertz, "Is Attacking Iraq Moral?"

37. Carnes, "Bush Doctrine," 38.

38. Ibid., 40.

39. Ibid.

40. Olsen, "Bush's 'Theological Perspective,'" 22.

41. Gushee, "Our Teachable Moment," 90.

Bibliography

Abbot, Elinor. "Unearthing Civil Dialogue: Human Rights Concern Brings Missionaries, Anthropologists Together." *Christianity Today*, 9 January 1995, 53.

Achebe, Chinua. "An Image of Africa." *Research in African Literature* 9 (1978): 1–15.

Adamson, Hazel. "The Power of God." *Missionary Tidings*, July 1950, 220–21.

Adeney, Miriam. "Do Your Own Thing (as Long as You Do It Our Way)." *Christianity Today*, 4 July 1975, 11–14.

———. "A Woman Liberated—for What?" *Christianity Today*, 13 January 1984, 28–30.

Ambrosius, Lloyd E. "Woodrow Wilson and World War I." In *A Companion to American Foreign Relations*, edited by Robert D. Schulzinger, 149–67. Oxford: Blackwell, 2006.

Anderson, Gerald H. "American Protestants in Pursuit of Mission: 1886–1986." *International Bulletin of Missionary Research* 12 (1988): 98–118.

———. "Who Will Evangelize the World in 2000 A.D." *Good News*, September–October 1990, 21–25.

Arcand, Bernard. "God Is an American." In *Is God an American? An Anthropological Perspective on the Missionary Work of the Summer Institute of Linguistics*, edited by Søren Hvalkof and Peter Aaby, 77–84. London: Survival International, 1981.

Asad, Talad, ed. *Anthropology and the Colonial Encounter*. New York: Humanities Press, 1973.

Augsburger, Myron S. "Beating Swords into Plowshares." *Christianity Today*, 21 November 1975, 7–9.

Axtell, James. *The Invasion Within: The Contest of Cultures in Colonial North America*. New York: Oxford University Press, 1985.

Bailey, Sarah Pulliam. "Intercontinental Divide: Global Pressure Mounts for Uganda to Defeat Anti-Gay Bill, and Puts Evangelicals at Odds with One Another." *Christianity Today*, February 2010, 17–19.

Balmer, Randall. *Grant Us Courage: Travels Along the Mainline of American Protestantism*. New York: Oxford University Press, 1996.

Banker, Jan Williams. "Mission Trip to Africa Turns Family's World Upside Down." *Tampa Tribune*, 15 November 1998, 4.

Barbira-Freedman, F. Review of *Is God an American? Man* 18 (1983): 420–21.

Barnett, Clifford R. "Is There a Scientific Basis in Anthropology for the Ethics of Human Rights?" In *Human Rights and Anthropology*, edited by Theodore E. Downing and Gilbert Kushner, 21–26. Cambridge, Mass.: Cultural Survival, 1988.

Barrett, Stanley R. *Anthropology: A Student's Guide to Theory and Method.* Toronto: University of Toronto Press, 1996.

Bassett, Paul Merritt. "The Theological Identity of the North American Holiness Movement." In *Variety of American Evangelicalism*, edited by Donald W. Dayton and Robert K. Johnston, 72–108. Knoxville: University of Tennessee Press, 1991.

Bates, Stephen. "Anglicans Warn U.S. Church." *Christian Century*, 1 November 2003, 12–13.

Bauer, Susan Wise. "Peretti Out-Grishams Grisham." *Christianity Today*, 9 August 1999, 70–72.

Bays, Daniel H., and Grant Wacker. "The Many Faces of the Missionary Enterprise at Home." In *The Foreign Missionary Enterprise at Home*, edited by Daniel H. Bays and Grant Wacker, 1–10. Tuscaloosa: University of Alabama Press, 2003.

Beecher, Lyman. *A Plea for the West.* 2nd ed. Cincinnati: Truman and Smith, 1835.

Beidelman, T. O. *Colonial Evangelism: A Socio-Historical Study of an East African Mission at the Grassroots.* Bloomington: Indiana University Press, 1982.

———. Review of *In the Way: A Study of Christian Missionary Endeavours. American Ethnologist* 21 (1994): 660–61.

———. "Social Theory and the Study of Christian Missions in Africa." *Africa: Journal of the International African Institute* 44 (1974): 235–49.

Bendroth, Margaret Lamberts. *Growing up Protestant: Parents, Children, and Mainline Churches.* New Brunswick: Rutgers University Press, 2002.

Benthall, Jonathan. "A.A.A. Annual Meeting, Phoenix, 1988." *Anthropology Today* 5, no. 1 (1989): 22–24.

———. "Missionaries and Human Rights." *Anthropology Today* 11, no. 1 (1995): 1–3.

Bergner, Daniel. "The Call." *New York Times Magazine*, 26 January 2006, 40–47, 72–76.

Berreman, Gerald D. "Is Anthropology Alive? Social Responsibility in Social Anthropology." *Current Anthropology* 9 (1968): 391–96.

Billings, Peggy. "Toward a New Missionary Age." *New World Outlook*, March 1987, 17–21.

"Bishop Sano Blasts New Mission Agency Pamphlet." *United Methodist Newscope*, 26 October 1984, 3.

"Blunders in Dominican Republic." *Christian Century*, 19 May 1965, 636–37.

Borneman, Jon. "American Anthropology as Foreign Policy." *American Anthropologist* 97 (1995): 663–72.

Bowden, Henry Warner. *American Indians and Christian Missions: Studies in Cultural Conflict*. Chicago History of American Religion. Chicago: University of Chicago Press, 1981.

Bowers, Joyce. "Women's Role in Mission: Where Are We Now?" *Evangelical Missions Quarterly* 21 (1985): 352–60.

Brands, H. W. *The Devil We Knew: Americans and the Cold War*. New York: Oxford University Press, 1993.

Brekus, Catherine A. *Strangers and Pilgrims: Female Preaching in America, 1740–1845*. Chapel Hill: University of North Carolina Press, 1998.

Brody, Jane E. "Books of the Times." Review of *No Graven Image*. *New York Times*, 27 July 1966, 37.

"Bully Culprit: Can a Pre-emptive Strike against the Tyrant of Bagdad Be Justified?" *Christianity Today*, 7 October 2002, 32–33.

Burridge, Kenelm. *In the Way: A Study of Christian Missionary Endeavors*. Vancouver: UBC Press, 1991.

Carnes, Tony. "The Bush Doctrine: The Moral Vision That Launched the Iraq War Has Been Quietly Growing in the President's Inner Circle." *Christianity Today*, May 2003, 38–40.

———. "Disappointed but Holding: While Overall Support for George W. Bush Has Plummeted, Evangelicals Remain Surprisingly Loyal." *Christianity Today*, 1 February 2006, 78–81.

Carpenter, Joel A. *Revive Us Again: The Reawakening of American Fundamentalism*. New York: Oxford University Press, 1997.

Carroll, Jackson W., Barbara G. Wheeler, Daniel O. Aleshire, and Penny Long Marler. *Being There: Culture and Formation in Two Theological Schools*. New York: Oxford University Press, 1997.

Case, Riley B. *Evangelical and Methodist: A Popular History*. Nashville, Tenn.: Abingdon Press, 2004.

"The Cause of Christ in East Asia." *World Outlook*, March 1954, 18–19.

"Chinese Y.P.M.S. Request Prayer." *Missionary Tidings*, January 1946, 20–21.

"The Christian Outlook in Africa." *Christian Century*, 7 January 1953, 6–8.

Christopher, Warren. "America's Leadership, America's Opportunity." *Foreign Policy*, Spring 1995, 6–28.

"Churchmen Look at Communism." *Christianity Today*, 23 June 1967, 6.

"C.I.A. Recruitment and the Church." *Christian Century*, 13 March 1996, 285–86.

Coggins, Ross. "Missions and Prejudice." *Christianity Today*, 17 January 1964, 3–5.

Colson, Charles W. "Just War in Iraq: Sometimes Going to War Is the Charitable Thing to Do." *Christianity Today*, 9 December 2002, 72.

Comaroff, Jean, and John L. Comaroff. *Of Revelation and Revolution: The Dialectics of Modernity on a South African Frontier*. 2 vols. Chicago: University of Chicago Press, 1991–97.

Connell, R. W. *Masculinities*. 2nd ed. Berkeley: University of California Press, 2005.

"The Converted Heathen Speaks." *Missionary Tidings*, September 1945, 1.

Coote, Robert T. "Taking Aim on 2000 A.D." In *Mission Handbook: North American Protestant Ministries Overseas*, edited by Samuel Wilson and John Siewert. Monrovia, Calif.: MARC, World Vision International, 1986.

Cotter, George. "Spies, Strings and Missionaries: The Church Cannot Play the Cloak for the C.I.A.'S Dagger." *Christian Century*, 25 March 1981, 321–24.

Crouse, Eric. "Popular Cold Warriors: Conservative Protestants, Communism, and Culture in Early Cold War America." *Journal of Religion and Popular Culture* 2 (2002), http://www.usask.ca/relst/jrpc/article-popcoldwar.html.

Cuordileone, K. A. *Manhood and American Political Culture in the Cold War*. New York: Routledge, 2005.

———. "Politics in an Age of Anxiety: Cold War Political Culture and the Crisis in American Masculinity, 1949–1960." *Journal of American History* 87 (2000): 515–45.

Daniels, Ella Maze. "The Missionary in Today's World." *Missionary Tidings*, April 1957, 104–5, 132.

Dart, John. "Gay Bishop Confirmed: Action in U.S. Triggers Worldwide Reaction." *Christian Century*, 23 August 2003, 10–11.

Davis, Joe, and Dorothy Davis. "The Call of the Central Congo." *World Outlook*, March 1953, 5–9, 49.

Dayton, Donald W. *Discovering an Evangelical Heritage*. New York: Harper and Row, 1976.

———. "The Search for the Historical Evangelicalism, George Marsden's History of Fuller Seminary as a Case Study." *Christian Scholar's Review* 23 (1993): 12–33.

———. "Some Doubts about the Usefulness of the Category 'Evangelical.'" In *Variety of American Evangelicalism*, edited by Donald W. Dayton and Robert K. Johnston, 245–51. Knoxville: University of Tennessee Press, 1991.

Dean, Robert D. *Imperial Brotherhood: Gender and the Making of Cold War Foreign Policy*. Amherst: University of Massachusetts Press, 2001.

"The Declaration of Barbados: For the Liberation of the Indians." *Current Anthropology* 14 (1973): 267–70.

Delfendahl, Bernard. "On Anthropologists vs. Missionaries." *Current Anthropology* 22 (1981): 89.

Delfendahl, Bernard, H. Dieter Heinen, and Claude E. Stipe. "On Anthropologists, Missionaries, and Indigenous Peoples." *Current Anthropology* 23 (1982): 338–40.

den Dulk, Kevin R. "Evangelical Elites and Faith-Based Foreign Affairs." *Review of Faith and International Affairs* 4, no. 1 (2006): 21–58.

————. "Evangelical 'Internationalists' and U.S. Foreign Policy during the Bush Administration." In *Religion and the Bush Presidency*, edited by Mark J. Rozell and Gleaves Whitney, 213–34. New York: Palgrave Macmillan, 2007.

Dennis, James. *Christian Mission and Social Progress: A Sociological Study of Foreign Missions*. New York: Fleming H. Revell, 1897.

Diefenbaker, John G. "Mission to the World." *Christianity Today*, 21 December 1962, 1.

"Dissent Is Not Treason." *Christian Century*, 18 November 1953, 1317–19.

Dodge, Ralph E. *The Unpopular Missionary*. Westwood, N.J.: Fleming H. Revell, 1964.

Donahue, Deirdre. "Spirit Moves Grisham's 'Testament.'" *USA Today*, 2 February 1999, D1.

Douglas, James D. "Lausanne's Extended Shadow Gauges Evangelism Progress." *Christianity Today*, 8 August 1980, 43–44.

Dowd, Maureen. "War Introduces a Tougher Bush to Nation." *New York Times*, 2 March 1991, 1, 7.

Dowie, William. *Peter Matthiessen*. Boston: Twayne, 1991.

Dowland, Seth. "'Family Values' and the Formation of a Christian Right Agenda." *Church History* 78 (2009): 606–31.

Ducat, Stephen. *The Wimp Factor: Gender Gaps, Holy Wars, and the Politics of Anxious Masculinity*. Boston: Beacon Press, 2004.

Dunch, Ryan. "Beyond Cultural Imperialism: Cultural Theory, Christian Missions, and Global Modernity." *History and Theory* 41 (2002): 301–25.

Dwight, E. W. *Memoirs of Henry Obookiah, a Native of Owhyhee, and a Member of the Foreign Mission School, Who Died at Cornwall, Conn., Feb. 17, 1818, Aged 26 Years*. New Haven: Published at the Office of the Religious Intelligencer, 1818.

Dyer, Richard. "In New Grisham, More Plotting." *Boston Globe*, 9 February 1999, D1.

"A Dynamic People." *Missionary Tidings*, January 1973, 6–8.

Eder, Richard. "Peril Called Inherent in Scholars' Work for C.I.A." *New York Times*, 28 June 1966, 5.

"Editors' Choice." *New York Times Book Review*, 6 December 1998, 6.

Edwards, Wendy J. Deichmann. "Forging an Ideology for American Missions: Josiah Strong and Manifest Destiny." In *North American Foreign Missions, 1810–1914: Theology, Theory and Policy*, edited by Wilbert R. Shenk, 163–91. Grand Rapids, Mich.: Eerdmans, 2004.

Elliot, Elisabeth. *Let Me Be a Woman*. Wheaton, Ill.: Tyndale House Publishers, 1976.

———. *The Mark of a Man*. Old Tappan, N.J.: Fleming H. Revell, 1981.

———. *No Graven Image: A Novel*. New York: Harper and Row, 1966.

———. *Passion and Purity*. Old Tappan, N.J.: Fleming H. Revell, 1984.

———. *The Savage My Kinsman*. New York: Harper, 1961.

———. *Through Gates of Splendor*. New York: Harper, 1957.

"Empire Is Justifiable If We Rule It!" *Christian Century*, 9 April 1947, 453.

"End of Strike Frees 400 Missionaries." *Christian Century*, 2 October 1946, 1171.

England, Nora. Review of *Is God an American? American Anthropologist* 85 (1983): 711–13.

"Episcopal Bishops Remain Defiant on Gay Bishop's Election." *Christian Century*, 8 February 2005, 14.

Eriksen, Thomas Hylland, and Finn Sivert Nielsen. *A History of Anthropology*. Sterling, Va.: Pluto Press, 2001.

Escobar, Samuel. "Missions' New World Order: The Twenty-First Century Calls for Us to Give Up Our Nineteenth-Century Models for Worldwide Ministry." *Christianity Today* 14 November 1994, 48–52.

———. "Social Concern and World Evangelism." In *Christ the Liberator*, 103–12. Downers Grove, Ill.: InterVarsity Press, 1971.

Feldman, Harry, and Claude E. Stipe. "More on the Antagonism between Anthropologists and Missionaries." *Current Anthropology* 24 (1983): 114–15.

Feldstein, Ruth. *Motherhood in Black and White: Race and Sex in American Liberalism, 1930–1965*. Ithaca, N.Y.: Cornell University Press, 2000.

Fernando, Ajith. "Bombs Away: How Western Military Actions Affect the Work of the Church." *Christianity Today*, 14 June 1999, 76–77.

Fousek, John. *To Lead the Free World: American Nationalism and the Cultural Roots of the Cold War*. Chapel Hill: University of North Carolina Press, 2000.

Fox, Richard Wightman. *Reinhold Niebuhr: A Biography*. Ithaca, N.Y.: Cornell University Press, 1997.

Fulton, Charles Darby. "Are We Going out of [the Missionary] Business?" *Christianity Today*, 30 March 1962, 8–9.

———. "Evangelism: The Heart of Missions." *Christianity Today*, 29 April 1966, 9–12.

Gaddis, John Lewis. *Strategies of Containment: A Critical Appraisal of American National Security Policy during the Cold War*. Rev. and expanded ed. New York: Oxford University Press, 2005.

"Getting Out of Vietnam." *Christian Century*, 23 December 1964, 1583.

Goerner, H. Cornell. "He Is Not without Love." Review of Ralph E. Dodge, *Unpopular Missionary*. *Christianity Today*, 17 July 1964, 26.

"Good News Executive Exchanges Heated Remarks with Bishop." *United Methodist Newscope*, 16 November 1984, 3.

Goodman, Ellen. "The New Model Male." *Chicago Tribune*, 17 March 1991, 6.

Gough, Kathleen. "New Proposals for Anthropologists." *Current Anthropology* 9 (1968): 403–35.

Graham, Billy. "Satan's Religion." *American Mercury*, August 1954, 41–46.

———. "Why Lausanne?" *Christianity Today*, 13 September 1974, 4–14.

Grisham, John. *The Testament*. New York: Doubleday, 1999.

"Guidelines for Mission." *Christianity Today*, 23 April 1976, 51–52.

Gushee, David P. "Our Teachable Moment: The Iraq War Calls for Some Serious Rethinking by Christians." *Christianity Today*, September 2007, 90.

Hall, Amy Laura. *Conceiving Parenthood: American Protestantism and the Spirit of Reproduction*. Grand Rapids, Mich.: Eerdmans, 2008.

Hankins, Barry. *Uneasy in Babylon: Southern Baptist Conservatives and American Culture*. Tuscaloosa: University of Alabama Press, 2002.

Harding, Susan Friend. *The Book of Jerry Falwell: Fundamentalist Language and Politics*. Princeton: Princeton University Press, 2000.

Harris, Paul. "Denominationalism and Democracy: Ecclesiastical Issues Underlying Rufus Anderson's Three Self Program." In *North American Foreign Missions, 1810–1914: Theology, Theory and Policy*, edited by Wilbert R. Shenk, 61–85. Grand Rapids, Mich.: Eerdmans, 2004.

Harrison, William K. "Search for Peace on Earth." *Christianity Today*, 13 April 1959, 7–9.

Hart, D. G. *Deconstructing Evangelicalism: Conservative Protestantism in the Age of Billy Graham*. Grand Rapids, Mich.: Baker Academic, 2004.

"Hemispheric McCarthyism." *Christian Century*, 20 October 1965, 1277.

Henry, Carl F. H. "A Nation in Trouble." *Christianity Today*, 12 September 1969, 37–38.

———. "Of Bicentennial Concerns and Patriotic Symbols." *Christianity Today*, 2 July 1976, 14–19.

Hersey, John. *The Call.* New York: Knopf, 1985.

Hertz, Todd. "Is Attacking Iraq Moral?" *Christianity Today,* 1 Septmeber 2002, www.christianitytoday.com/go/iraq. 11 October 2010.

Hertzke, Allen D. "An Assessment of the Mainline Churches since 1945." In *The Role of Religion in the Making of Public Policy,* edited by James E. Wood Jr. and Derek Davis, 43–79. Waco, Tex.: Baylor University, 1991.

Hill, Patricia R. "The Missionary Enterprise." In *Encyclopedia of the American Religious Experience: Studies of Traditions and Movements,* edited by Charles H. Lippy and Peter W. Williams, 1683–96. New York: Scribner, 1988.

———. *The World Their Household: The American Woman's Foreign Mission Movement and Cultural Transformation, 1870–1920.* Ann Arbor: University of Michigan Press, 1985.

Hodges, Olive I. "Citizen of an Enemy Country." *Christian Century,* 5 September 1945, 1005–6.

"Honest Intervention." *Christian Century,* 5 June 1963, 731–32.

Hooper, Charlotte. *Manly States: Masculinities, International Relations, and Gender Politics.* New York: Columbia University Press, 2001.

———. "Masculinist Practices and Gender Politics: The Operation of Multiple Masculinities in International Relations." In *The "Man" Question in International Relations,* edited by Marysia Zalewski and Jane Parpart, 28–53. Boulder, Colo.: Westview Press, 1998.

Horton, Michael Scott. "Reflection: Is Evangelicalism Reformed or Wesleyan? Reopening the Marsden-Dayton Debate." *Christian Scholar's Review* 31 (2001): 131–55.

Howard, D. M. "Fishers of Men or Founders of Empire: The Wycliffe Bible Translators in Latin America." *Missiology* 12 (1984): 380.

Howard, Thomas T. Letter to the editor. *Christianity Today,* 2 September 1966, 18.

Huber, Mary Taylor. Review of *In the Way: A Study of Christian Missionary Endeavours. Man* 28 (1993): 388–89.

Hughes, Daniel T. "Mutual Biases of Anthropologists and Missionaries." In *Mission, Church, and Sect in Oceania,* edited by James A. Boutilier, Daniel T. Hughes, and Sharon W. Tiffany, 65–82. Ann Arbor: University of Michigan Press, 1978.

"The Hunger of the Masses." *Christianity Today,* 16 March 1962, 24–25.

Hunt, Rosalie Hall. *Bless God and Take Courage: The Judson History and Legacy.* Valley Forge, Pa.: Judson Press, 2005.

Hunter, Jane. *The Gospel of Gentility: American Women Missionaries in Turn-of-the-Century China.* New Haven, Conn.: Yale University Press, 1984.

Hunter, Stanley Armstrong. "Sea Strike Delays 400 Missionaries." *Christian Century*, 2 October 1946, 1186–87.

Hutchison, William R., ed. *Between the Times: The Travail of the Protestant Establishment in America, 1900–1960.* New York: Cambridge University Press, 1989.

———. *Errand to the World: American Protestant Thought and Foreign Missions.* Chicago: University of Chicago Press, 1987.

Hvalkof, Søren, and Peter Aaby. "Introducing God in the Devil's Paradise." In *Is God an American? An Anthropological Perspective on the Missionary Work of the Summer Institute of Linguistics*, edited by Søren Hvalkof and Peter Aaby, 9–15. London: Survival International, 1981.

———, eds. *Is God an American? An Anthropological Perspective on the Missionary Work of the Summer Institute of Linguistics.* London: Survival International, 1981.

Hvalkof, Søren, Claude E. Stipe, and David Stoll. "On the Summer Institute of Linguistics and Its Critics." *Current Anthropology* 25 (1984): 124–26.

Immerman, Richard H. *John Foster Dulles: Piety, Pragmatism, and Power in U.S. Foreign Policy.* Wilmington, Del.: Scholarly Resources, 1999.

Inboden, William. *Religion and American Foreign Policy, 1945–1960: The Soul of Containment.* New York: Cambridge University Press, 2008.

"India Veers Away from Religious Liberty." *Christian Century*, 21 April 1954, 485.

"Interview: John Stumbo." *New World Outlook*, May 1988, 22–23.

Iverson, Lalla. "For Those Who Live Alone." *Together: The Mid-Month Magazine for Methodist Families*, September 1962, 30–31.

Jeffords, Susan. *The Remasculinization of America: Gender and the Vietnam War.* Bloomington: Indiana University Press, 1989.

Jenkins, Philip. *The Next Christendom: The Rise of Global Christianity.* New York: Oxford University Press, 2002.

Johnston, Robert K. "American Evangelicalism: An Extended Family." In *Variety of American Evangelicalism*, edited by Donald W. Dayton and Robert K. Johnston, 252–72. Knoxville: University of Tennessee Press, 1991.

Jones, Malcolm. "Grisham's Gospel." *Newsweek*, 15 February 1999, 65–67.

Kaplan, Amy. *The Anarchy of Empire in the Making of U.S. Culture.* Cambridge, Mass.: Harvard University Press, 2002.

Kato, Byang H. "Christian Surge in Africa, Part 1." *Christianity Today*, 26 September 1975, 4–7.

Kearns, Doris. *Lyndon Johnson and the American Dream.* New York: Harper and Row, 1976.

Kellar, Jeanne. "Mission United." *World Outlook*, August 1947, 5–8.

Kelly, Katy. "Brazilian 'Testament' to Faith." *USA Today*, 11 February 1999, D8.

Kennedy, Gerald. "Defender and Invader." *Christianity Today*, 21 December 1962, 2.

Kennedy, John F. "The Soft American." *Sports Illustrated*, 26 December 1960, 13, 15–17, 26.

Kingsolver, Barbara. *The Poisonwood Bible: A Novel*. New York: HarperCollins, 1998.

Klausler, Alfred P. Review of *The Call*. *Christian Century*, 14 August 1985, 742–43.

Klein, Christina. *Cold War Orientalism: Asia in the Middlebrow Imagination, 1945–1961*. Berkeley: University of California Press, 2003.

Knight, George W., III. "Can a Christian Go to War?" *Christianity Today*, 21 November 1975, 4–7.

Kornfield, William. "Fishers of Men or Founders of Empire: The Wycliffe Bible Translators in Latin America." *Evangelical Missions Quarterly* 19 (1983): 308–15.

Kucheman, Clark. "Churches and the Viet Nam Issue." *Christianity Today*, 23 October 1970, 15–16.

Lahr, Angela M. *Millennial Dreams and Apocalyptic Nightmares: The Cold War Origins of Political Evangelicalism*. New York: Oxford University Press, 2007.

Lamson, Byron S. *To Catch the Tide*. Winona Lake, Ind.: Light and Life Press, 1963.

Landau, Paul S. "Hegemony and History in Jean and John L. Comaroff's *Of Revelation and Revolution*." *Africa* 70 (2000): 501–19.

Larson, Janet K. "Wolf in the Shepherd's Frock." *Christian Century*, 18 August 1976, 699–700.

"The Lausanne Covenant." *Christianity Today*, 16 August 1974, 22–24.

Layne, Christopher, and Benjamin Schwarz. "American Hegemony— without an Enemy." *Foreign Policy*, Fall 1993, 5–24.

Lelyveld, Joseph. "India Still Wary of U.S. Scholars." *New York Times*, 14 August 1968, 7.

Lewis, Diane. "Anthropology and Colonialism." *Current Anthropology* 14 (1973): 581–602.

Lian, Xi. *The Conversion of Missionaries: Liberalism in American Protestant Missions in China, 1907–1932*. University Park: Pennsylvania State University Press, 1997.

Lindsell, Harold. "One Doesn't Tell God." *Christianity Today*, 8 July 1966, 29.

Long, Kathryn T. "In the Modern World but Not of It: The 'Auca Martyrs,'

Evangelicalism, and Postwar American Culture." In *The Foreign Missionary Enterprise at Home*, edited by Daniel H. Bays and Grant Wacker, 223–36. Tuscaloosa: University of Alabama Press, 2003.

Luce, Henry. "The American Century." *Life*, 17 February 1941, 61–65.

MacKay, John A. "Latin America and Revolution—I." *Christian Century*, 17 November 1965, 1409–12.

————. "Latin America and Revolution—II." *Christian Century*, 24 November 1965, 1439–43.

Makdisi, Ussama. *Artillery of Heaven: American Missionaries and the Failed Conversion of the Middle East*. Ithaca, N.Y.: Cornell University Press, 2008.

Malinowski, Bronislaw. *A Diary in the Strict Sense of the Term*. London: Routledge & Kegan Paul, 1967.

Mariscal, George. "In the Wake of the Gulf War: Untying the Yellow Ribbon." *Cultural Critique*, no. 19 (1991): 97–117.

Marsden, George M. *Fundamentalism and American Culture: The Shaping of Twentieth-Century Evangelicalism, 1870–1925*. New York: Oxford University Press, 1980.

Martin, Steven C., Robert M. Arnold, and Ruth M. Parker. "Gender and Medical Socialization." *Journal of Health and Social Behavior* 29 (1988): 333–43.

Marty, Martin E. "Peace and Pluralism: *The Century*, 1946–1952." *Christian Century*, 24 October 1984, 979–83.

Mason, Francis. *The Karen Apostle; or, Memoir of Ko Thah-Byu, the First Karen Convert, with Notices Concerning His Nation*. Boston: Gould, Kendall and Lincoln, 1843.

Matthiessen, Peter. *At Play in the Fields of the Lord*. New York: Random House, 1965.

May, Elaine Tyler. *Homeward Bound: American Families in the Cold War Era*. New York: Basic Books, 1988.

Mayer, Enrique. Review of *Is God an American? American Ethnologist* 10 (1983): 618.

McAlister, Melani. *Epic Encounters: Culture, Media, and U.S. Interests in the Middle East since 1945*. Updated ed. Berkeley: University of California Press, 2005.

McConnell, Dorothy. "Energy and Hot Countries." *World Outlook*, April 1948, 25–26.

McDougall, Walter A. *Promised Land, Crusader State: The American Encounter with the World since 1776*. New York: Houghton Mifflin, 1997.

McGavran, Donald A. "The Lions in Missions." *Christianity Today*, 3 December 1971, 20–22.

Meacham, Jon. "How Colin Powell Plays the Game." *Washington Monthly*, December 1994, 33.

Mead, Walter Russell. *Special Providence: American Foreign Policy and How It Changed the World*. New York: Alfred A. Knopf, 2001.

Meeman, Edward J. "Christianity and Profits." *Christian Century*, 20 February 1952, 219–21.

Mercer, Charles E. *Rachel Cade*. New York: Putnam, 1956.

"Methodist Women around the World: A Picture Story." *World Outlook*, January 1954, 27–31.

Michener, James A. "'Aloha' for the Fiftieth State." *New York Times*, 19 April 1959, SM 14.

———. *Hawaii*. New York: Random House, 1959.

Mintz, Steven, and Susan Kellogg. *Domestic Revolutions: A Social History of American Family Life*. New York: Free Press, 1988.

"Mission Study Themes for 1955–56." *Missionary Tidings*, June 1955, 186–87.

Montgomery, John Warwick. "Should We Export the American Way?" *Christianity Today*, 23 April 1976, 57–58.

Moore, P. C. "Missions Reassessed." Review of James A. Scherer, *Missionary, Go Home*. *Christianity Today*, 8 May 1964, 35–37.

Moore, Thomas R. "SIL and a 'New-Found Tribe': The Amarakaeri Experience." In *Is God an American? An Anthropological Perspective on the Missionary Work of the Summer Institute of Linguistics*, edited by Søren Hvalkof and Peter Aaby, 133–43. London: Survival International, 1981.

Morrison, C. C. "Protestantism and the Lordship of Christ." *Christian Century*, July 3 1946, 833–35.

Morrison, John. "Too Little and Too Late." *Christianity Today*, 4 February 1957, 10–11.

Mouw, Richard. "Awakening the Evangelical Conscience." *Christianity Today*, 1 October 2006, http://www.christianitytoday.com/ch/2006/issue92/8.39.html. 1 October 2010.

Nader, Laura. "Up the Anthropologist—Perspectives Gained from Studying Up." In *Reinventing Anthropology*, edited by Dell Hymes, 284–311. New York: Vintage Books, 1974.

Nason, James D. "Civilizing the Heathen: Missionaries and Social Change in the Mortlock Islands." In *Mission, Church, and Sect in Oceania*, edited by James A. Boutilier, Daniel T. Hughes, and Sharon W. Tiffany, 109–38. Ann Arbor: University of Michigan Press, 1978.

"National Purpose and Christian Mission." *Christian Century*, 6 January 1960, 3–5.

Neuhaus, Richard John. "Christianity and Democracy: A Statement of the Institute on Religion and Democracy." *Center Journal* 1 (1982): 9–25.

Niebuhr, Reinhold. *The Children of Light and the Children of Darkness: A Vindication of Democracy and a Critique of Its Traditional Defense.* New York: Charles Scribner's Sons, 1944.

"1990/91 Mission Study Books Reviewed." *Good News*, September–October 1990, 27.

Ninkovich, Frank A. *The Wilsonian Century: U.S. Foreign Policy since 1900.* Chicago: University of Chicago Press, 1999.

Niva, Steve. "Tough and Tender: New World Order Masculinity and the Gulf War." In *The "Man" Question in International Relations*, edited by Marysia Zalewski and Jane Parpart, 109–28. Boulder, Colo.: Westview Press, 1998.

Olsen, Ted. "Bush's 'Theological Perspective': U.S. Presence in Iraq Is 'Allowing for the Inevitable to Happen.'" *Christianity Today*, September 2007, 22.

"On Foreign Policy." *Christian Century*, 7 July 1965, 863.

"100 Leading Christian Ethicists Oppose Iraq War." *Sojourners*. http://www.sojo.net/index.cfm?action=action.ethicists_statement. 11 October 2010.

"One Hundred Years in China." *World Outlook*, November 1947, 5.

"One Year After." *New York Times*, 14 August 1946, 20.

Padilla, C. René. "The Church and Political Ambiguity." *Christianity Today*, 26 July 1974, 41–42.

———. "Peru: Evangelicals under Attack." *Christianity Today*, 11 April 1975, 46–47.

———. "The Theology of Liberation." *Christianity Today*, 9 November 1973, 69–70.

———. "What Is the Gospel?" *Christianity Today*, 20 July 1973, 34–35.

Parshall, Gerald. "Powell & Schwarzkopf." *U.S. News & World Report*, 16 March 1998, 76.

Pate, Nancy. "In Grisham's Latest, Not All of the Predators Are Two-Legged." *Journal Star*, 11 February 1999, C4.

Patterson, James Alan. "The Loss of a Protestant Missionary Consensus: Foreign Missions and the Fundamentalist-Modernist Conflict." In *Earthen Vessels: American Evangelicals and Foreign Missions, 1880–1980*, edited by Joel A. Carpenter and Wilbert R. Shenk, 73–91. Grand Rapids, Mich.: Eerdmans, 1990.

Patteson, Richard F. "*At Play in the Fields of the Lord*: The Imperialist Idea and the Discovery of Self." *Critique* 21 (1979): 5–14.

"The Peace Drive in the Churches." *Christianity Today*, 13 April 1959, 20–21.

Pereira, Luis A. "Go Forth to Every Part of the World and Make All Nations My Disciples: The Bolivian Instance." In *Is God an American? An Anthropological Perspective on the Missionary Work of the Summer Institute of Linguistics*, edited by Søren Hvalkof and Peter Aaby, 109–20. London: Survival International, 1981.

Petersen, Glenn T. "Reply to Stipe." *Current Anthropology* 21 (1980): 173.

Pierard, Richard V. "Billy Graham and Vietnam: From Cold Warrior to Peacemaker." *Christian Scholar's Review* 10 (1980): 37–51.

———. "From Evangelical Exclusivism to Ecumenical Openness: Billy Graham and Sociopolitical Issues." *Journal of Ecumenical Studies* 20 (1983): 425–46.

Plowman, Edward E. "The View from Lausanne." *Christianity Today*, 16 August 1974, 35–37.

Porter, Andrew. "'Cultural Imperialism' and Protestant Missionary Enterprise, 1780–1914." *Journal of Imperial and Commonwealth History* 25 (1997): 367–91.

"President Barack Obama's Inaugural Address." http://www.whitehouse .gov/blog/inaugural-address/. 24 October 2011.

"President Bush's Remarks on September 11, 2002." CNN.com, http:// articles.cnn.com/2002-09-11/us/ar911.bush.speech.transcript_1_attacks-deepest-national-conviction-life?_s=PM:US. 24 October 2011.

"Problems of Peace." *New York Times*, 16 August 1945, 17.

"Protestant Freedom and Italian Law." *Christian Century*, 1 October 1952, 1117.

"Protestants Petition the Colombia President." *Christian Century*, 4 November 1953, 1252.

Qalo, Aminiasi. "Partnership in Missions: New Patterns of Teamwork." *Christianity Today*, 18 September 1981, 21, 31.

Rappaport, Joanne. Review of *Fishers of Men or Founders of Empire? American Anthropologist* 86 (1984): 442–43.

"Rebirth Offers Opportunity for Realigning Relationships." *Christian Century*, 27 December 1950, 1541–42.

Reed, James. *The Missionary Mind and American East Asia Policy, 1911–1915*. Cambridge, Mass.: Harvard University Press, 1983.

"Rein in Women's Group, Say SBC Conservatives." *Christian Century*, 21 April 1993, 423–24.

Renda, Mary A. *Taking Haiti: Military Occupation and the Culture of U.S. Imperialism, 1915–1940*. Chapel Hill: University of North Carolina Press, 2001.

"Retrospect." *Christian Century*, 29 December 1954, 1575–77.

Robb, Edmund W. "Christian Scandalmongering." *Christian Century*,
6 January 1982, 27–30.

Robb, James S. "Missions Derailed." *Good News*, May–June 1983, 6–29.

Robbins, Joel. "Continuity Thinking and the Problem of Christian
Culture: Belief, Time, and the Anthropology of Christianity." *Current
Anthropology* 48 (2007): 5–38.

Robert, Dana L. *American Women in Mission: A Social History of Their
Thought and Practice*. Macon, Ga.: Mercer University Press, 1997.

———. "The Crisis of Missions: Premillennial Mission Theory and the
Origins of Independent Evangelical Missions." In *Earthen Vessels:
American Evangelicals and Foreign Missions, 1880–1980*, edited by
Joel A. Carpenter and Wilbert R. Shenk, 29–46. Grand Rapids, Mich.:
Eerdmans, 1990.

———. "From Missions to Mission to Beyond Missions: The
Historiography of American Protestant Foreign Missions since World
War II." In *New Directions in American Religious History*, edited by
Harry S. Stout and D. G. Hart, 362–93. New York: Oxford University
Press, 1997.

———. *Occupy Until I Come: A. T. Pierson and the Evangelization of the
World*. Grand Rapids, Mich.: Eerdmans, 2003.

Roberts, Steven V., and Bruce B. Auster. "Colin Powell Superstar." *U.S. News
& World Report*, 20 September 1993, 48.

Robinson, James H. "Awakening Africa." *Christian Century*, 11 January 1956,
41–43.

Robinson, Scott S. "Fulfilling the Mission: North American Evangelism in
Ecuador." In *Is God an American? An Anthropological Perspective on the
Missionary Work of the Summer Institute of Linguistics*, edited by Søren
Hvalkof and Peter Aaby, 41–50. London: Survival International, 1981.

Rogers, Richard L. "'A Bright and New Constellation': Millennial Narratives
and the Origins of American Foreign Missions." In *North American
Foreign Missions, 1810–1914: Theology, Theory and Policy*, edited by
Wilbert R. Shenk, 39–60. Grand Rapids, Mich.: Eerdmans, 2004.

Roof, Wade Clark, and William McKinney. *American Mainline Religion: Its
Changing Shape and Future*. New Brunswick: Rutgers University Press,
1987.

Rosaldo, Renato. *Ilongot Headhunting, 1883–1974: A Study in Society and
History*. Stanford, Calif.: Stanford University Press, 1980.

Rosell, Garth. *The Surprising Work of God: Harold John Ockenga, Billy
Graham, and the Rebirth of Evangelicalism*. Grand Rapids, Mich.: Baker
Academic, 2008.

Rosenberg, Emily S. "'Foreign Affairs' after World War II: Connecting Sexual and International Politics." *Diplomatic History* 18 (1994): 59–70.

Sachs, William L. "Anglican Disunion: The Global Response to a Gay Bishop." *Christian Century*, 16 November 2004, 8–9.

Said, Edward W. *Orientalism*. New York: Pantheon Books, 1978.

———. "Representing the Colonized: Anthropology's Interlocutors." *Critical Inquiry* 15 (1989): 205–25.

Sanneh, Lamin O. "Christian Missions and the Western Guilt Complex." *Christian Century*, 8 April 1987, 330–34.

———. "Global Christianity and the Re-education of the West." *Christian Century* 19 July 1995, 715–18.

———. "Particularity, Pluralism and Commitment." *Christian Century*, 31 January 1990, 103–8.

"SBC Women Find a *Via Media*." *Christian Century* 27 January 1993, 80.

"SBC Women's Group Asked for 'Clarification.'" *Christian Century*, 17 February 1993, 167–68.

Schapera, Isaac. "Christianity and the Tswana." In *Cultures and Societies in Africa*, edited by Simon Ottenberg and Phoebe Ottenberg, 489–503. New York: Random House, 1960.

Schlesinger, Arthur Meier, Jr. "The Missionary Enterprise and Theories of Imperialism." In *Missionary Enterprise in China and America*, edited by John K. Fairbank, 336–73. Cambridge, Mass.: Harvard University Press, 1974.

Schmitz, David F. *The United States and Right-Wing Dictatorships, 1965–1989*. Cambridge: Cambridge University Press, 2006.

Scofield, Willard A. "What Is the Missionary's Message?" *Christianity Today* 6 November 1964, 16–17.

Seamands, David A. "Missions without Salvation." *Good News*, April–June 1972, 23–30, 37.

"Self-Respect after My Lai." *Christian Century*, 10 December 1969, 1569.

Settje, David E. "'Sinister' Communists and Vietnam Quarrels: The *Christian Century* and *Christianity Today* Respond to the Cold and Vietnam Wars." *Fides et historia* 32 (2000): 81–97.

Shacklock, Floyd. *This Revolutionary Faith*. New York: Friendship Press, 1955.

Shaw, R. Daniel. "Ethnohistory, Strategy, and Bible Translation: The Case of Wycliffe and the Cause of World Mission." *Missiology* 14 (1986): 47–53.

Shenk, Wilbert R. "Missions in Retrospect and Prospect." *Christianity Today*, 28 July 1972, 8–12.

Shepherd, George W., Jr. "The West vs. Asia and Africa." *Christian Century*, 13 March 1957, 326–27.

Sider, Ronald J. *The Chicago Declaration*. Carol Stream, Ill.: Creation House, 1974.

Sidey, Kenneth H. "An Overdose of Glasnost." *Christianity Today*, 20 August 1990, 34–36.

Siegel, Lee. "Sweet and Low." *New Republic*, 22 March 1999, 30–37.

Silver, Miriam. "Kingsolver Writes for Social Change." *Press Democrat*, 25 October 1998, G1.

Skeete, F. Herbert. "Embracing the Future in Mission." *New World Outlook*, January–February 1993, 5–7.

Skinner, Tom. "The U.S. Racial Crisis and World Evangelism." In *Christ the Liberator*, 189–210. Downers Grove, Ill.: InterVarsity Press, 1971.

Skow, John. "Hearts of Darkness." *Time Magazine*, 9 November 1998, 113.

Smith, Tony. *America's Mission: The United States and the Worldwide Struggle for Democracy in the Twentieth Century*. Princeton: Princeton University Press, 1994.

Spain, David. Review of T. O. Beidelman, *Colonial Evangelism*. *American Anthropologist* 86 (1984): 205.

"Spies in Missionary Guise." *Christian Century*, 7 August 1968, 985–86.

Stafford, Tim. "Poisonous Gospel." *Christianity Today*, 11 January 1999, 88–90.

Stearman, Allyn MacLean. *No Longer Nomads: The Sirionó Revisited*. Lanham, Md.: Hamilton Press, 1987.

————. *Yuquí: Forest Nomads in a Changing World*. San Francisco: Holt, Rinehart and Winston, 1989.

Steers, Tom. "Asians Consider Asia." *Christianity Today* 1 February 1974, 40.

Steinfels, Peter. "Christianity and Democracy: Baptizing Reaganism." *Christianity and Crisis*, 29 March 1982, 80–85.

Steinmetz, David C. "Gay Episcopal Ordination Smacks of Arrogance to World." *Knight Ridder Tribune News Service*, 11 November 2003, 1.

Stephanson, Anders. *Manifest Destiny: American Expansionism and the Empire of Right*. New York: Hill and Wang, 1995.

Stipe, Claude E. "Anthropologists versus Missionaries: The Influence of Presuppositions." *Current Anthropology* 21 (1980): 165–79.

Stipe, Claude E., and Harry Feldman. "Further Thoughts on Anthropologists and Missionaries." *Current Anthropology* 22 (1981): 297–98.

Stoll, David. *Fishers of Men or Founders of Empire? The Wycliffe Bible Translators in Latin America*. Cambridge, Mass.: Cultural Survival, 1982.

————. "Higher Power: Wycliffe's Colombian Advance." In *Is God an American? An Anthropological Perspective on the Missionary Work of the Summer Institute of Linguistics*, edited by Peter Aaby and Søren Hvalkof, 63–76. London: Survival International, 1981.

———. *Is Latin America Turning Protestant? The Politics of Evangelical Growth.* Berkeley: University of California Press, 1990.

———. "What Should Wycliffe Do?" *Missiology* 14 (1986): 37–45.

———. "Words Can Be Used in So Many Ways." In *Is God an American? An Anthropological Perspective on the Missionary Work of the Summer Institute of Linguistics,* edited by Søren Hvalkof and Peter Aaby, 23–40. London: Survival International, 1981.

Strickland, Eunice Jones. "Power of the Glad Heart." *World Outlook,* February 1951, 27–28.

Strong, Josiah. *Our Country: Its Possible Future and Its Present Crisis.* New York: Published by Baker & Taylor for the American Home Missionary Society, 1885.

Struchen, Donald E. "Q&A about Missions." *New World Outlook,* January 1984, 44.

Svelmoe, William L. "The General and the Gringo: W. Cameron Townsend as Lazaro Cardenas's 'Man in America.'" In *Foreign Missionary Enterprise at Home,* edited by Grant Wacker and Daniel H. Bays, 171–86. Tuscaloosa: University of Alabama Press, 2003.

———. *A New Vision for Missions: William Cameron Townsend, the Wycliffe Bible Translators, and the Culture of Early Evangelical Faith Missions, 1896–1945.* Tuscaloosa: University of Alabama Press, 2008.

Sweeney, Douglas A. "The Essential Evangelicalism Dialectic: The Historiography of the Early Neo-evangelical Movement and the Observer-Participant Dilemma." *Church History* 60 (1991): 70–84.

———. "Historiographical Dialectics: On Marsden, Dayton, and the Inner Logic of Evangelical History." *Christian Scholar's Review* 23 (1993): 48–52.

Taber, Charles R. "Fishers of Men or Founders of Empire: The Wycliffe Bible Translators in Latin America." *International Bulletin of Missionary Research* 8 (1984): 34–35.

Taylor, Robert B. "Reply to Stipe." *Current Anthropology* 21 (1980): 174.

Thatcher, Floyd W. Letter to the editor. *Christianity Today,* 2 September 1966, 18.

"There Is Good News." *Good News,* Winter 1967, 2–3.

Tipton, Steven M. *Public Pulpits: Methodist and Mainline Churches in the Moral Argument of Public Life.* Chicago: University of Chicago Press, 2007.

Toulouse, Mark G. "Days of Protest: The *Century* and the War in Vietnam." *Christian Century,* 8 November 2000, 1154–57.

———. *The Transformation of John Foster Dulles: From Prophet of Realism to Priest of Nationalism.* Macon, Ga.: Mercer University Press, 1985.

Tucker, Ruth. "Female Mission Strategists: A Historical and Contemporary Perspective." *Missiology* 15 (1987): 73–89.

———. *Guardians of the Great Commission: The Story of Women in Modern Missions.* Grand Rapids, Mich.: Academie Books, 1988.

"UM Evangelist Warns against Segregation Plan for UMC." *UMAction Brief*, Spring 2008. http://www.theird.org/Document.Doc?id=103. 6 July 2010.

"United Methodist General Conference, April 23–May 2." *UMAction Brief*, Spring 2008. http://www.theird.org/Document.Doc?id=103. 6 July 2010.

"The United States and World Government." *Christian Century*, 25 February 1948, 231.

Vickers, William T. "The Jesuits and the SIL: External Policies for Ecuador's through Three Centuries." In *Is God an American? An Anthropological Perspective on the Missionary Work of the Summer Institute of Linguistics*, edited by Peter Aaby and Søren Hvalkof, 51–62. London: Survival International, 1981.

———. Review of *Fishers of Men or Founders of Empire? American Ethnologist* 11 (1984): 200–201.

Wacker, Grant. "Second Thoughts on the Great Commission: Liberal Protestants and Foreign Missions, 1890–1940." In *Earthen Vessels: American Evangelicals and Foreign Missions, 1880–1980*, edited by Joel A. Carpenter, 281–300. Grand Rapids, Mich.: Eerdmans, 1988.

———. "The Waning of the Missionary Impulse: The Case of Pearl S. Buck." In *The Foreign Missionary Enterprise at Home*, edited by Daniel H. Bays and Grant Wacker, 191–205. Tuscaloosa: University of Alabama Press, 2003.

Wagner, C. Peter. "Lausanne Twelve Months Later." *Christianity Today*, 4 July 1975, 7–9.

———. "A New 'Graven Image'?" *Evangelical Missions Quarterly* 3 (1967): 228–33.

Wald, Kenneth D. "The Religious Dimension of American Anti-Communism." *Journal of Church and State* 36 (1994): 483–506.

Walker, Tom. "Grisham Concocts Improved Formula; 'Testament' Provides Welcome Twists." *Denver Post*, 21 February 1999, H1.

Wall, James M. "Anticommunism Binds IRD to White House." *Christian Century*, 28 November 1984, 1115–16.

Warmbold, Carolyn Nizzi. " 'Poisonwood Bible' Preaches Wrongs of U.S. Policy." *Atlanta Journal Constitution*, 18 October 1998, K12.

Warner, R. Stephen. *New Wine in Old Wineskins: Evangelicals and Liberals in a Small-Town Church.* Berkeley: University of California Press, 1988.

Watson, Elizabeth. "Kambini's New Jerusalem." *World Outlook*, April 1948, 27–28.

Welter, Barbara. "She Hath Done What She Could: Protestant Women's Missionary Careers in Nineteenth-Century America." *American Quarterly* 30 (1978): 624–38.

Westad, Odd Arne. *The Global Cold War: Third World Interventions and the Making of Our Times.* Cambridge: Cambridge University Press, 2005.

"What Have We Learned from China?" *Christian Century,* 27 June 1951, 756–57.

Wheeler, Rachel M. *To Live upon Hope: Mohicans and Missionaries in the Eighteenth-Century Northeast.* Ithaca, N.Y.: Cornell University Press, 2008.

"Where Have the China Missionaries Gone?" *Christian Century,* 26 November 1952, 1371–72.

Whitfield, Stephen J. *The Culture of the Cold War.* 2nd ed. Baltimore: John Hopkins University Press, 1996.

Wiley, David. "The Fire *This* Time." *Christian Century,* 17 February 1965, 200–203.

"Will Colombia Become a Theocracy?" *Christian Century,* 21 April 1954, 484–85.

Williams, Peter W. *America's Religions: Traditions and Cultures.* Urbana: University of Illinois Press, 1998.

Williamson, René de Visme. "The Theology of Liberation." *Good News,* March–April 1980, 18–30.

Wills, Anne Blue. "Mapping Presbyterian Missionary Identity in the Church at Home and Abroad." In *The Foreign Missionary Enterprise at Home: Explorations in North American Cultural History,* edited by Daniel H. Bays and Grant Wacker, 95–105. Tuscaloosa: University of Alabama Press, 2003.

Wirt, Sherwood Eliot. "World Mission Situation." *Christianity Today* 1 August 1960, 6–7.

Woodward, David B. "Missionary Calling." *Christianity Today,* 8 May 1964, 9–10.

Wuthnow, Robert. *Boundless Faith: The Global Outreach of American Churches.* Berkeley: University of California Press, 2009.

———. *The Restructuring of American Religion: Society and Faith since World War II.* Princeton: Princeton University Press, 1988.

Zoba, Wendy Murray. "The Testament." *Books & Culture,* September–October 1999, 36.

Index

Capitalism, 48, 102–3, 105, 107

Carnes, Tony, 164–65

Carpenter, Joel, 13

Catholicism, 30–31, 91

Central Intelligence Agency (CIA), 39–40, 83, 105

Chicago Declaration of Evangelical Social Concern (1973), 146–47

Chile, 83

China, 27–28, 32, 33, 60

China Inland Mission, 13

Christian Century, 15, 24, 39–40, 49, 59; on American Protestantism, 4, 20, 23; on Catholicism and Hinduism, 30–31; Cold War stance of, 26–27, 28, 29, 32; on missionaries' work, 21, 28, 30–31, 33; on national purpose, 36–37; on U.S. military interventions, 37–39; on U.S. world leadership, 4, 52; on women in missions, 121, 122–23

Christianity and Democracy, 47

Christianity Today, 15, 56, 84, 115, 154–55; on American military power, 61–62; on Cold War fight against communism, 57, 61, 62; on Elliot book, 63, 64–65, 74–75; on evangelism, 62, 85; as flagship magazine, 14, 59; on Gulf and Iraq wars, 89, 163, 164–65; on internationalization of Church, 68, 77, 82; on Lausanne congress, 78, 87, 108; on missionary work abroad, 66–67, 70–71, 81, 86; on other religions, 56, 88; on rise of nationalism, 57, 65; on Vietnam War, 79; on Western culture, 77–78; on women in missions, 147–48

Christopher, Warren, 7–8

Christ the Liberator, 84

Church-state separation, 31

Clinton, Bill, 7, 8

Co Chien, Harvey T., 82

Coggins, Ross, 67

Cold War, 20, 32, 36; evangelicals and, 57, 60–63, 65; gender and, 126, 127–28, 135–36; ideological side to, 7, 8, 25–26; missionaries seen as part of, 156–57; moralist mainline during, 24–25, 28–29; rhetoric of, 5, 25

Colombia, 30–31

Colonial Evangelism (Beidelman), 113

Colonialism, 69, 71, 89, 95, 98; anthropologists and, 92–93, 98, 110, 111; Matthiessen's critique of, 130–34; missionaries and, 52, 66, 73, 95, 98, 103, 108, 113–14. *See also* Imperialism

Colson, Charles, 159, 163

Comaroff, Jean and John, 113–14, 115, 116–17

Communism, 25, 36, 126; *Christian Century* on, 26, 28, 29, 32; evangelicals and, 57, 60–61, 62–63; Protestantism and, 29, 33, 61; victory of in China, 27–28, 33

Congo, 36, 37–38, 42, 153–54

Connell, R. W., 149

Conrad, Joseph, 145

Consultation on World Evangelization (COWE), 147–48

Containment strategy, 25

Cranston, Bob, 55–56, 75–77

Cross-cultural ministering, 81, 82

Cultural imposition, 3

Cultural relativism, 100–101

Cultural Survival, 101, 103

Cultural Survival Quarterly, 107
Culture: American, 9, 11, 57, 58, 77, 79, 86, 89; Evangelical Christianity and, 78–79; indigenous, 52, 95, 98; Western, 77–78, 83–84, 87–88, 95
Current Anthropology, 93–94, 98, 101–2, 111, 112

Daniels, Ella Maze, 65, 67
Davis, Joe and Dorothy, 127
Dean, Robert, 135–36
"The Declaration of Barbados: For the Liberation of the Indians," 101–2, 107
Delfendahl, Bernard, 96
Democracy and freedom, 7, 20, 29; and American values, 6, 22–23, 36, 43; Christianity and Protestantism and, 11–12, 20, 33, 43, 47–48, 52–53; missionary work and, 43, 48–49, 52–53
Dennis, James, 12
Denominationalism, 47, 66
Diefenbaker, John G., 62
Dissent: theological, 78, 89–90; and treason, 32
Dodge, Ralph E., 66–67
Dominican Republic, 36, 38
Dowie, William, 130
Drew Theological School, 51, 70–71
Dulles, John Foster, 24, 25

Economist, 150
Ecumenical Program for Inter-American Communication Action, 45
Eisenhower, Dwight D., 25, 154
Elliot, Elisabeth Howard, 63–64, 71–75, 109, 148

Episcopal Church, 158, 159, 169 (n. 3)
Ericksen, Thomas Hylland, 100
Escobar, Samuel, 84, 87, 88
Ethnocentrism, 94, 98, 114
Evangelical Christianity: *Christianity Today* and, 14, 59, 62, 85; and Cold War consensus, 57, 60–63, 65; conservative advocacy of, 12–13, 19; gender roles in, 146–47; on homosexuality, 158–60; and indigenous churches, 56–57, 76; as international movement, 68–69, 80–81, 85, 88, 176 (n. 102); and Lausanne congress, 4, 78, 87, 108; neo-evangelicals in, 58–59; normativity of, 57–58; portrayed as ethnocentric and imperialist, 83, 90, 102; postwar growth of, 59; Reformed, 58–59; priority of evangelism in, 59, 62, 68–71, 75; response to nationalism by, 87, 88; and social concerns, 70, 84; *The Testament*'s depiction of, 142–45; ties to right-wing governments, 104–5, 107; Wesleyan-Holiness movement as part of, 59, 173 (n. 5). See also *Christianity Today*; Protestantism
Evangelical Coalition for United Methodist Women (ECUMW), 46–47, 48
Evangelical Missions Quarterly, 74–75, 109

Faith missions, 13, 122
Falwell, Jerry, 47, 147
Federal Council of Churches Commission to Study the Bases of a Just and Durable Peace, 24

Feldman, Harry, 96
The Feminine Mystique (Friedan), 136
Feminism, 121, 124, 129, 147, 149
Fernando, Ajith, 89–90
Fine, Robert M., 68, 69
The Fire Next Time (Baldwin), 37
Fishers of Men or Founders of Empire? (Stoll), 103, 107
Foreign Missions Conference (FMC), 121
Foreign Policy, 7–8
Fousek, John, 22–23
Free Methodist Church, 14–15, 59, 77, 173 (n. 5); and missionary work, 57, 70, 71, 169 (n. 22); on United States' world role, 55–56, 59–60; Women's Missionary Society of, 65; and World Free Methodist Fellowship, 67–68
Friedan, Betty, 136

Gender: norms of, 126, 127–29; *At Play in the Fields of the Lord* on, 134–40; *The Testament* on, 145–46, 148–49, 151; and U.S. power, 123, 135, 151–52. *See also* Masculinity; Women
General Board of Global Ministries (GBGM), 19, 44, 45, 46, 51
God's will, 64, 73–74, 75
Goerner, H. Cornell, 66–67
Goodman, Ellen, 150
Good News (Methodist reform movement), 19, 20, 47, 157; on liberation theology, 44–45; Women's Task force of, 46
Good News: A Forum for Scriptural Christianity, 43–47, 48
Gough, Kathleen, 111

Graham, Billy, 61, 87, 89, 90; at Lausanne congress, 78, 108
Grenada, 45
Grisham, John, 140–42
Griswold, Frank, 159
Guiart, Jean, 94
Gulf War (1991), 89, 150
Gushee, David, 165
Gutiérrez, Gustavo, 85

Haiti, 86–87
Harrison, Benjamin, 12
Harrison, William K., 61
Hawaii (Michener), 1–2, 3–4
Headland, Thomas, 91
The Heart of Darkness (Conrad), 145
Heidinger, James V., 19–20
Heinen, H. Dieter, 95
Henry, Carl F. H., 63, 79, 80, 147
Hersey, John, 49
Hinduism, 31
Historical particularism, 100
Hodges, Olive I., 24
Holmberg, Allan, 115
Homosexuals and homosexuality, 126, 158–60
Hooper, Charlotte, 150–51
Howard, David M., 108–9
Howard, Thomas, 64, 75
Huber, Mary Taylor, 116
Hughes, Daniel T., 99–100
Hvalkof, Søren, 103

Ilongot Headhunting, 1883–1974 (Rosald), 114
Imperialism: anthropologists and, 111–12; cultural, 102, 103, 165, 167–68 (n. 13); missionaries and, 28, 52, 83, 102, 167–68 (n. 13); *The Testament*'s critique of,

142–45; Wilsonian, 159. *See also*
Colonialism
Inboden, William, 25–26, 61
India, 28
Indigenous churches, 42, 56–57, 68,
76, 104
Indigenous peoples and cultures, 52,
77–78, 93; anthropologists and,
95, 101, 106, 115, 116–17, 118–19;
missionaries and, 95, 98, 102–7,
109, 111
Institute on Religion and Democ-
racy (IRD), 45, 46–47, 157
*International Bulletin of Missionary
Research*, 108
International Congress on World
Evangelization (Lausanne, 1974),
4, 78, 87, 108
*International Journal of American
Linguistics (IJAL)*, 97
InterVarsity Christian Fellowship, 59
*In the Way: A Study of Christian Mis-
sionary Endeavours* (Burridge),
116
Iraq War (2003), 163–65
Is God an American?, 97, 103, 105,
110
Is Latin America Turning Protestant?
(Stoll), 110
Isolationism, 7, 22
Iverson, Lalla, 127

Jenkins, Phillip, 176 (n. 102)
Jessup, David, 45–46
Johnson, Lyndon B., 136
Jones, Lora M., 60
Judson, Sarah Boardman, 125

Kane, J. Herbert, 78
Kato, Byang H., 81, 86
Kearns, Doris, 136

Kennan, George, 25
Kennedy, Gerald, 62
Kennedy, John F., 135–36
Kennedy, Robert, 136
King, Martin Luther, Jr., 35
Kingdom of God, 53; and social
change, 44; U.S. identification/
nonidentification with, 20, 47,
78, 89, 108
Kingsolver, Barbara, 153–56
Kirkpatrick, Charles, 70
Kissinger, Henry, 117
Knippers, Diane, 46
Kornfield, William, 109

Lamson, Byron, 68, 69, 174 (n. 39)
Land, Richard, 163, 164
Landau, Paul, 116–17
Latin America, 36–37, 38
Lewis, Diane, 111
Liberation theology, 19, 44–45, 46,
85
Life (magazine), 22
Lindsell, Harold, 64, 74
Long, Kathryn, 72
Luce, Henry, 21, 22
Lumumba, Patrice, 37

Mair, Lucy, 94
Makdisi, Ussama, 11, 17
Malinowski, Bronislaw, 92, 99
Mao Zedong, 27
Maples, Rick and Carrie, 160–62
Marriage, 127, 180 (n. 10); gay, 158
Marshall Plan, 25
Marxism, 44, 48, 61, 63, 126
Maryknoll movement, 39
Masculinity: hegemonic, 150–51;
periodic "crises" of, 125; *At Play
in the Fields of the Lord* on, 134–
40; in post–Cold War period,

149–50; and power, 123, 129, 135, 151–52

Matthew 28:19, 35

Matthiessen, Peter, 130–40, 141

Maybury-Lewis, David, 101

McAlister, Melani, 17

McCarthy, Joseph, and McCarthyism, 32, 63, 126

McConnell, Dorothy, 128

McGavran, Donald, 84

McKinley, William, 12

Mead, Walter Russell, 6

Meeman, Edward J., 27–28

Methodists, 20, 23, 40, 43, 45–46. *See also* Free Methodist Church; United Methodist Church

Michener, James A., 1–2, 3–4

Missiology, 109

Missionaries: in Africa, 28, 29–30, 59–60, 112–13, 160–62; as allies of anthropologists, 114–16; anthropologists' bias against, 92, 94–95, 96, 97, 101; attitude of cultural superiority, 32, 67, 73, 81, 95, 96; call for moratorium on, 81, 86; and capitalist economic policies, 102–3, 106; in China, 27–28, 32; CIA and, 39–40, 83, 105; and colonialism, 52, 66, 73, 95, 98, 103, 108, 113–14; and cross-culturalism, 82; and cultural imperialism, 102, 103, 167–68 (n. 13); dialogue with anthropologists by, 91–92, 108; differentiation with U.S. policy by, 20, 33, 36, 66, 110; duplicity charged against, 104; and ethnocentrism, 94–95, 98, 102, 113, 114, 153; filmstrips on, 34–36, 40–42, 129; and fracturing of mission movement, 12–13; and freedom and democ-

racy, 43, 48–49, 52–53; harvesting souls as priority of, 69–70, 71; in Hawaii, 1–2, 3; and history of mission movement, 10, 12; and indigenous peoples and cultures, 95, 98, 102–7, 109, 111; literature on, 167–68 (n. 13); as naïve, 95, 113; and national churches, 42, 68, 76, 104; no longer Western monopoly, 82; number of, 20, 46, 50, 105; and oppressive regimes, 94, 102–3, 104–5, 107; and power relationships, 77, 82, 87, 88, 159; and social ills, 40–41, 69, 71, 84, 129; in Solomon Islands, 114; studies of, 101, 112, 115–16; ties to U.S. policy and interests, 36–37, 99, 104, 110, 156–57; and U.S. power, 2, 9, 10–13, 22, 86, 156–57; and Wilsonian paradox, 9, 16, 157–58; women as, 11, 72, 121–23, 125, 129, 147–48

Missionary, Go Home (Scherer), 66, 174 (n. 32)

Missionary Tidings, 14–15, 55, 59–60, 81

Missionary to Chile, 34

Mission, Church and Sect in Oceania, 114, 116

Mission Is . . . , 34–36, 40, 41–42

Mission Perspective, 40

Mission Society for United Methodists, 19, 46, 47

Mluanda, Martin, 95

Monroe Doctrine, 6

Montgomery, John Warwick, 80

Moore, P. C., 66

Moore, Thomas R., 107

Morgan, Barney and Caroline McAffee, 24

Morrison, C. C., 23, 32

zation, 12, 23, 32; world tasks for
Christianity as seen by, 23–24,
53. *See also* Evangelical Christianity; *specific denominations*
Puritans, 10

Qalo, Aminiasi, 82

Racism, 37, 67, 87
Reader's Digest, 46
Reagan, Ronald, 57
Religious liberty, 32
Robb, Edmund W., 46, 47
Robb, James S., 45, 46
Robbins, Joel, 117
Robert, Dana, 122
Robertson, Walter R. S., 61
Robinson, Gene, 158
Robinson, James, 29–30
Robinson, Scott S., 105
Roosevelt, Franklin, 22
Roosevelt, Theodore, 12
Rosaldo, Renato, 114
Rugamba, Mark, 86
Rusher, Jerry and Wanda, 86
Russian Orthodox Church, 88

Said, Edward, 118
Salvation, 85, 106; through faith in
Jesus Christ, 13, 49; through liberation from oppression, 44, 45,
48, 85; missionaries' focus on, 13,
102, 136; United States conceived
as carrier of, 80
Sanneh, Lamin, 52
Sano, Roy I., 19–20
The Savage My Kinsman (Elliot),
71–72
Schapera, Isaac, 92, 99
Scherer, James A., 66
Schlesinger, Arthur, Jr., 102, 126

Schwarzkopf, Norman, 150
Scofield, Willard A., 70–71
Seamands, David A., 44
September 11, 2001, 162–63
Settje, David, 63
Sexuality, 158–60, 161–62
Shacklock, Floyd, 65
Shaw, R. Daniel, 110
Shenk, William, 82
Shepherd, George W., 26, 29
Shoemaker, Esther, 124, 127, 179
(n. 4)
Siegel, Lee, 155–56
60 Minutes, 46
Skeete, F. Herbert, 51–52
Skinner, Tom, 84
Skow, John, 155
Slessor, Mary, 147
"Social Theory and the Study of
Christian Missions in Africa"
(Beidelman), 112
Southern Baptist Convention, 147,
148
Soviet Union, 25, 88, 150
Spain, David, 93
Stafford, Tim, 154–55
Stearman, Allyn, 114–16
Steinfels, Peter, 48
Stephanson, Anders, 7
Stipe, Claude, 93–95, 96–97
Stoll, David, 97, 104, 105, 108; *Fishers
of Men or Founders of Empire?*,
103, 107; *Is Latin America Turning
Protestant?*, 110; "What Should
Wycliffe Do?," 109–10
Strickland, Eunice, 124
Strong, Josiah, 11–12
Struchen, Donald, 50
Structural functionalism, 99–100
Stuart, John Leighton, 24
Stumbo, John, 51

Williams College, 10

Williamson, René de Visme, 44–45

Wilson, Woodrow, 6, 22

Wilsonianism, 165–66; about, 6–7,
167 (n. 11); mainline and evangelical groups and, 21, 89, 157–
58; paradox of, 9, 16, 157–58;
and U.S. world role, 7–9, 16,
36, 123, 157

Winthrop, John, 10

Wirt, Sherwood Eliot, 69–70

Women: femininity of, 124, 127,
128; feminism and, 121, 124, 129,
147, 149; and gender roles, 125,
127–29, 146–47; leadership by,
147; and marital status, 127; and
masculinity "crises," 126; as missionaries, 11, 72, 121–23, 125, 129,
147–48; as physicians, 124, 179

(n. 4); in workforce, 125–26.
See also Gender

Women's Missionary Society
(WMS), 65, 174 (n. 32)

Woodward, David B., 68, 69

World Free Methodist Fellowship,
67–68, 69, 87

World Outlook, 24, 27, 124, 127, 128

World Vision, 59

Wuthnow, Robert, 47, 176 (n. 102)

Wycliffe Bible Translators (WBT),
96, 106–7; criticisms of, 83, 97,
103, 104, 109–10; Statement of
Doctrine, 106; and U.S. interests,
104, 105

Young Men's Christian Associations, 12

Yuquí, 115–16